THE AGONY OF
GALLIPOLI

To my Mother, Sister Nellie Alfreda Laffin (née Pike), 1888–1980, who served with the 3rd Australian General Hospital on Lemnos Island off the coast of Gallipoli during the campaign, in Egypt and in France and England
and
To my Father, Lieutenant Charles George Laffin, 1894–1948, of 20th Battalion Australian Imperial Force, who served on Lemnos, in Egypt and on the Western Front.

THE AGONY OF
GALLIPOLI

JOHN LAFFIN

SUTTON PUBLISHING

This book was first published in 1980 by
Osprey Publishing Limited

First published by Sutton Publishing Limited in 1989 under
the title *Damn the Dardanelles!*

This new edition first published in 2005

British Library Cataloguing in Publication Data
A catalogue record for this book is available from the British
Library.

ISBN 0 7509 3639 8

Typeset in 11/13.5pt Galliard.
Typesetting and origination by
Sutton Publishing Limited.
Printed and bound in Great Britain by
J.H. Haynes & Co. Ltd, Sparkford.

Contents

The Arena

The Gallipoli peninsula of Turkey, about forty miles long and twelve miles across at its widest point, has a spiny backbone rising to a peak of nearly a thousand feet. Largely barren or scrub-clad, it is fiercely hot and stifling in summer and bitterly cold in winter, with a torturous terrain of razor-backed ridges and deep ravines.

Outside the few settlements – Gallipoli town itself and Eceabat (formerly Maidos) – the peninsula has a last-place-in-the-world atmosphere. Not that it is ugly; it radiates a strange, siren beauty, as many men with reason to hate the place have acknowledged. In the morning and at sundown the forbidding coast has a compelling beauty – the gullies are deeply blue, and the sea and sky are multi-tinted. Then you can love it. When you struggle, sweat-soaked and panting, through the spiky bush and up the heart-breaking cliffs and hills, you hate it.

The Straits of the Dardanelles – known in ancient times as the Hellespont – run as a strong south-flowing current between the peninsula and Asiatic Turkey. From its mouth at Cape Helles to the Sea of Marmara, the narrow waterway is overlooked by the Gallipoli heights and by lesser hills on the Asiatic shore. At one point, the Narrows, just fourteen miles from the entrance, the width of the channel is less than 1,600 yards from shore to shore between Chanakkale (Chanak) and Kilid Bahr.

Few places have so many natural advantages for defence. Yet it was this harsh finger of land and this blue beguiling waterway which the British and French proposed to master in order to snatch the glittering prize to the north, Istanbul (Constantinople).

The campaign, in 1915, ended in defeat at a shocking cost in life.

The purpose of this book is to explain the defeat, to apportion the blame and to let the soldiers speak. Only in this way can some justice be done to the soldiers and sailors who went to their deaths in as pitiless a place of war as history can produce. One soldier called it 'hell heaped up'; another described it as 'sacred ground of lost endeavour'.

The kinfolk of the men of Gallipoli deserve to be told that they did all that could be expected of them in the face of merciless climate, unyielding enemy and their own shameful political and military leadership.

1

Outplayed in Diplomatic Chess

Turkey and Britain should never have been at war with each other, for they were traditional allies. Had they remained so in 1914 the idea of capturing the Gallipoli peninsula and forcing the Straits of the Dardanelles would not have arisen.

The two powers became enemies because Britain lost to Germany a deadly game of diplomatic chess played in Constantinople. Through their ambassadors, attachés, and heads of missions they had been engaged in this game since the 1870s. From 1897 Germany gained a major advantage because its principal player was Baron Marshal von Bieberstein, who held the post of ambassador until 1912. Bieberstein had been carefully chosen as 'right' for the Turks. A huge man with a scarred face and an aggressive personality, he impressed them by his sheer force. Bieberstein's main task was to convince the Turks that Germany was a stronger friend and a more dangerous enemy than Britain, and a single conversation with the massive, thunderous German convinced most Turks that this was true.

To Turkish officers and officials, von Bieberstein personified German might, and during his last five years he did with them what he liked. In private he despised them as weak, and boasted about his ability to make them dance like puppets.

Turkey had built up such an appalling record of atrocities against minorities that even its most ardent supporters were disgusted. The British Press labelled the Turks 'beastly', 'unspeakable', 'barbaric' and 'decadent'. Even though it paid British interests to maintain the *status quo* in Turkey, the British public lost all patience. Oddly enough, the Turks continued to regard Britain as their hereditary friend – just as the Russians were hereditary enemies. But gradually the Turks became aware that the British were no longer friendly; the signing of the Anglo-Russian agreement in 1907 made this politically clear.

The watchful Germans exploited the opportunity. Bieberstein explained to the Turks how Britain had betrayed them and was working against them. This was the climax of the patient and thorough groundwork. Now the Germans could point out that when the Turks had needed a new government loan Britain and France had refused it – the Germans had raised the money. When Britain and France had declined to receive Turkish officers at their military academies, the Germans had encouraged them to come to Berlin. And who had reorganized the Turkish Army? Why, the Germans.

The British ambassador during the vital years, Sir Louis Mallet, was a charming man with neither prestige nor forcefulness, yet Britain had a mature power built on centuries of diplomatic, economic and military strength and was more then Germany's match. Mallet did nothing to convince the Turks of this. One Englishman could perhaps have countered von Bieberstein's influence and beaten him in his own game – Lord Kitchener. Kitchener quietly coveted the post of ambassador to Turkey, but apparently was never seriously considered for it. He would have been ideal, with his international military reputation and his prestige in the Mohammedan world.

Von Bieberstein's successor as ambassador, Baron Wangenheim, was cast in the same mould, a huge, solid man, with a bold Teutonic head, piercing eyes and aristocratic manner. Aged fifty-four and an overwhelming mixture of amiability and force, Wangenheim was experienced, shrewd and ruthless – and he had personal orders from the Kaiser, his friend, to build on Bieberstein's sound foundations and win Turkey.

When the so-called Young Turks, led by Taalet, Enver and Djemal, came to power through a brutal *coup d'état* on 26 January 1913, the Germans at once saw their opportunity. These new young rulers – Enver, who became Minister of War, was only thirty-two – were vain and ambitious, and the older, experienced German flattered and fêted and fooled them into compliance. In his own home Enver received visitors while seated between outsize portraits of Napoleon and Frederick the Great. Wangenheim and his aides knew exactly how to exploit this kind of egotism.

The British Embassy knew what was happening but seemed unable to play the same game. The American ambassador, Morgenthau, describes Mallet as 'a high-minded and cultivated English gentleman'. Bompard, the French ambassador, was 'charming and honourable' and Giers, the Russian ambassador, was 'a proud and scornful diplomat of the old aristocratic regime'. Mallet and Bompard were constitutionally incapable of taking part in the murderous intrigues of Turkish politics, while Giers was too contemptuous of them to be bothered.

Early in 1914 the Germans sent their new and impressive battle cruiser, *Goeben*, on a 'goodwill visit', which was really a calculated compliment to the impressionable Young Turks and a shrewd demonstration of modern naval might. *Goeben* lay at anchor off the Golden Horn on the Bosporus for several weeks, while Wangenheim and his attachés incited the traditional Turkish fear of Russia. 'The Russians want the Dardanelles straits,' they said, 'and without our protection they will take them.'

Through the Treaty of Paris, 1856, and the Treaty of

London, 1871, England, France, Russia, Austria and Prussia had agreed that foreign warships would be prohibited from entering the Straits while Turkey was at peace. The Turks' acceptance of the *Goeben*'s presence was an implicit statement that Turkey was no longer 'at peace'.

Anchored off the palatial German Embassy, the *Goeben*, dressed in bunting and at night a blaze of light, was an impressive emblem of Germany. The officers gave receptions for the flattered Turks and carefully chosen foreigners while German agents encouraged the little ferries that plied up and down the Bosphorus to sail close to the *Goeben* and its friendly crew. British naval prestige, formerly pre-eminent in Constantinople, was virtually destroyed. The British Admiralty did nothing to counter the German move, yet no peace-time naval demonstration was ever more pointed and portentous.

Also significant, though less spectacular, had been the arrival in December 1913 of a reputedly clever general, Liman von Sanders, with several hundred German military personnel under him. Von Sanders was made a kind of inspector-general of the Turkish Army, a post arranged by the German Embassy so that it gave him virtual control over every aspect of the Turkish Army without offending senior Turkish officers.

British Intelligence, though at that time weak on prediction and deduction, knew from messages intercepted between the German Embassies in Constantinople and Berlin that Turkish claims to be still neutral were quite false. A month before the outbreak of the European war Germany was exercising the powers of sovereignty in Constantinople, and the whole Turkish Press had come under German direct ownership or indirect control.

Enver, in his position as War Minister, was certain of war between Germany and Russia, and he asked Wangenheim, on 27 July, for a secret alliance against Russia. The Germans were graciously pleased to consent to the treaty, which was signed within a few days, though it was kept secret from most of the Turkish cabinet. On 3 August the first mines were laid in the Dardanelles. British and French Intelligence knew almost at once of this treaty. Astonishingly, Enver also offered the Russians an alliance, which they rejected without informing their allies.

The Turks had been eagerly awaiting delivery of their first two modern battleships, largely financed by money raised among the common people, and being built in Britain. One was virtually complete. On 3 August, as the Turks were laying their mines in the Straits, Britain announced that it was taking over the Turkish ships for the Royal Navy. The Turks were shocked and accused Britain of betrayal, bad faith and dishonesty. The depth of feeling can be understood. Turkey was longing for a new war with Greece to get back the islands of Lemnos, Imbros and Mitylene, lost in the war of 1912. The new warships were to be the instrument of recovery.

The British seizure was militarily justifiable, legally sound and, in the circumstances of the period, politically right, but the Turks were in no mood for rational argument.

Turkish anger was at its height when news came of Britian's declaration of war on Germany on 4 August. This brought back into the Turkish scene the battleship *Goeben*, which had been in the Mediterranean with its escort, the cruiser *Breslau*. Chased by the Royal Navy, the German ships sought sanctuary through the narrow neck of the Dardanelles not only because it was one of the few places open to them but because Wangenheim had arranged it that way. The forts at the entrance to the Dardenelles asked Constantinople for instructions: Should the German warships be allowed to enter?

Significantly, it was a German staff officer, Lieutenant-Colonel von Kress, who brought Enver this request for orders while he was at a top-level meeting. Cleverly pressed by von Kress, Enver gave his permission. Pursuing his advantage, Kress said, 'And if British warships follow the

Germans they are to be fired on if they attempt to enter the Dardenelles?'

It was a statement framed as a question, and Enver concurred. In effect, he had gone to war.

In mid-August Winston Churchill proposed that a British squadron should steam up the Dardanelles and sink the *Goeben* and *Breslau* since Turkish neutrality, he pointed out, was now publicly a fiction. The Prime Minister, Asquith, rejected Churchill's 'most bellicose' proposition.*

Kitchener, all powerful as Secretary of State for War, was also against taking the initiative against the Turks, on the grounds that the British Empire had a vast Muslim population which might react badly to military action against their co-religionists, the Turks. The fact that the Turks held millions of Muslims in oppressive subjection seems to have had no influence on Kitchener's thought, nor did his knowledge of the Turkish intention to become allies of the Germans.

To allay the fears of the more apprehensive members of the Turkish cabinet and to get around international law – a neutral country was not supposed to give sanctuary to belligerents' warships – Enver and his German friends arranged the 'sale' of the *Goeben* and *Breslau* to Turkey, and they were re-named *Sultan Selim* and *Medilli*. The Germans succeeded in one coup after another – the German crews were kept for the *Goeben* and *Breslau*, and the German Admiral Souchon was appointed to command the Turkish Navy. The British Naval Mission lost all influence and was humiliated.

The Germans took over the Constantinople dock of the British firm of Armstrong and Vickers. Wangenheim told the Young Turks that the German naval engineers had found that the British had left the Turkish ships in a deplorable and

---

* In 1898 Churchill had written a novel with a climax in which a fleet of powerful ships forced its way through 'a sort of Dardenelles' to quell a rebellious capital.

deliberate state of disrepair; it was part of Britain's plot to ruin Turkey. The Turks believed him.

Conciliatory when it should have been forceful, the British Admiralty committed one folly after another. It had announced its intention of appointing Admiral Limpus, former Chief of the Naval Mission to Turkey, to command the British Dardanelles Squadron. The appointment was cancelled – in case the Turks might be offended and because it was 'unfair and unduly provocative' to place in command a man with an inside knowledge of the Turkish fleet.

The Limpus decision has been defended on the grounds that with him in command the Turks would not believe in the British ambassador's protestations of England's continuing friendship for Turkey. In fact, that point had long been passed; the Turks believed only what the Germans told them.

By the end of September Turkey had violated all treaty rights concerning the Dardanelles; no vessel of any kind was allowed to enter. Britain, France, America and other nations protested, but took no action. By closing the Straits, the Germans separated Russia from its allies and destroyed it economically and militarily, for it could no longer be supplied from abroad.

The Germans tried to induce Britain to attack Turkey by arranging Turkish army raids across the border into British Egypt, but this provocation failed. Through a cleverly contrived plot known to few of the Turkish leaders, Wangenheim and Admiral Souchon then took a much more decisive step. On 28 October, Souchon led the Turkish fleet to bombard Odessa, Sebastopol and other Russian Black Sea ports. This might bring about the final rupture between Britain and Turkey. Wangenheim told the United States ambassador Henry Morgenthau, 'We have our foot on Russia's corn and we propose to keep it there.'

Britain and Russia should now have taken up the German gauntlet and made war instantly and decisively on Turkey.

The Dardanelles was as easy to pluck as a plum, for the Turkish defences were obsolete, incomplete and poorly manned – facts known in Whitehall and St Petersburg. Turkey had only two munitions factories – both on the Bosphorus close to Constantinople; a few naval shells would have blown them to pieces. Between the Russian Black Sea fleet from the north and the British Mediterranean fleet from the south, the *Goeben* and *Breslau* would have been trapped. The Turkish leaders, now aware of the German trickery which had led them into the Black Sea bombardments, and appalled by the possible consequences, were incapacitated by the lethargy of fear. This, too, was known in Whitehall and St Petersburg.

The time was past for friendly British gestures and conciliation, but the shortsighted Russians and the indecisive British did nothing except to enter a state of official but passive hostility on 31 October. Thus they set the stage for 'the great adventure' of Gallipoli, in which British and Turks were equally German victims.

2

The Pre-Campaign Intelligence Failure

To be successful, any military operation needs accurate information and a competent Intelligence staff. Intelligence work before the invasion of Turkey was lamentable; much information readily available was either not passed through to those competent to deal with it, or was ignored, misinterpreted or simply not collected.

In the year preceding the landing at Gallipoli, certain Intelligence failures stand out as particularly deplorable. This opinion is not a matter of hindsight and it is not the result of being able to research records not available in 1914–15. The following case studies in lax military Intelligence make interesting though exasperating reading, and taken in conjunction with blunders in political Intelligence they go some way towards explaining the failure of the Gallipoli campaign.

THE CASE OF THE AMERICAN MILITARY ATTACHÉ

In March 1914, the American military attaché in Constantinople was Major John Taylor, who was generally considered to be well informed about Turkish intentions. In

March, Taylor lunched in Cairo with the British Minister of War, Lord Kitchener, and other officers. Taylor briefed them on the current situation in Turkey and said, 'When the big war comes Turkey will be the ally of Germany. If she is not in direct alliance, at least she will mobilize on the line of the Caucasus Mountains and thus divert three Russian army corps away from the European front.' This would be disastrous for the other members of the Tripple Entente – Britain and France – who would need the Russians to apply as much pressure as possible against Germany.

Taylor's view was valuable, and Kitchener thought about it. Then he said, in his deliberate way, 'I agree with you.'

If Kitchener reported Taylor's first-hand observations to his Intelligence staff there is no record of it. More than that, a few months later Kitchener rejected the idea of taking the initiative against Turkey, though by then Taylor's prediction was coming true.

THE CASE OF THE BRITISH MILITARY ATTACHÉ

Between 1911 and 1914, successive British military attachés at Constantinople and vice-consuls at Chanak on the Dardanelles had sent reports on the Dardanelles defences to the War Office. The attaché in 1914 was the enterprising and energetic Lieutenant-Colonel Charles Cunliffe-Owen. In the spring of that year Cunliffe-Owen, on his own initiative, made a detailed survey on the spot of the Dardanelles and the Gallipoli peninsula.

He sent frequent reports to the War Office, including information on gun sites, minefields and the topography of the peninsula. With the possible exception of the vice-consul at Chanak, Cunliffe-Owen probably knew as much about the Dardanelles and the Turkish Army as any German Intelligence officer. Returning to London when Britain's relations with Turkey deteriorated, he made himself available in case operations against Turkey were contemplated – which he assumed would happen. He was never consulted. When a team of staff officers were scratched together, many of them unsuitable, Cunliffe-Owen was not included, though he was in London and available. He was probably the only officer who had seen Gallipoli on the ground, but his reports were never seen by the Commander-in-Chief of the invading army, General Sir Ian Hamilton, or his Chief-of-Staff, Major-General Braithwaite, both of whom were ignorant about the Straits and the peninsula. (Cunliffe-Owen was later posted to Gallipoli and for a time commanded the Anzac artillery.)

NAVAL INTELLIGENCE AND ITS GRAND DELUSION

On 3 November 1914, on the authority of Winston Churchill as First Lord, the Admiralty ordered the bombardment of the outer Dardanelles forts at Sedd-el-Bahr and Kum Kale. In itself, this decision was an Intelligence failure; J.F.C. Fuller calls it a 'senseless operation of war', because it alerted the Turks to the Allies' intentions and therefore destroyed the element of surprise. The German advisers in Constantinople exploited the attack to frighten the Turks into greater efforts to strengthen their defences.

But an equally significant result of the naval attack was that it made the British overconfident. The warships had destroyed the shore guns with such ease that the Navy assumed it could pick off any Turkish gun position or ammunition magazine at will. As it turned out, the ships' guns caused more damage in this one brief bombardment than during the rest of the naval campaign, but the devastation was more a matter of luck than skill. Naval Intelligence, as excited as anybody about the fleet's shooting, did not take into consideration the basic weakness and inefficiency of the Turks' coast artillery; like the gunnery officers, they imagined they had knocked out powerful shore batteries. But the Turkish guns – four long-range and twenty medium-range – were badly sited and uncovered, and they were crewed by incompetent, half-trained soldiers, while the magazines were dangerously close to the guns and unprotected by concrete or camouflage. Ammunition supply, telephone communications and range-finding were woefully poor. Practically everything the Turks possessed was visible from the sea.

The Royal Navy had merely had target practice against antiquated and ill-served guns. Intelligence should have made this clear and should have drawn the obvious inference that the Turks would not again be so easily caught – if only because their German advisers would insist on improvements. The British and French navies went on believing that their great guns would quickly reduce the defence to rubble.

THE RAILWAY DEMOLITION INCIDENT

On 18 December 1914, the light cruiser HMS *Doris* was sent to a point north of Alexandretta in Asiatic Turkey, with orders to cut the railway line that supplied the Turkish armies in Arabia, then under Turkish domination.

A party of bluejackets was landed near the town and to their surprise they found the Turks co-operative. While the sailors blew up a station and bridge, the helpful Turks hurriedly shunted the locomotives together for destruction. The Turkish officers explained to the lieutenant in charge of the British party that they would like to assist him but that a matter of 'face' was involved. If he would consent to become a Turkish officer for the day he would be their superior and they would have to obey him; in that way they could not be held responsible. Under the orders of the 'Anglo-Turk' naval officer, the Turkish soldiers then blew up their own locomotives. The operation was entirely successful and the British withdrew without a casualty. The officers shook hands in parting.

This absurd incident convinced Churchill and many British politicians and naval officers that the Turks would not be formidable enemies. No serious Intelligence study was made of the episode, and this one incident was assumed to indicate a general comic opera attitude to war.

THE TURKISH INVASION OF THE CAUCASUS

In December 1914, a Turkish army of 100,000 moved into the Caucasus against the Russians, just as American Major John Taylor had foreseen. In severe winter weather the Turks made rapid progress across difficult country in an operation that required much skill from the officers and great fortitude from the men. Even General von Sanders, who had advised against the invasion, was impressed.

On December 29, Enver's army met the Russian General Vorontzov in the battle of Sarikamish. Enver had already lost 15,000 men through desertion and frostbite before the battle began and the ferocious conflict took place in a blizzard, with a temperature of thirty degrees below zero, at an altitude of 10,000 feet. At one point it seemed that the Turks' plan for a wide envelopment of the Russians would succeed, but a Russian counter-attack killed 30,000 Turks and smashed Enver's army. Many more froze to death in the retreat, and about 18,000 effective Turkish soldiers reached Erzerum.

This Turkish reverse was never properly analysed by Allied Intelligence. It was again assumed that here was further evidence of Turkish military incompetence. The Turks had undeniably lost the battle, but the rank and file, ill-clad and ill-fed, had fought with immense courage and tenacity. Had they been well-led they might have won. Nobody in authority on the Allied side gave a thought to what the Turkish armed multitudes might accomplish if led by German generals, a feasible eventuality.

BLINDLY INTO BATTLE

Hamilton was not given any Intelligence officers until 18 March. Pitched into a strange theatre of war so close to the time of invasion, it was not surprising that they were not clear about the number of Turks on the peninsula. The closest they could come was 'between 40,000 and 80,000', an enormous margin. In addition, 30,000 were 'said to be' on the Asiatic side of the Straits, and 60,000 more within 'close call'. (We know now that about 60,000 Turks in all were on the peninsula at the time of the landing, 25 April.) All information was imprecise and unreliable, and next to nothing was known about the disposition of Turkish forces. (Only two battalions and one engineer company were in position to oppose the landing at Helles – about 1,000 fighting men in all.) Yet Turkish and Arab spies could be easily bought and their information checked against that of the well-informed Greek traders, who were constantly moving among the Aegean islands and along the Turkish Asiatic coast.

While I am mostly concerned here with the failure of Intelligence before the landing, it must be said that throughout the campaign the British failed to make use of a constant stream of information from the Turkish side. It came from American journalists, who were often allowed to visit the Turkish lines, even at the front; subsequently they wrote detailed reports about conditions and the German–Turkish conduct of the war on the peninsula. Notable among the correspondents were those of the *New York Times* and the American Associated Press, but even a staff correspondent of the *Brooklyn Eagle* was allowed into Krithia. Their reports contained much of Intelligence value – but they were not sent to Hamilton's GHQ at Gallipoli. No military or naval Intelligence appreciation of the Gallipoli–Dardanelles situation was ever made – not even at the strategic level. It is one of the strangest omissions of the whole affair. Had such an analysis been attempted, the officers concerned might well have asked themselves if a serious naval or military attack was really necessary. And they may have concluded, as did Major-General Sir Charles Callwell, Director of Military Operations, that 'so long as they were merely more or less threatened, the Dardanelles and Constantinople placed a trump card in the hands of the Allies'.

Callwell's point was that without risking a ship or a soldier the Entente Powers could have kept great Turkish forces occupied. The weapon would have been bluff. The British and French navies dominated the Aegean, and large numbers of British, Australian, New Zealand and Indian soldiers were in Egypt. Skilfully planted rumours about impending naval or military attacks would reach the Turks through the islands of Tenedos, Imbros and Lemnos. Now and then the fleet would carry out just enough bombardment, not only at the Dardanelles, to add credence to the idea of invasion and breakthrough. Callwell believed that great pressure could have been placed on Turkey. In this way Russia would be helped, Turkish armies pinned down, and unrest and confusion created in Turkey.

But the threat would cease to be a powerful asset for Allies if they really did undertake a breakthrough and landing – and failed. A sober Intelligence assessment that it was better to go on threatening than to attack and fail would almost certainly have had the great effect of forcing careful preparation for the campaign upon Churchill, with his impetuous, rapier mind, and on Kitchener, with his stolid, bludgeon mind; then the failure factor would have diminished.

3

Ships Against Forts – First Period

The idea of the Dardanelles/Gallipoli campaign might have started life in Winston Churchill's mind, but the first practical move came from Eleutherios Venizelos, the Greek Prime Minister, on 20 August, only a few weeks after the outbreak of war. With King Constantine's agreement, he offered to the Entente Powers – Britain, France and Russia – Greece's military and naval resources. This was a considerable offer, but the Foreign Secretary, Sir Edward Grey, rejected it on the grounds that acceptance would antagonize Turkey. By now this was an irrelevancy, but Grey was still pursuing the dead trail of friendship with Turkey.

The Greeks had an ambitious and detailed plan. Sixty thousand men would land near the outer tip of the peninsula to capture from the rear the forts guarding the Straits, while another 30,000 would land near Bulair to capture the narrow isthmus.

Despite Grey's stance, in August Churchill discussed the matter with Lord Kitchener and the next day asked the Chief of the Imperial General Staff to appoint two officers who, with two naval officers, would produce a plan for seizing the Gallipoli peninsula 'by means of a Greek Army of adequate strength' with a view to admitting a British fleet to the Sea of Marmara.

The elderly Admiral Fisher, appointed First Sea Lord on 30 October, challenged the Gallipoli plan and proposed a landing in the Baltic, but this operation would require British troops and Kitchener had none to spare. The Dardanelles project gained ground, but the Greeks now hedged; Bulgaria must join them in declaring war on Turkey. The proposal was shelved, but remained very much alive in the hothouse of Churchill's mind.

The irresponsible prelude to the Dardanelles campaign took place on 3 November. The Admiralty – which at that date really meant Churchill – ordered Rear-Admiral Sackville Carden to bombard the outer forts at the entrance to the Dardanelles, at 12,000 to 14,000 yards' range. He was not to run any risks, but was to retire before the Turkish fire became effective. Because of these restraints it was said that the purpose of the naval attack was to ascertain the maximum range of the Turks' coastal guns – information any efficient naval Intelligence department could have produced in a few minutes. When this message passed through the hands of Admiral Limpus in Malta he telegraphed to Admiralty that the first stage in opening the Dardanelles should be the landing of an army. Also, he said, from his personal knowledge of the Turks, they would exploit the fleet's retirement by spreading the news that the British had been repulsed with heavy losses. The experienced and shrewd Limpus was ignored, and Carden was told to go ahead as ordered.

The ships opened up on forts at Sedd-el-Bahr and Kum Kale with spectacular results. A chance shot hit a magazine, which blew up with such force that many naval officers felt satisfied that they had virtually demolished the outer defences. As ordered, the fleet turned away as some Turkish guns sent shells splashing into the Aegean and, as predicted, the Turks scored good propaganda – 'the British fleet had been frightened off'. More than that, the Turks and their

German masters were now alerted to the possibility of even more serious attack.

Late in November, Churchill heard that two Australian divisions had arrived in Egypt. He ordered that the transports which had brought them must be held in Egypt, 'in case they are required for an expedition'. The idea of forcing the Dardanelles more than interested Churchill; it fascinated and then obsessed him. To him the occupation of Constantinople was 'the shortest path to a triumphant peace'. In theory, it appeared to be no less than this. By dominating Constantinople, Britain could shape history: Russia would be relieved of Turkish pressure; the Balkan States would swing to the Entente; Germany would be demoralized by having the British and French in their rear; the Austrians would have their hands full fighting the Balkan States, and would be virtually out of the war on the Western Front; Italy would almost certainly come in on the side of Britain and France; Turkish armies in Arabia, their communications cut, would wither on a dead vine. . . . The list of advantages to a successful Dardanelles campaign was almost limitless. But they could only be achieved by early decisive action. One such action was taken on 13 December by a British submarine commander Lieutenant Holbrook of the *B-11*, who dived his tiny ship under the Turkish mines and sank a ship, the battlecruiser *Messudieh*, near the Narrows. Such an exploit, while winning the Victoria Cross for the submariner, was no substitute for planned action on a large scale, and again it warned the Turks to expect trouble.

On the Western Front the British Army had lost half its strength by the end of 1914. Open warfare had been replaced by pointless fighting in a muddy battlefield of trenches and barbed wire. Enterprise was needed, and one of the few soldiers with any strategic horizon and insight, Lieutenant-Colonel Maurice Hankey, Secretary of the War Council, was suggesting, like Churchill, that Germany could be best struck through her allies, especially Turkey. Three new British army corps, hopefully co-operating with Greek and Bulgarian troops, would attack Constantinople. He detailed the obvious advantages, including the release of 350,000 tons of shipping now bottled up in the Black Sea.

Almost simultaneously with the Hankey report came a plea from the Russian Grand Duke Nicholas for a British 'demonstration' to relieve the pressure on his forces in the Caucasus. Kitchener's first choice, an attack on Alexandretta, was abandoned after the Navy reported that harbour facilities were inadequate. He then suggested that the Dardanelles would be ideal for such a demonstration.

On 3 January, Fisher, informed of the Grand Duke's telegram, wanted a more ambitious 'demonstration', and wrote to Churchill to urge an immediate combined attack on Turkey. He suggested that the Indian Corps and 75,000 seasoned troops be taken from France and placed ashore at Besika Bay. At the same time the Greeks were to be persuaded to attack the peninsula, the Bulgarians to march upon Constantinople, the Russians to join the Serbs and Romanians in an attack on Austria–Hungary. While all this was happening a squadron of old British and French battleships would force its way through the Dardanelles. And he quoted Napoleon's maxim: 'Celerity – without it, failure.' It was almost as if Fisher knew that among the war planners of the time celerity was the last quality to expect.

Churchill knew that the possibility of obtaining troops for a large-scale attack was remote, but he seized on Fisher's support for the naval possibility, and with Fisher's consent he telegraphed the Admiral on the spot, Carden: Do you consider the forcing of the Straits by ships alone a practicable operation?

As always with Churchill, the framing of the question was calculated to produce a predetermined response. In this case Churchill's loaded query gave the impression that an idea was being tested, not that a plan was being made. Carden replied:

I do not consider Dardanelles can be rushed. They might be forced by extended operations with large numbers of ships. He was speculating, and did not realize that Churchill would use this speculation as a lever to draw from him a detailed plan.

Churchill took this plan with him to the War Council meeting on 13 January, and waited patiently while the members became weary and depressed from interminable and inconclusive discussion. Then he produced 'the Carden plan'. His timing and dramatic presentation were superb, and everybody seized on this means of doing something, *anything*. Even the dour, dull Sir John French, so preoccupied with the Western Front that nothing else existed, expressed enthusiasm.

And a conclusion rather than a decision emerged: To prepare for a naval expedition in February, to bombard and take the Gallipoli peninsula with Constantinople as the objective. The impossibility of 'taking' any piece of land with ships alone must have occurred to some members of the council, but this amateurish phraseology was permitted to remain, and with it the inbuilt tactical weakness of the plan.

Despite his enthusiasm, Churchill complained that the plan was too petty, while Fisher feared that it might become too grand – with consequent damage to his Baltic invasion project. A deep quarrel split the two men – theirs had always been a love-hate relationship – and at the next War Council meeting on 28 January, Fisher rose to tender his resignation. Kitchener quickly intervened and, drawing the old admiral aside, persuaded him to join with the others in a compromise plan. Fisher was obviously greatly disturbed about something, but neither the Prime Minister nor any other member of the Council asked for his opinions or objections.

It is not possible to understand why the War Council made so many serious errors of omission and commission, and why it was ineffectual, without knowing how it operated. It might be expected that senior army and navy officers of great sagacity and experience would attend these meetings as 'experts' – and indeed they did. But they were never asked for their opinions. Neither did the experts volunteer their views. If they disagreed with their Minister they 'loyally' kept their mouths shut. The War Council assumed the silence of the experts to imply agreement with what had been said, when it was really obedience to Service etiquette. The experts were, therefore, useless. The War Council was dominated by the Secretary of State for War, Kitchener, and the First Lord of the Admiralty, Churchill – and from them only did it get technical information and deductions to be drawn from that information. That the War Council met so infrequently is not surprising, since Kitchener and Churchill each knew what they wanted, even when the means to their ends were sometimes not even visible. Both concealed much from the War Council and the Cabinet. Kitchener is reported to have once said, 'It is repugnant to me to have to reveal military secrets to twenty-three gentlemen [of the Cabinet] with whom I am hardly acquainted.' He was so secretive that he even concealed vital information from Grey. For instance, when the French Minister of War, Alexandre Millerand, suggested a conference on 22 March 1915, Kitchener did not pass on this request.

In effect, Kitchener was his own General Staff, making all the decisions and brooking no disagreement. This was graphically shown on 16 February 1915, when he brought Captain Wyndham Deedes to his office. Deedes, a capable officer who had served with the Turkish Army and knew the Dardanelles, was then an Intelligence officer at the War Office. Kitchener wanted to know whether a purely naval attack on the Dardanelles would succeed. Deedes gave a military direct answer: The operation must fail. When Kitchener gave no immediate response, Deedes went on to argue his case. Kitchener, who had been bewitched by Churchillian rhetoric, became angry and dismissed him.

Churchill could not be so authoritarian and dictatorial in the Admiralty, partly because of Fisher but also because other naval commanders had forthright opinions. But he often imposed his will by wearing down any opposition with a mixture of eloquence, enthusiasm and bullying.

However, he received the same advice as Kitchener had from Deedes. In Churchill's case the advice came from the old French Minister for the Navy, Victor Augagneur, who told Churchill, at a meeting in London on 26 January, that French naval Intelligence had reported that a purely maritime operation to force the Dardanelles was unlikely to achieve any useful purpose. To be effective, the French Intelligence officers insisted, the way must first be cleared by land operations.

Augagneur, like others, was spellbound by Churchill's pictures of the tremendous military and political results that would follow the successful naval breach of the Dardanelles, and quickly put out of his mind the French Intelligence report. In any case, he was under the impression that Churchill had the unanimous backing of the British naval and civil authorities.

All decisions regarding the Dardanelles–Gallipoli enterprise were reached without a French voice in strategy and tactics. They were mostly kept informed, but all plans were presented as finished, not as the basis for discussion and possible amendment. Vice-Admiral Aubert, Chief of the French Naval Staff, saw the weaknesses of Carden's plan, and made the sharp point that the British scheme had a beginning but that no end could be foreseen. Aubert, the first naval expert to express misgivings, might have pointed to more weaknesses than this, but did not. For instance, Carden assumed that his task was merely to destroy the forts. He suggested no means of dealing with mobile howitzers, and apparently did not consider it likely that the Turks would rebuild their forts and replace their guns.

Augagneur, now dominated by Churchill, did not show Aubert's report to his cabinet colleagues, and wrote to Churchill on 9 February: 'The provisions . . . appear to me to have been conceived with prudence and foresight. . .' Having employed an expert, Augagneur was now ignoring him.

Whatever Augagneur's opinion, there was some doubt in the mind of the French President, Raymond Poincaré, who wrote at the time:

> The thing is going to be thoroughly done, but there is considerable risk and no great certainty of success. However, as there is to be no announcement, if the attack does not come off it can be said out loud that there was no question of forcing the Dardanelles and that the only object was bombardment of the forts.

Churchill's own experts, Admiral Oliver, Chief of Naval Staff, and Captain Richmond, Assistant Director of Operations, advised Churchill to send the entire Royal Naval Division – sailors turned infantry – to support the fleet. Confident of a naval victory, Churchill merely sent enough marines to land and complete the destruction of the guns at the Narrows.

The naval attack began with bombardment of the outer forts on 19 February. Bad weather held up the operation until the 25th, when the forts were outranged and the Turks withdrew. The second phase, destruction of the intermediate defences, was more difficult because the forts were inside the mouth of the Straits. Perhaps the most significant act was to land a party of marines on the tip of the peninsula; without hindrance, they destroyed the guns in the abandoned outer forts. At this exact spot two months later, thousands of British soldiers fell dead or wounded.

The Straits, which could have been so easily passed in August and even as late as November 1914, were a different proposition by February 1915. Under German direction, the defensive system had improved dramatically. The minefields had been laid with care and forethought and were the principal defence; the main role of the guns was to protect the minefields. The British and French battleships could not even get close to the Narrows, let alone steam through them, until the mines were swept. The vicious circle was that the minesweepers could not get rid of the mines until the guns were put out of action. The Turks by themselves could never have evolved such an efficient system of defence, but in Whitehall the planners persisted in thinking that they were dealing only with Turks. The destruction of the outer defences was given much publicity, but it meant little, for the twenty-four heavy Turkish mobile howitzers brought in as support artillery could not be located. The astute Germans planted dummy batteries, which emitted black smoke to draw the warships' fire.

Reconnaissance was an acute problem. A merchant ship was converted into a seaplane carrier, but the planes were unreliable, and their gallant crews were so inexperienced they could tell Carden little about the Turkish defences. The fleet bombarded the inner forts on three other days, but with little effect. Naval officers were becoming frustrated and confused, but on 2 March Carden reported to Admiralty that he hoped to be in the Marmara in about a fortnight. Only Kitchener and Lloyd George did not share the general elation about this forecast. The previous day the Greeks, scenting an Allied victory, proposed to land three Greek divisions on the Gallipoli peninsula – only to be told by Russia that in no circumstances would it allow Greek forces to participate in the Allied attack on Constantinople.

This stupidly suicidal attitude drove Churchill to desperation and he wrote to Grey:

. . . You must be bold and violent. You have a right to be. Our fleet is forcing the Dardanelles . . . yet we seek nothing here but victory of the common cause. Tell the Russians we will meet them in a generous spirit about Constantinople. But no impediment must be placed in the way of Greek co-operation. . . . I am so afraid of your losing Greece and yet playing all the future into Russian hands. If Russia prevents Greece helping I will do my utmost to oppose her having Constantinople. She is a broken power but for our aid. . . .

But the Russians preferred their own destruction to the idea of allowing the Greeks any territorial rewards. With this diplomatic failure, the Venizelos government was thrown out of power and an openly pro-German government took over, just as Churchill had predicted that it would. For his part Grey, having justified earlier inactivity on the grounds of antagonizing the Turks, now rationalized lack of resolution on the grounds of not antagonizing the Russians.

On 5 March, HMS *Queen Elizabeth* took up station off Gabe Tepe and fired its 15-inch shells over the peninsula's spine at the Narrows forts. This indirect fire from such great guns demoralized the Turks, who could not reply to it at such a range – 14,000 yards. But the hapless British seaplanes and their crews were again unable to spot, so Carden was unaware of his one touch of success. The Germans rushed a battery to Gabe Tepe overnight, and when *Queen Elizabeth* arrived next morning she was shelled and had to move so far out to sea that her gunnery deteriorated.

By 11 March, the fleet was still making no progress – and Turkish morale was high. Conversely, the morale of the minesweepers' crews was depressed. Manned by civilian seamen, under a naval officer with no experience of minesweeping, the minesweepers were only converted fishing trawlers. Their task was desperately difficult and they faced dangers which those who maligned them could not comprehend. The current was strong, the trawlers were exposed by strong sunlight during the day and by searchlight at night, and they were under the fire of more than seventy guns at close range. They swept in pairs, hooking the mines with a wire linking the sweepers. Once on the minefield the trawlers might easily be blown up, since their hulls were deeper than the mines. After repeated attempts the minesweeping flotilla reached a major minefield, but when one blew up on a mine the others retreated. The crews had lost their nerve completely and the following night, when enemy shells splashed near them, they ran.

Commodore Roger Keyes, Carden's dynamic Chief-of-Staff and a man of the Churchill style, took over the minesweepers and manned them largely with naval volunteers. On the night of 13 March, he sent six trawlers with the cruiser HMS *Amethyst* as escort to clear the Kephez Bay minefield. Within minutes four little ships were out of action from shellfire, while HMS *Amethyst* was also hit and for a time was useless.

Churchill was anxious and impatient, as his numerous telegrams showed. Under great strain, Carden decided that on 17 March he would send in the fleet and by sheer weight pound the enemy guns out of existence, after which he could deal with the mines at will. Then he collapsed from exhaustion and anxiety. His successor, Vice-Admiral J.M. de Robeck, after assuring Churchill of his support for Carden's plans, made the great attack on 18 March. In a tremendous spectacle of naval might, eighteen battleships and an armada of cruisers and destroyers squeezed themselves into the mouth of the Straits, and did what generations of naval officers knew they must never do – brought themselves under close-range fire of shore batteries.

The ships' own gunfire was heavy, and grew even more intense as one line of ships after another steamed within range and opened fire on the forts. The battle began at 11.30 a.m.; an hour later a shell damaged the French *Gaulois* below the waterline and she had to be beached. Then HMS *Inflexible* was forced to retire for a few hours to put out fires and repair damage. *Lord Nelson*, *Agamemnon*, *Charlemagne* and *Albion* were hit, but carried on. Ashore, the Turkish batteries had suffered some direct hits; others were buried by debris, and communications were non-existent.

Then the French *Bouvet* blew up with a great explosion and sank in less than a minute with most of her crew; the Turks said that she struck a mine and was then hit by a shell. The minesweepers, though urged on under cover of the naval bombardment, ran into a rain of shells dropping from howitzers that warships could not locate; they fled in disorder. *Inflexible* struck a mine and took on a heavy list; *Irresistible* was also in a bad way from hull damage, and *Suffren* was hit and damaged. *Ocean* suffered an internal explosion and sank several hours later. The anxious de Robeck called off the battle. The British and French had not even reached the Narrows, and had lost three battleships sunk and three crippled, and 700 men. The Turks' setback was that they had fired most of their ammunition.

On his flagship *Queen Elizabeth*, on 22 March, de Robeck told the Army Commander, General Sir Ian Hamilton, and General Sir William Birdwood – according to these two officers – that he could not take the fleet through the Dardanelles without the help of the troops. He cabled the Admiralty that it would be better to undertake a combined military and naval attack about the middle of April. Just what these combined operations were supposed to be was so vague that the Naval Commander and the Army Commander had different conceptions. De Robeck's decision, never clarified to Hamilton, was that until the Army occupied the peninsula, his ships would not again venture into the Straits. Hamilton's belief, never clarified to de Robeck, was that his army would assist the Navy in another assault. Neither commander gave a thought to integrating their plans; by using the term 'combined operations' they had done all that was necessary.

Part of Hamilton's understanding was that the Navy would harass the Turks until the Army was ready; and de Robeck promised a vigorous offensive against the forts and the minefields and sustained intense reconaissance. The Navy did nothing for three weeks.

Back in London, on 23 March, Churchill, after a heated meeting with the Admiralty War Staff Group, reported the unhappy end of the naval operations to the Cabinet. The unruffled Kitchener told the Cabinet that the Army would not carry through the capture of the peninsula. The Prime Minister, with an almost childlike faith in Kitchener, was content to leave the matter there. The Cabinet discussed the campaign eleven times in the next few months, but Hamilton was given no indication of Government policy, priorities or plans. The Cabinet members, in effect, had conversations about Gallipoli; direction and management could be left to the War Council. But that did not meet again until 19 May, after a lapse of two months. The only man worried about this and the lack of planning was Colonel Hankey.

Meanwhile the Turks and Germans, still deaf from the vast explosions which had shaken them, watched the sea apprehensively for a renewal of the attack. Most gun positions were quickly restored, but the ammunition was desperately scarce and everything hinged on how long the howitzers could keep the trawlers away from the mines. The enemy officers had not been impressed by the minesweepers' performance, so they reasoned that the British and French would be back with a more definite minesweeping plan. When they did not come back, the Turks' attitude changed from fear to wonder and then to excitement and triumph; they had stopped the two largest and most renowned fleets in the world – and Christian fleets at that.

Ambassador Morgenthau, from his privileged position of

observation, saw 'the hesitating and fearful Ottoman' now becoming 'an upstanding almost dashing figure, proud and asserting . . . and contemptuous of his Christian foes.' In this mood the Turks embarked on a savage massacre of the Christian Armenians – a sad by-product of the Allied naval defeat.

The bombardments of 19–25 February and of 18 March destroyed all hopes of surprise, and were directly responsible for strengthening the enemy's defences and increasing his power to resist a military landing. The Germans and Turks knew that the next Allied step must be a military landing. The public reviews of British troops in Cairo and Alexandria, and spies' reports of the development of a base on the island of Lemnos, off the Gallipoli coast, were evidence of that. In any case, Liman von Sanders, putting himself in Allied shoes, knew that he would now go for a landing. His only worry was whether time was on his side.

4

Planning for Defeat

Much more than time was on the side of the Turks and Germans. There was also British incompetence. The British had considered neither tactics nor logistics and, until 12 March, were without a commander for the contemplated field force. The choice of Ian Hamilton, the manner of his appointment and the personality of the man, are decisive factors in the Gallipoli defeat.

The cultured, wealthy and gifted Hamilton was sixty-two, and had more active service on his record than any other senior serving officer in the British Army. He had bled for his country in India, South Africa and the Sudan, and he was popular with his men. In 1914 he was Commander of Central Force in Britain, but he had not been to France – the enmity of Sir John French and others had seen to that. Still, his command was important and reasonably satisfying for an officer nearing retirement.

For the period Hamilton was an unusual general. He had tastes and interests outside the Army, he could write lucidly and he was at home with politicians – Churchill was a close friend. All this did not endear him to his brother generals, most of whom distrusted a 'brainy' officer. His publications, *A Staff Officer's Scrap Book* and *The Fighting of the Future*, as well as a report he had written on compulsory service, were regarded as controversial – and he was, therefore, in many eyes a dangerous man to know.

But Hamilton was too personally charming, too balanced and too lacking in ruthlessness to be dangerous. These qualities meant, almost automatically, that he was not the man for a high and independent command abroad. That he and Kitchener encountered each other frequently in London may have had something to do with his selection. Another reason may well have been that Kitchener knew he was offering Hamilton nothing less than his last chance to win a campaign by himself, and perhaps to retire a field-marshal. Many another fighting general would have demanded more than Hamilton was satisfied to accept when Kitchener summoned him to his office on 12 March. In describing the occasion, Hamilton may be telling us even more than he knew:

Opening the door I bade him good morning and walked up to his desk, where he went on writing like a graven image. After a moment he looked up and said in a matter-of-fact tone, 'We are sending a military force to support the fleet now at the Dardanelles and you are to have command.'

At that moment K wished me to bow, leave the room and make a start as I did some thirteen years ago. . . . But the conditions were no longer the same. In those old Pretoria days I had known the Transvaal by heart, the number, the value and disposition of the British forces, the characters of the Boer leaders, the nature of the country. But my knowledge of the Dardanelles was nil, of the Turk nil, of the strength of my own forces next to nil.

. . . K, after his one tremendous remark, went on writing. At last he looked up again with, 'Well?'

'We have run this sort of thing before, Lord K,' I said, 'and you know without saying that I will do my best – but I must ask you some questions.'

K frowned, shrugged his shoulders; I thought he was going to be impatient, but although he gave me curt answers at first he slowly broadened out until no one else could get a word in edgeways.

Hamilton was not the only general startled by his appointment. Wolfe Murray, Chief of the Imperial General Staff, and Archibald Murray, Inspector of Home Forces, came into Kitchener's office – and heard the news for the first time. Hamilton also met Major-Geneneral Walter Braithwaite, arbitrarily appointed his Chief-of-Staff. Braithwaite volunteered the opinion that it was vital for Hamilton's army to have a better air service than the Turks; whatever else the force got or did not get, could Hamilton please have a squadron of modern aircraft, with experienced pilots and observers. Hamilton describes Kitchener's reaction: 'K turned on him with flashing spectacles and rent him with the words, "Not one!"'

Major-General C.E. Callwell, Director of Military Operations, gave Hamilton a cursory briefing and commented that the Greeks, who knew the problems, reckoned that 150,000 men would be necessary. Kitchener testily disputed this. 'Half that number will do you handsomely – the Turks are busy elsewhere. I hope you will not have to land at all; if you do have to land, why then the powerful fleet at your back will be the prime factor in your choice of time and place.'

With one British submarine in the Sea of Marmara, the Dardanelles defences would collapse, Kitchener assured Hamilton. Hamilton was not well informed enough at the time to point out that the B-11 had blown up a Turkish battleship without causing a military collapse. Kitchener went on: 'Supposing one submarine pops up opposite the town of Gallipoli and waves a Union Jack three times, the whole Turkish garrison on the peninsula will take to their heels and make a bee line for Bulair.'

Nothing more clearly indicates Kitchener's contempt for

the Turkish enemy. But he had not always held the Turks in such low regard; in 1877, after seeing them in action against the Russians, he described the Turkish soldier as 'always ready to fight and never conquered by anything except overwhelming numbers'.

Hamilton asked for a Chief-of-Staff of his own choosing, was curtly refused and had to resign himself to Braithwaite, a man with a knack of antagonizing people and a conviction that the staff always knew best. Nevertheless, he was an able officer and set about finding staff for Hamilton in the forty-eight hours at his disposal. He personally went to Military Intelligence to get whatever background he could on Gallipoli, the Dardanelles and the Turks. He was given two small tourist guidebooks on western Turkey, an out-of-date map not intended for military use – it was soon found to be inaccurate – and a 1905 textbook on the Turkish Army. Intelligence had no information about weather in the Aegean, and nobody gave a thought to ocean currents.

So inadequate was the Intelligence briefing that not until after the landings did anybody on the British side – except the unconsulted Cunliffe-Owen – know that the southern end of the peninsula was not an even, gentle slope, but deeply cut with many watercourses and scarred by erosion. Nobody Braithwaite met at the War Office could tell him how many enemy troops were on the peninsula, or the names of the Turkish or German commanders.

Hamilton set off at once for the Mediterranean, equipped with little more than his enthusiasm – which blinded him to the difficulties and magnitude of the task. Even his scratch staff, some of whom did not know how to put on their uniforms, amused rather than worried him – yet only one had seen active service in the war. Only a general in the twilight of his career would have gone off with so much boyish ardour to fight an unknown foe in an unknown place with an unknown army.

He had only two known assets; General Sir William Birdwood, who had expected to be given command of the Gallipoli force, and the tested and experienced 29th Division, though it was only on loan until Hamilton had established himself on Gallipoli.

Having personally witnessed the defeat of the fleet, Hamilton went to Alexandria in his efforts to come to grips with the complexities of his command. He had no firm control of anything because his army was scattered over much of the Mediterranean in a state of confusion and exasperation. Battalion commanders could not even trace some of their companies; guns were on one ship and their shells on another, and nobody knew where the fuses might be. Wagons were separated from horses. Some ships' captains had been given such poorly phrased orders that they did not know which port was their destination.

Many put in at Mudros, which Rear-Admiral R.E. Wemyss was struggling to convert into the expedition's base. To do this he had to build jetties, anchor pontoons, make roads and erect buildings, mostly with whatever materials he could scrape together in Egypt.

The Royal Naval Division, now an army formation put together with contingents of men culled from ships and shore establishments, was unfortunate enough to be dumped at Mudros for weeks before Wemyss could get them off to Cairo. The division's equipment included armoured cars and motor cars, none of which could possibly be used on Gallipoli.

Security was non-existent, especially in Egypt, where the Press made easy the job of Turkish spies by announcing the arrival of each new unit. Editorials and articles analysed the forthcoming campaign, while small boats trading in the Aegean, many of them calling regularly at Lemnos, passed on news in Turkey about the growing preparations for invasion.

Hamilton's task was further complicated by the Commander-in-Chief Egypt, General Sir John Maxwell, who did not approve of the expedition, mainly because he feared it would rob him of troops. Kitchener sent Maxwell a telegram ordering him to supply Hamilton with any troops that could be spared, and certainly with particular officers and men Hamilton might need. He was told to show Hamilton the telegram, but did not do so. Instead, he wrote to Kitchener painting a black picture of the danger he was facing from Turks in Sinai. He gave the false impression then and later that he had just enough men to cope with this desert menace. Maxwell at no time helped Hamilton, and gave up troops only when Kitchener gave him a direct order about a particular unit. One of the 'hate-Hamilton' school of generals, Maxwell considered that Hamilton was being too generously treated. He did his best to counterbalance the situation by withholding co-operation; for instance, when asked to provide a suitable headquarters building for Hamilton's staff in Alexandria, he allotted a former brothel without light, water or drainage. Somehow, Maxwell, could not find the necessary engineers and signallers to make the place serviceable, so Hamilton's officers had to endure the hideous place.

Through much hard work and enthusiasm the army was put together in two weeks. Units were reassembled, guns and shells brought together, trench equipment collected, supply problems rectified. Enterprising and hard-pressed officers scoured the Middle East to find horses, mules and stores, though serious defects remained – the army had few grenades, for example.

Hamilton at last had an organized body of men – infinitely better men than he yet knew, especially the Australians and New Zealanders. Not yet fully trained, the colonials had the reputation of being undisciplined and hard to lead, so they were to be given the easiest part of the landing.

One grave organizational fault remained: GHQ officers, working with Hamilton and having coped with the initial problems, were in no mood to pass over their assumed tasks to the specialist administrative staff who had come out from England. Such vital officers as the Director of Medical Services, the Quartermaster-General and the Adjutant-General were left behind in Cairo when GHQ moved to Imbros, slighted at best and ignored at worst. How Hamilton proposed to fight a campaign without a Quartermaster-General by his side is not clear. This senior officer and his trained staff were needed to ensure a continuous supply of water, food, ammunition and the thousand other things needed by an army on active service. One reason for Hamilton's lack of interest in the logistical officers is that he disliked a large staff, preferring to handle everything through just a few people. Also, he did not expect the campaign to take so long as to need vast quantities of supplies. The fleet was expected to reach the Sea of Marmara within a few days of the army landing, and nobody gave any thought to a long campaign.

The subject of likely casualties came up quite late in the preparations, so the losses incurred at the battle of Mons at the end of 1914 was taken as a basis. There, the two divisions (or 20,000 men) engaged had suffered a seven and a half per cent loss in killed, wounded and missing. Hamilton's staff increased their likely losses for the first divisions ashore to ten per cent in wounded alone. Yet they provided only two hospital ships with a total capacity of 700 for taking the wounded to hospital in Cairo, Alexandria and Malta.

The Director of Medical Services, Surgeon-General W.G. Birrell, had to go to extreme lengths to find out what plans had been made to handle the wounded. This took him several days – and what he found out worried him desperately. Unable to talk to anybody at GHQ, Birrell wrote a detailed report explaining why the arrangements were wholly inadequate. By then it was too late to make any major changes. At last, arriving at Mudros, he ordered more ships, which did not arrive until after the landing had begun.

Co-operation, that most vital factor in combined

operations, was always woefully lacking, and because of this imaginative ideas came to nothing. A British engineer officer, Colonel Joly de Lotbinière, designed eight floating piers for use in the landings, four at Helles and four at Anzac. He went to much trouble to have them built in Egypt, and arranged for the Navy to tow them to Gallipoli. As ballast, each pier would carry 4,000 sealed tins of water. Thus the colonel's plan gave the armies a good landing stage within a few hours of landing, and reduced the difficulty of getting adequate fresh water to the thirsty troops. The naval officers who had promised that the piers would reach the peninsula gave the transport job to merchant-ship captains; seven of them abandoned their tows in the Mediterranean, the other reached Mudros and was taken no farther.

From the little liaison between the British and French over the Gallipoli campaign, they might not have been fighting as allies. Yet the French had contributed a large part of the fleet, and a French division was to take part in the operation. Kitchener had not wanted French soldiers to be involved. 'I have just seen Grey,' he wrote to Churchill on February 20, 'and hope that we shall not be saddled with a French contingent.' Marshal Joffre, the French Commander-in-Chief, felt the same; he was profoundly opposed to the whole Dardanelles operation, and needed all the troops he could find for the slaughters on the Western Front. But political expediency won the day – the French feared that the absence of French troops would enable the British to establish themselves in the Levant, which the French considered their territory.

Millerand selected a commander for the French corps more or less as Kitchener had selected Hamilton – apparently on the basis that no other general was available or would want the command. Yet his choice, General Albert d'Amade, had already shown that he was unfitted for a difficult role. As Commander of the Allied line in France between Dunkirk and the British Army, he had lost his nerve and without orders withdrawn his force. The withdrawal became a retreat and then almost a rout, and enormous confusion followed. Joffre, on the grounds that d'Amade had been guilty of gross dereliction of duty, relieved him of his command. This was the officer subsequently placed in command of 400 officers and 18,000 men to fight at the Dardanelles. More than this, the French War Office wanted him to be in overall command of land operations.

When he left for Bizerte, where his division was assembling, d'Amade had practically no information and only a vague outline of his responsibilities. On March 8 he was moved to write to Birdwood (Hamilton had not then been appointed), 'begging to be informed' about the plan of operations. Birdwood was unhelpful:

> There is up to now no order from Admiral Carden and the only instructions that I have received are to stand ready to leave when told to do so; neither one of us can do anything for the moment – I might receive my instructions from Lord Kitchener when all the plans are finished.

Despite his lack of information, d'Amade made himself important by consenting to an interview with an Alexandrian newspaper. He kept back nothing, presenting the enemy with a virtual blueprint for a landing. His staff had prepared detailed plans for a landing in the Bay of Adramyti, to be followed by an advance into Asia. He wanted to leave Gallipoli entirely alone, partly because his own Intelligence had reported that a force prepared to move fast could head for Constantinople on the Asian side, take or neutralize enemy defences from the rear and capture the capital.

The French general had a capable staff, and they got their Chief and the first convoy away from Bizerte on March 10. At Mudros, the frustrated d'Amade managed to get a message to Carden asking if he had any plans for the French division. Carden replied that this was Hamilton's decision, and soon after Wemyss told d'Amade that Hamilton had been appointed to command the Allied army. Up to this point d'Amade had been under the impression – one fostered by his superiors in Paris – that he was to lead the combined force. His plans for a landing were now useless.

Hamilton, on seeing the peninsula for the first time – from the deck of a ship – began to understand that the task facing him was even more difficult than he had anticipated. He wrote to Kitchener, 'Gallipoli looks a much tougher nut to crack than it did over the map in your office.' It is not difficult to detect a note of mild reproach.

Hamilton had 75,000 men, and his object was to open a path for the fleet through the Narrows. In theory, the landings open to him to achieve this object were these:

The Asiatic Coast near Besika Bay. Here movement would be easy and the British could threaten the Turkish rear. The landing would be relatively simple because the Turks had few heights from which to threaten the invaders.

One well-informed officer who wanted the landing to be at Besika Bay was Lieutenant-Colonel Maucorps, Chief of the French Military Mission in Egypt and a former military attaché in Constantinople. Knowing the Dardanelles and the real fighting qualities of the Turks, he submitted a well-reasoned report to both the English and French authorities. The fleet had practically no chance of getting through, he wrote, and even if the fighting ships successfully ran the gauntlet the troop transports could come under fire from concealed batteries. The best line of attack was through Besika Bay. Maucorps was supported in this by the Chief of the General Staff in Paris, General Graziani.

High ground on the coast would provide excellent viewing for artillery observation officers so that the guns could support the infantry advancing across the plain. The area had rivers and marshes, but they were insignificant obstacles from

April onwards, and the roads in this part of Turkey were good. Most vital of all, the more important defences were on the Asiatic side, and could readily be taken from the rear by infantry. Certainly the army would have to cover a greater distance, but as it moved it could spread. It would be vulnerable to a flank attack from Anatolia, but if the defences were quickly overrun the most significant part of the battle would be over, and the troops could then be easily supplied by sea.

The Peninsula neck in the Gulf of Saros. At Bulair the peninsula is a mere three and a half miles across and the terrain is not difficult. It was the most obvious place to attack, and a landing here would cut off the defenders of the peninsula from Thrace and Constantinople. But the capture of a corridor could result in having two fronts on which to fight, a disadvantage. Hamilton decided against a landing here because the beaches near Bulair appeared to be strongly defended, and because even if he got ashore in force and enlarged his territory, he could not directly threaten the Narrows forts from such a distance.

Gaba Tepe. At this point the width of the peninsula is still only six miles and a low valley runs right across to Maidos at the Narrows. It would provide an excellent line of approach if the heights on either side could be held. The beaches, though small, were considered adequate.

Cape Helles. From a landing on the tiny beaches at the southern tip the enemy might be rolled up systematically and steadily, while his positions on the gradual ascent to the heights of Achi Baba could be swept by the guns of the fleet.

Suvla Bay. Here a long, crescent shaped and gently sloping beach was available for a landing and a push south-east. It was overlooked by hills near Gaba Tepe and behind it was a salt lake, dry in summer but containing water when Hamilton saw it in April.

While Hamilton had these five options in theory, in combination or with subsidiary operations, in practice he was restricted to the peninsula. Kitchener had told him not to attack on the Asiatic side; he gave no reasons for this and Hamilton apparently asked for none. In fact, it was potentially the best approach because it was indirect and it would outflank the peninsula. Neither Kitchener nor Hamilton, in their South African, Sudanese and Indian service, had experience of the strategy of indirect approach. In all their previous theatres of war the practice had been to locate the enemy and attack him, generally head on. This is what had been happening, too, on the Western Front in 1914 and 1915, without any advantage being gained.

Hamilton decided on a double blow in the southern half of the peninsula, plus three feint attacks. The 29th Division would land on the four beaches at the toe of Gallipoli, and the Australians and New Zealanders would go ashore near Gaba Tepe. The Royal Naval Division would make a feint attack near Bulair, a French regiment would land at Kum Kale, on the Asiatic side, to provide a distraction for the Turks, and another French force would take a landing in Besika Bay. It was the best Hamilton thought he could do.

Not long before the attack began Hamilton added two more landings – at Y Beach on the Aegean coast, and S Beach at the northern end of Morto Bay. Three battalions in all were involved, and would come under the command of the GOC 29th Division, Major-General Sir A.G. Hunter-Weston.

All the time Hamilton was looking over *his* shoulder at Kitchener, and was conscious of Kitchener looking over his shoulder. The degree of his fear of his chief can be guaged from a comment he made in his diary on 25 March, about his request for a brigade of Gurkhas. 'Really, it is like going up to a tiger and asking for a small slice of venison.' Hamilton's trepidation was based on experience. In South Africa he had seen Kitchener respond to an officer's appeal for reinforcements by taking half his troops away from him.

On the day (25 March) that Hamilton was asking for

Gurkhas, Enver, in Istanbul, decided at last to agree to a German request for a separate army for the defence of the Dardanelles. Von Sanders, asked to command this force, told his aide, Hans Kannengiesser, that everything depended on the British leaving him alone for eight days. The English gave him a clear four weeks, which enabled him to bring the 3rd Division from Constantinople. He then had six divisions, or 84,000 men, on the peninsula – six times the army strength present before the naval attack began.

He placed two divisions near Besika Bay, two near Bulair, and one in the south under Colonel Mustapha Kemal. The other was stationed near the waist as a general reserve. While the troops were moving into their positions, von Sanders gave orders for new roads to be made and the old ones improved. Much, he believed, would depend on mobility.

Without knowing it – though better field Intelligence might have told him – Hamilton planned to strike where the Turkish troops were fewest. In this sense von Sanders' dispositions justify Hamilton's plan.

Since total surprise was impossible, the attackers sought oblique forms of surprise that might provide a tactical advantage. The most dramatic was suggested by Commander E. Unwin, who suggested that a collier packed with troops could be run ashore at V Beach, Cape Helles; the soldiers would then run out from openings cut in the sides. In this way a large number of men could be put ashore in a short time. The notion of a wooden seahorse was poetically appropriate, since Troy was only a few miles from Helles across the Straits in Asiatic Turkey. The *River Clyde* was hurriedly prepared for the part.

Hamilton had decided on the overall plan, and his staff on a mass of trivial details, but Hamilton did not impose his will on the landings to be made by his subordinates. Birdwood planned to land at dawn in the hope that he would get his first Australian and New Zealand units ashore before the Turks spotted them, or at least before they could aim accurately. Hunter-Weston preferred a daylight landing to obviate the risk of confusion. In allowing his subordinate generals great latitude, Hamilton was planning for failure rather than success.

He believed that his multi-pronged attacks and fake attacks would keep von Sanders guessing long enough to allow his own troops to fight and win the decisive battles within forty-eight hours. Such a conception called for incisive execution, but Hamilton did not stress urgency to Hunter-Weston. While urging him to get his division ashore, he did not insist that his battalions must move rapidly inland – yet this was the most vital factor of all. And no commander was provided with contingency plans should the advance be held up.

Back in London Colonel Hankey was still worried. Unable to get Churchill to see any difficulties, two days before the great naval attack on the Narrows Hankey had sent a professional and perceptive note to the Prime Minister which said, in part:

> It must be remembered that combined operations require more careful preparation than any other class of military enterprise. All through our history such attacks have failed when the preparations have been inadequate and the successes are in nearly every case due to the most careful preparation beforehand. . . . It must be remembered also that one of the greatest advantages to be obtained from this class of operation has been lost – surprise. . . . The military enterprise, therefore, will be of a most formidable nature. It is suggested that the War Council ought to cross-examine the naval and military authorities on the extent of the preparations.

Hankey listed ten points to be clarified, and concluded with a warning: *Unless details such as these are duly thought out before the landing takes place it is conceivable that a serious disaster will occur.*

Asquith raised only one of Hankey's points with Kitchener: Had a scheme for a possible disembarkation been worked out? Kitchener replied that there was inadequate information at home; the general and admiral on the spot would plan any disembarkation. He gave no instruction for a scheme to be worked out. In fact, he had already told Hamilton in writing that 'having entered on the task of forcing the Dardanelles there can be no idea of abandoning the enterprise'.

The Prime Minister took Hankey's worried memorandum no further; Field-Marshal Lord Kitchener obviously knew more about war in general, and this operation in particular, than a mere lieutenant-colonel.

At the end of March, on a day when Hamilton was writing to Kitchener to beg for more guns and shells, Fisher came out vehemently against the Dardanelles as an area of combat. Having had time to reconsider his earlier enthusiasm for the project, he now said that whether or not the British and French won the battle for the Dardanelles was inconsequential. No longer under Churchill's spell, he wrote to the younger man on 5 April, 'You are simply eaten up with the Dardanelles and cannot think of anything else. Damn the Dardanelles! They will be our grave!'

This prophecy did not reach Hamilton. On 21 April he issued a general address and ordered that it be read to all troops.

SOLDIERS OF FRANCE AND OF THE KING

Before us lies an adventure unprecedented in modern war. Together with our comrades of the fleet we are about to force a landing upon an open beach in face of positions which have been vaunted by our enemies as impregnable.

The landing will be made good, by the help of God and the Navy; the positions will be stormed, and the war brought one step nearer to a glorious close.

'Remember,' said Lord Kitchener, when bidding adieu to your Commander, 'Remember, once you set foot upon the Gallipoli Peninsula you must fight the thing through to a finish.'

It sounded almost like an exhortation from God.

Birdwood, as befitted a corps commander in closer touch with the troops, was more pragmatic in his special order to the Anzacs.

Officers and men – In conjunction with the Navy we are about to undertake one of the most difficult tasks any soldier can be called upon to perform, and a problem which has puzzled many soldiers for years past. That we will succeed I have no doubt, simply because I know your full determination to do so. . . . Before we start there are one or two points which I must impress on you, and I most earnestly beg every single man to listen attentively and take these to heart.

We are going to have a real hard and rough time of it until . . . we have turned the enemy out of our first objective. Hard, rough times none of us mind but to get through them successfully we must keep before us the following facts: [Here Birdwood urged discipline with food, water and ammunition, and concluded]:

Remember:

Concealment wherever possible

Covering fire always

Control of fire and control of your men

Communications never to be neglected.

Hunter-Weston was much more blunt than Birdwood, and in his special orders to the 29th Division he told his men to expect 'heavy losses by bullets, by shells, by mines and by downing'.

Other special orders were in the heroic mould, like that of

Brigadier-General S.W. Hare to his 86th Infantry Brigade of the 29th Division.

Fusiliers,

Our brigade is to have the honour to be the first to land and to cover the disembarkation of the rest of the Division. Our task will be no easy one. Let us carry it through in a way worthy of the traditions of the distinguished regiments of which the Fusilier Brigade is composed; in such a way that the men of Albuhera and Minden, of Delhi and Lucknow may hail us as their equals in valour and military achievement, and that future historians may say of us as Napier said of the Fusilier Brigade at Albuhera, 'Nothing could stop this astonishing infantry.'

While the British generals were writing their special orders, von Sanders was making final inspections of the Turkish defences. On 24 April, he announced that he was pleased enough with them. He was now ready for the British.

They arrived the very next morning.

5

'Thou'st Given Me
a Bloody Job'

Liman von Sanders' headquarters was on the isthmus, near
Bulair, and here too he kept the III Corps, since he
considered the neck the most likely point of British attack.
From 6 a.m. onwards on 25 April, urgent messages streamed
into HQ, reporting that several landings had begun and that
others were imminent.

According to these reports, many of them written in fear
and panic, British warships and transports were disembarking
troops near Gaba Tepe in an obvious move to strike overland
to Maidos. These invaders already held the cliffs at Ari Burnu
(Anzac). In the south, British units were storming ashore at
places near Sedd-el-Bahr, while warships were heavily shelling
the whole Helles end of the peninsula. From Kum Kale, the
Turkish 3rd Division reported that warships had bombarded
its positions and its men were facing combat with French
troops. Farther south, a large fleet was entering Besika Bay
'and would land in strength'. Yet other messages came from
posts on the Gulf of Saros, close to where von Sanders had
his HQ – warships were pounding the Bulair lines and a
dozen transports were approaching the shore.

Von Sanders knew that not all of these attacks could be

genuine – the British did not have enough troops for so many thrusts – but he hesitated to take troops away from the Bulair neck. If anything, he would have to move reinforcements towards this region or risk, tactically speaking, having his throat cut. Posting himself on the heights of Bulair, the German general resisted all pleas for help until the position became clearer. By the evening of the 25th he was confident enough of the safety of Bulair to despatch five battalions from there to reinforce the areas where landings had taken place.

By then history had been made, especially by the Australians and New Zealanders, who were going into action for the first time in the war. They did not know quite what to expect, but they were keen and confident and their officers anticipated success. The CO of the 4th Battalion, Lieutenant-Colonel Onslow Thompson, paraded his men on their ship on the eve of battle and, as recorded by Sergeant-Major G. Scott, 'told us in a gentlemanly and fatherly manner to behave like gentlemen and uphold the good name of Australia when we reached Constantinople.'

Their first step towards this distant goal was taken at 1.30 a.m., when the 1,500 soldiers of the Australian 1st Division, each laden with eighty-eight pounds of equipment and ammunition, climbed down the sides of the battleships into the waiting open boats. They had not slept, but they were buoyed up with a strangely silent tension as they took their places in the crowded boats. Every man was aware that these boats were prime targets if the Turks were alert, though as it happened many of the Turks had been on night exercises and were asleep from weariness.

The big ships dropped their tows two and a half miles out, and the soldiers were then in the hands of the young midshipmen and the sailors who were to get them to the enemy shore. Twelve steam pinnaces each towed four boats, and the noise the pinnaces made as they drew closer and closer to the shore should have roused the Turks in their trenches on the hills, which to the Australians seemed frighteningly ominous and high in the gloom. First dawn would break at 4.05 a.m., and the sun would rise at 5.15.

At 4.25 the pinnaces cast off the open boats about fifty yards from the beach, and the sailors manning them dug in their oars. At that moment a flare went up and panicky, ill-aimed fire broke out from near Ari Burnu headland. With the natural light becoming clearer every minute the boats landed where they could, and the Turkish fire became more accurate.

Fifteen-year-old Midshipman Eric Bush, from HMS *Bacchante*, had some of his soldier passengers hit before they reached shore, but most reached the beach safely. With the troop-laden destroyers pressing close behind, Bush collected his boats and was distressed by the plight of the wounded men. 'Unfortunately there is nothing we can do to help them,' he wrote. 'One Australian is wounded in the wrist and is clutching his arm in a desperate endeavour to check the flow of blood. Another sits in the bottom of the boat with a bullet sticking out of his cheek. . . .'

There was no time to take the wounded out of the boats before fresh troops came clambering into them; some wounded men had to make several trips between ship and shore before anybody could attend to them.

The Australians had been repeatedly told that they must get off the beach at once, and this they did. But something had gone wrong and the boats had landed in the wrong place – too far north. Some soldiers were facing steep cliffs instead of the expected low sandbanks. It was a disastrous mistake. Had it not been made, the 4,000 Australians who disembarked before 5 a.m., and the 4,000 who followed them between 6 and 8 a.m., could have pushed back the Turkish outposts and established themselves on the vital Gun Ridge and dominating Chunuk Bair before the arrival of enemy reinforcements.

Great confusion occurred as men of various battalions became intermixed, but junior leadership was so competent that small groups of Australians made rapid progress up the tangle of ravines and cliffs. The ground was covered with thick green or blackish scrub, mostly prickly oak, which in some places was six feet high and difficult to penetrate.

Few casualties had occurred in the landing and by 6 a.m. the landing was already successful, a tribute as much to the skill of naval crews as to the soldiers' determination. The cliffs above Ari Burnu are steep and difficult, but panting and resolute Australians had taken the first ridge by 6 a.m. and an hour later some were at the Third Ridge. They outnumbered the Turks in the vicinity by five or six to one, though they were not to know this. Lieutenant N.M. Loutit, with two men, climbed Scrubby Knoll to see, only three miles away, the waters of the Narrows. The landing at Anzac seemed at that moment to justify Hamilton's hopes for it, although serious trouble had occurred on the extreme left, where the transport *Galeka* arrived with men of the 6th and 7th Australian battalions. About 600 yards off Ari Burnu the commander anchored, and waited for some time for tows to disembark the troops. When none arrived, and with shrapnel shells bursting above the crowded decks, six of the ships' own boats were used to ferry a company of the 7th ashore. The first four steered for what appeared to be the left flank of the troops already ashore; in fact, it was a Turkish post. The Turks held their fire until the boats were 200 yards away; then their fusilade killed or wounded more than a hundred of the men before they reached land. Only eighteen of the 140 men who left the *Galeka* rejoined their battalion that day.

Soon after the Australians reached the beach at Ari Burnu, a similar operation was taking the 29th Division towards its beaches on the Helles coast. The sea was calm, the air balmy and a beach mist softened the sharp edges of the promontory. The roar of the naval bombardment shattered this peace and demoralized the Turks, who in several places had no artillery and only a few machine-guns. At that moment fewer than

1,000 Turks held the Helles sector, and many watched the approaching armada of small boats in paralytic stupefaction.

At Y Beach on the west side of the peninsula, nearly 3,000 British troops (King's Own Scottish Borderers, a company of South Wales Borderers, the Plymouth Battalion of Royal Marines) landed without opposition, and by 6 a.m they were firmly established.

At X Beach the landing party of two companies of Royal Fusiliers, backed by the heavy guns of HMS *Implacable*, was atop the cliffs by 6.30 a.m. and had suffered few casualties. The men advanced nearly half a mile before being checked by enemy fire, but the way was now safely open for the main body to land on the beach.

At S Beach the other companies of South Wales Borderers went ashore and consolidated themselves at the tip of Morto Bay, where Hunter-Weston, from his HQ on HMS *Euryalus*, told them to dig in.

The situation at W Beach was starkly different. Here, about ninety Turks with a few machine-guns survived the naval bombardment, and though shocked they stayed at their posts in the trenches. W Beach was a death trap for the invaders. The Turks, under orders to hold their fire, saw the British troops – the Lancashire Fusiliers – being rowed ashore by sailors in a calm and ordered way. They were heading straight towards barbed wire, some of it under water, and as the boats touched bottom the Turks opened up at close range. It was a target that could not be missed. Men fell dead on the wire and others, agonizingly wounded, writhed on the sand. Some just sank into the bloodied water. The Turks, emboldened by lack of return fire, even stood to aim. Gradually the Lancashires fought their way forward in ones and twos. Brigadier-General Hare, having exhorted his men to do the impossible, set his own example. He found a safer landing under the cover of a bluff and personally directed his men there. The official history records that one Lancashire man said laughingly to his officer, 'Thou'st given me a bloody job,' as he went on pulling up the stakes of the wire entanglement though bleeding from seven different wounds.

Some Lancashires clawed their way to the higher ground to fire at the Turks from the flank, and gradually the resistance weakend – but not before 533 casualties had been suffered out of the 950 officers and men who had left the *Euryalus*. Still, tactically the victory lay with the British, for the Turks withdrew and a vital point, Hill 138, was ready for the taking. But now no senior leader was available to point the way: the gallant Hare was badly wounded and his successor lasted only a few minutes before he fell dead. The Lancashire men could do little more than pull themselves together and give what help they could to the wounded, many of whom were lying helpless under the weight of other wounded and dead on top of them. In the small area the carnage seemed immense to the next wave of troops from the ships. Some of the boats collided with floating bodies. Other dead men sat upright in the boats, their bodies kept in place by the crush of those still living.

An Army Service Corps officer, Major John Gillam, saw another wave of troops set off from the transport *Dongola*, and wrote in his diary at 8 a.m.:

> The Essex are disembarking now, going down the rope ladders with difficulty. One slips on stepping into a boat and twists his ankle. An onlooking Tommy is heard to remark, 'Somebody will get hurt over this job soon.' . . . Tug after tug takes these strings of white open boats towards land [W Beach, after being diverted from V Beach] with their overweighted khaki freight. Slowly they wind their way towards the green shore in front of us, winding in and out among transports, roaring battleships and angry destroyers, towards *the land of the Great Adventure*.* Never, surely, was

---

* My italics, Gillam's capitals.

Army and Navy so closely allied. I go below to get breakfast ... I feel ashamed to be there. ... The steward calmly hands the menu around, just as he might on a peaceful voyage. What a contrast! Two boiled eggs, coffee, toast and marmalade. Here we are sitting down to a good meal and men are fighting on the cliffs a few hundred yards away.

The V Beach landing was a simultaneous two-part operation. The *River Clyde*, with its 2,000 soldiers of the Munster Fusiliers and the Hampshire Regiment, was to ground itself under the battered Sedd-el-Bahr castle, while the Royal Dublin Fusiliers came ashore in ships' boats. This landing, with so many men landing at once, was the key to the success of the whole Helles plan. At 6.20 the ship nosed firmly but gently onto the shore. There was no sign of the enemy, though firing could be heard from W Beach. A small steamboat was to have put together a bridge of lighters from the ship to the beach, but when it was swept away by the current, Commander Unwin and Able Seaman W.C. Williams dived into the water, lashed some of the lighters together and held them in place. Then Unwin shouted the order for the landing to begin.

The sally-port doors swung open and the soldiers ran excitedly down the gangways – straight into concentrated Turkish small-arms fire. In seconds the gangways were blocked with dead and wounded men whose blood stained red the water around the ship. A few men reached the shore and found shelter under a ridge. About 1,000 stayed aboard *River Clyde*, where they were safe but impotent. From *River Clyde* the only real threat to the Turks were the machine-guns in the ship's bows, which prevented the Turks from coming down to annihilate the landing party.

In their open boats the Dublins too were caught by the intense fire, and the ghastly scenes at W Beach were repeated: many men died in the cutters or drowned when the smashed boats sank. The beach was the scene of sustained butchery, and only forty or fifty men managed to get to the low cliff and dig themselves in.

The firing at V Beach was audible on board *Euryalus*, off W Beach, but Hunter-Weston did not ask to be taken there to see what was developing. At 8.30, two hours after the beginning of the carnage on *River Clyde* and V Beach, the General gave the order for the main body to land from the ships. This order was obeyed by the commander of the main force, Brigadier-General H.E. Napier, who with his staff headed for the beach in a small boat. Aghast, officers still penned on the *River Clyde* yelled to him to go back; nobody could land on V Beach and live, they shouted. Napier jumped onto a lighter already full of dead men and called, 'I'll have a damned good try!' He and his staff died minutes later.

Major G.S. Adams of the Lancashire Fusiliers, writing the very next day, describes the scene vividly. 'As the boats touched the shore a very heavy and brisk fire was poured into us, several officers and men being killed and wounded in the entanglements through which we were trying to cut a way. Several of my company were with me under the wire, one of my subalterns was killed next to me, also the wire-cutter who was lying on the other side of me. I seized his cutter and cut a small lane myself, through which a few of us broke and lined up under the only cover available, a small sand ridge covered with bluffs of grass. I ordered fire to be opened on the crests but . . . the rifles were clogged with sand. The only thing left to do was to fix bayonets and charge up the crests, which was done in a very gallant manner,* though we lost heavily in doing so. However, this had the effect of driving

---

* The gallantry was recognized by the award of the Victoria Cross to six members of the Lancashire Fusiliers.

the enemy from his trenches which we occupied. . . . In my company alone I have 95 casualties out of 205 men.'*

By now the flagship and Hamilton's battle HQ, HMS *Queen Elizabeth*, was off V Beach and Hamilton, de Robeck and Commodore Roger Keyes, among many others, could see what was happening. They held an immediate council of war with the result that *Queen Elizabeth* opened fire on the Turkish positions. This bombardment was spectacular and noisy, but when it ceased the surviving Turks returned to their posts and again prevented the pinned down British troops from advancing. Hamilton considered diverting to Y Beach the other troops destined for V Beach, but Braithwaite questioned the propriety of GHQ interfering with Hunter-Weston's operation: 'Would you like to get some more men ashore on Y Beach? If so trawlers are available.'

When there was no reply Hamilton repeated the message. This time Hunter-Weston replied that Admiral Wemyss believed that to try to land men at Y Beach would 'interfere with present arrangements' and delay disembarkation. Hamilton, though on the spot and with a clearer understanding of the situation than Hunter-Weston, nevertheless let his subordinate have his head. Seven hours elapsed before Hunter-Weston knew what had happened on V Beach, though he was only five minutes' steaming time away from it.

Hamilton cannot be criticized for remaining on board *Queen Elizabeth* with his staff. There was no place for him ashore, where communications were poor and liable to disruption. On the ship he could quickly move from one place to another, and he could get a more accurate picture of the overall operation than at any place on land. He was also accessible to his subordinates, who knew where they could find him by wireless or messenger sent off by boat. He

* Maj Adams was himself killed two days later.

himself believed that he was more accessible than any commander of a major force in history, and claimed that at no time was he more than forty-five minutes away from any battle front. From his position of vantage on a ship he could see, sometimes with the naked eye, situations and crises not visible to the divisional generals on land. All this being so he should have exercised more direct control, even taking over when necessary.

At 12.40 p.m., a report reached *Queen Elizabeth* that Turkish prisoners at Anzac were saying that their forces south of Gaba Tepe – that is, where the Helles landings were taking place – consisted of only two regiments, about 2,000 men. This news was considered so important at Anzac that it was repeated to *Queen Elizabeth* at 5 p.m. and at 10.30 p.m. It is not clear if Hamilton himself read this information, but as it reached his HQ three times it seems likely. Nobody believed the information, which was, in fact, accurate.

While noisy slaughter had been going on elsewhere, at Y Beach all was calm and peaceful in the cliff-top positions of the Scottish Borderers and Royal Marines. The officer in command, Lieutenant-Colonel G.E. Matthews of the Marines, had been given vague orders 'to advance some little distance inland . . . and interfere with Turkish reinforcements for the positions further south.' Lieutenant-Colonel A.S. Koe of the Borderers, believing that he was in command, now asked Hunter-Weston and divisional HQ for advice and orders, but none came. Matthews, with his adjutant, actually walked to the deserted village of Krithia, later the objective of three major battles, and the dominating hill of Achi Baba. His troops could have taken it without opposition on the morning of 25 April.

As the Y Beach force waited for orders, the Turks were hurrying a battalion to the threatened area. It reached Y Beach about 3 p.m., just as the British had decided to dig trenches. By evening the two sides were locked in siege combat and no advance was possible. Hunter-Weston boarded *Queen Elizabeth*, and Hamilton was able to ask him in person about the situation at Y Beach. Hunter-Weston 'understood' that the troops there were being hard-pressed, but as he had heard nothing more he assumed they were 'all right'. In fact, as the Y Beach operation had been tacked onto Hunter-Weston's command, Hamilton was not particularly interested in it. He took no further action, despite having written in his diary that day: 'If this Y Beach lot press their advantage they may cut off the enemy troops on the toe of the peninsula.'

Across the Straits at Kum Kale the French part of the operation lacked incisiveness. Warships pounded the Turkish positions at 5.15 a.m., but the French soldiers did not go ashore until after 10 a.m., when 3,000 of them occupied Kum Kale without opposition. The single Turkish platoon stationed there simply withdrew. This advantage was not pressed, and it was 5.30 p.m. before all d'Amade's force was ashore. French hesitancy gave the Turks more stomach for fighting, and the area commander, goaded and threatened by Army HQ, pushed his men in against the invaders. The Turkish soldiers, cowed early in the day, now began to fight with the same dogged, fatalistic courage being displayed on the peninsula.

A French surgeon on the transport *Savoie*, a former luxury liner, describes the scene as the casualties were brought off Kum Kale:

> The convoys of wounded follow each other rapidly. From twilight of the 25th till the first rays of dawn the next day we are leaning over wounded in an atmosphere of blood, of groans, and of indescribable horrors. We do not stop for a single minute. . . . The wounded still come in. They are mounted on the deck from the bottom of the boats, and form a long line of stretchers. We are able to put six wounded at a time on the big tables of the children's playroom of the *Savoie*. The wounds of the night are

frightful. A sergeant-major comes back to us only to die. His chest was crushed . . . and for a moment we saw his heart, almost bare, still beating. There is a Senegalese with his head torn, a foot missing and three fingers gone. Another, waiting his turn on a chair, is asked, 'Beaucoup malade?' 'Non, il y en a un peu.' Both legs have been torn off by a shell.

At Anzac that evening the situation was critical. Nobody will ever know all the details of the savage fighting that took place on those narrow, jagged heights, where the remnants of seven Australian and New Zealand battalions cut down wave after wave of screaming, charging Turks screaming 'Allah!' Yet still the Turks came on, stumbling over the bodies of those butchered before them. So far as is known nobody offered to surrender, but in any case neither Turks nor Anzacs were taking prisoners; entire Turkish units were wiped out. The fighting went on incessantly for hours, and the outnumbered, exhausted Anzacs clung in separated groups to their crests and hillocks. If they prayed at all it was for darkness.

At nightfall the position was as it would remain for the next three months; the whole area was hardly more than a mile and a half long by three-quarters of a mile deep. It was impossible to realize how small the area was because its heights are so steep and its valleys and ravines are so tortuous and tangled. Little information was coming back from the 'front', and in their efforts to assess the crisis staff officers resorted to asking the wounded and stragglers for information, though it is a military axiom that both will exaggerate the dangers. The Australian divisional commander, Major-General W.T. Bridges, and the New Zealand divisional commander, Major-General A. Godley, could see for themselves that at Anzac Cove the situation was chaotic. The beach was crowded with wounded waiting evacuation, wreckage and masses of disorganized stores; the sea was getting rough and rain was falling. Everybody anticipated a Turkish counter-attack at dawn, and the tension was acute. Bridges and Godley, two constitutionally calm generals, asked Birdwood to come ashore for consultation. He was astounded when they told him the situation was desperate and that evacuation was inevitable. With great reluctance, but impressed by the force with which Bridges and Godley advanced their arguments – which were supported by the brigade commander – Birdwood sent an urgent message to Hamilton. The key sentence was: If troops are subjected to shellfire again tomorrow morning there is likely to be a fiasco as I have no fresh troops to replace those in the firing line. I know my representation is most serious but if we are to re-embark it must be at once.

The senior officers were victims of a psychological crisis. The Anzacs had proved their fighting quality, but their ability to hang on was still an unkown quantity. Bridges, who had virtually created the Australian Imperial Force, had great confidence in the Australians' ability to develop into fine soldiers after battle experience, but at this moment he seemed to underestimate their capacity to withstand the heavy counter-attack he anticipated.

Hamilton was awakened to receive the startling message and a conference took place on *Queen Elizabeth*. The Commander-in-Chief had much less of a decision to make than most historians have understood; it was made for him by Rear-Admiral Thursby, in charge of the landings, who said that an evacuation was administratively impossible. Nevertheless, Hamilton's rejection of the idea of withdrawal was reinforced by a telegram from the submarine *AE2*, with its Australian–English crew, that it had passed through the Narrows and had sunk an enemy ship. This was tremendous news and Hamilton included the morale-raising information to his message to Birdwood:

Your news is indeed serious. But there is nothing for it but to dig yourselves right in and stick it out. It would take at least two days to re-embark you as Admiral Thursby will explain to you. Meanwhile, the Australian submarine has got up through the Narrows and has torpedoed a gunboat. . . . Hunter-Weston despite his heavy losses will be advancing tomorrow which should divert pressure from you. Make a personal appeal to your men . . . to make a supreme effort to hold their ground.

Ian Hamilton

PS You have got through the difficult business, now you have only to dig, dig, dig until you are safe. Ian H.

This was the only order Hamilton gave during the day of the landing – and by the time it arrived the Anzac leaders had changed their minds in any case. They were not alone in their apprehensions. At every point of landing, officers during that wet and dreadful night must have pondered on and hoped for evacuation.

Before he went to bed that night Hamilton wrote:

One thing is sure. Whatever happens to us here we are bound to win glory. There are no other soldiers quite of the calibre of our chaps in the world; they are *volunteers* every one of them; they are *for it*; our Officers – our rank and file – have been so *entered* to this attack that they will all die – that we will all die – sooner than give way before the Turk. . . . Should the Fates so decree the whole brave army may disappear during the night . . . but assuredly they will not surrender; where so much is dark, where many are discouraged, in this knowledge I feel both light and joy.

There was not much joy on the peninsula, as the many spectators of the battle could attest. The crews of the naval vessels and merchant transports, the Corps and GHQ staffs, some newspaper correspondents, other troops waiting to land – all could see and hear the fighting. Many observers were so close inshore that they saw men fall and struggle to rise, they watched bayonet charges, and soldiers trying to claw their way up sheer cliffs, and boats full of dead and wounded caught by the Dardanelles currents and drifting aimlessly away from the shore. Because much of the fighting took place on rising ground and in natural amphitheatres, there was an element of violent drama in the fighting. Some spectators were even close enough to see the blood spurt and to hear the wounded cry out.

If the day had been desperate for the invaders it was disastrous for the Turks. In the X–W Beach area they were outnumbered by ten to one, and counter-attacks at X Beach had been beaten back with heavy loss. No reserves were left and the local commander received no reply to his frantic calls for reinforcements and more ammunition; fresh troops did not arrive until after 9 p.m. But at Anzac the defence, under the direction of Colonel Mustapha Kemal, had hardened. During the afternoon he brought in the whole 19th Division, an almost overwhelming reinforcement. Holding the high ground, Kemal was confident that no breakthrough would be made on *his* front, although he lost probably 2,000 men killed that first day.

The day of 25 April 1915, did not come to an end on the Gallipoli peninsula – it hardly seemed like a normal day, with the usual number of hours. The troops had had practically no sleep on the night of the 24th and they were active and in danger throughout the day. Nightfall was only a relative consolation, for there was still much backbreaking work in digging trenches and graves and in carrying stores. The men were dirty, most were blood-stained and all were strained; any sleep they had on the night of the 25th was fitful and miserable. So the day did not end; it simply stretched into the next.

For the British, the 'tone' of the campaign had been set on the first day. Its principal elements were a degree of indecision in high command bordering on irresponsibility; a marked detachment between staff and fighting troops that was as much intellectual as physical; a distinct air of theatre; and a prodigal, vaunting and contemptuous courage among the soldiers and sailors which somehow invests the Gallipoli peninsula with an atmosphere to this day.

6

'The Beautiful Battalions are Wasted Skeletons'

On the morning of 26 April, aboard *Euryalus*, Hunter-Weston was told that at Y Beach the situation was 'desperate'. This beach was directly under his command, but he merely passed the message to Hamilton, saying that he had no reserves to spare. This was untrue; he had at least six battalions of French troops. Completely occupied with the battles on Helles the bovine Hunter-Weston had no understanding of the significance of the Y Beach operation. Hamilton, in contrast, did understand and was worried about it. But etiquette was more important to him than decision, and it still prevented him from taking over command himself or from appointing another commander.

Thus two different types of stupidity combined to create a crisis of command – which, aggravated by repetition, would lead within a few weeks to total failure in the southern sector of Gallipoli.

At 9.30 a.m. on 26 April, Hamilton, in *Queen Elizabeth*, reached Y Beach, but could not find out what was happening – reason enough for a Commander-in-Chief to have given some incisive orders on his own account. He saw soldiers coming down the cliffs to the beach, where groups of other men stood around – but nobody was going *up* the cliffs. 'I mistrusted and disliked the look of those aimless dawdlers by the sea,' he wrote.

During the night the Turks had gallantly pressed their counter-attacks and had inflicted fairly heavy casualties on the British, who were running short of ammunition. But the outnumbered Turks had also suffered under the intense British small-arms fire, and at dawn they withdrew. The British position was not really desperate, but, on the authority of an officer no more senior than a lieutenant, men started to leave the beach by courtesy of some obliging naval boats' crews. Long before Hamilton reached Y, many hundreds of troops were already on the warships. Witnessing this evacuation, Hamilton assumed that the order had come from Hunter-Weston's HQ; Colonel Matthews, in command at Y and tired from a night of combat, made the same assumption – quite unwarrantedly as he had received no message from Hunter-Weston in about thirty hours. Hunter-Weston did not reply to any of Matthews' urgent appeals, and sent no officer to visit him – though this would have been a simple journey.

In landing a force at Y Beach Hamilton had taken a step that could have won the southern end of the peninsula, had the troops there been clearly directed by Hunter-Weston and resolutely led. Hamilton was frustrated, exasperated and angry. 'To see a part of my scheme, from which I hoped so much, going wrong before my eyes is maddening,' he wrote. But he did nothing, largely because he allowed Braithwaite to dissuade him from intervening. It was indefensible, in Braithwaite's opinion, for the Commander-in-Chief to make decisions over Hunter-Weston's head. Yet by this time it was clear to Braithwaite as to everybody else that Hunter-Weston had divorced himself from Y Beach.

The Turks, because they were either asleep or re-forming, and in any case anxious not to provoke a naval bombardment, kept out of the way and had no idea that the British were evacuating. It was well into the afternoon before they made that heartening and surprising discovery – and came across the great heaps of ammunition and equipment left ashore. Then they were rushed farther south to reinforce their hard-pressed comrades.

While in the process of condoning the evacuation of Y Beach, Hamilton came under pressure from the panicky d'Amade, who wanted to evacuate Kum Kale. On this occasion Braithwaite urged Hamilton to reject d'Amade's request, and was supported by de Robeck, whose Intelligence through his naval patrols was probably the best available. Both men said that the French could and should hold. Accepting d'Amade's version of the fighting, apparently without question, Hamilton reluctantly agreed to disembarkation.

General d'Amade had either no idea what was happening, or he believed that as a 'demonstration' his landing had run its course and should be terminated. But though planned only as a demonstration, the operation was so successful that by evening the French troops had killed or wounded 1,700 Turks while suffering 800 casualties of their own, and they had taken 500 prisoners. The Turks were beaten and the French held the Kum Kale area. When Admiral Guépratte came aboard *Queen Elizabeth* and told Hamilton about the French success, the Commander-in-Chief immediately withdrew his permission for d'Amade to evacuate. It was too late – the men were already streaming back.

Hamilton's vacillation on this second day of the campaign was enough to lose it, without any other factors.

The situation was better at Helles, where the Turkish defences had been reduced to little more than outposts. Von Sanders tried to provide some kind of defensive system for Krithia, but by mid-afternoon on 26 April the courageous and costly British attacks had just about smashed the Turkish resistance. The British were in no state to exploit their advantage; food, water and ammunition were getting ashore, but their distribution lacked organization and the place was clogged with wounded.

At Anzac, too, the Australians and New Zealanders had dug and fought and dug, and were holding firm under almost ceaseless small-arms fire. Hearteningly for Birdwood, four mountain guns had been heaved to Plugge's Plateau, from where they could give some support to the men clinging to the cliff faces. Anzac was a more dangerous front than Helles. A soldier could be mortally wounded unloading a cart, drawing water for his unit or directing a mule convoy. He could lose life or limb when off duty – returning from a bathe or washing a shirt. An Australian, Hector Dinning, describes* the death of a mate while reading his just-delivered mail from home. 'He is retiring to his dugout when struck by shrapnel. The wound gapes in his back. There is no staunching it. Every thump of the aorta pumps out his life. Practically he is a dead man when struck. He lives but a few minutes – with his pipe still steaming, clenched in his teeth.'

Shells sometimes burst in the middle of a burial party and fresh graves would be dug at once for the newly dead. As Dinning wrote: 'To die violently and be laid in this shell-swept area is to die lonely indeed.'

One of the most blameworthy aspects of the campaign was now unfolding. Some thought had been given to the handling of wounded men – but it was inexpert thought. GHQ had estimated casualties for the first few days at 3,000, but this was a figure reached without reference to Surgeon-General Birrell or to the Adjutant-General and Quartermaster-General. Birrell was on Lemnos desperately trying to co-ordinate medical services, while the other two administrators were aboard the headquarters staff ship *Arcadian* unable to get off it and out of touch with the

* In *The Anzac Book*, 1915–16.

battle. Despite the poor planning, the 3rd Australian General Hospital was on Lemnos and ready for work, with a highly skilled staff of surgeons, nursing sisters, orderlies, an operating theatre and even X-ray equipment. The hospital had a capacity of 400 seriously wounded, but could if necessary take more for short periods. At anchor somewhere off Helles was a well-equipped hospital ship, *Hindoo*, but neither its captain nor its chief medical officer had any orders and did not know of the heavy casualties ashore. Birrell's estimate of 10,000 casualties was close to the mark, and his fears about their sufferings had not been exaggerated.

All observers agree that the situation was worst on the small congested beach of Anzac, where men lay tightly packed in rows, waiting to be taken off. But that was more often than not just the beginning of their most appalling period of suffering. Sailors and soldiers on beach duty would pack a boat with wounded and row from transport to transport, pleading to have their cargo taken aboard. Some captains refused on the grounds that they were not equipped to deal with wounded. The most infamous case was that of a lighter with several hundred wounded aboard which was turned away by seven transports. A naval patrol found it drifting in rough seas in the deep darkness of early morning, and somehow got the men transhipped.

A little later a fleet-sweeper crowded with Australian wounded wandered from ship to ship in vain, and at last lashed itself to the Headquarters ship *Arcadian*; the staff and crew turned out to do what they could while Hamilton sent a signal to a hospital ship to join *Arcadian* at once.

Some of the transports had brought animals to the peninsula – now their stalls, still uncleaned, became 'wards'. Soldiers told to act as orderlies on these casualty ships were so aghast at the serious hideousness of some of the wounds that they refused to lift the men from their stretchers; this produced a chronic shortage of stretchers on land.

Some transports had been fitted to double on the return journey as reasonably well-equipped hospital ships, but when they were only half full – mostly with lightly wounded men – somebody ordered them to steam for Egypt. Others, packed with seriously wounded, were denied permission to leave. And, for several days, nobody brought in the *Hindoo*.

One transport took 1,600 wounded, including 300 stretcher cases, to Alexandria, while just four doctors worked heroically to treat them. On another small ship the wounded lay uncovered on the deck all the way to Egypt – a journey of three nights – and in other ships the wounded were accommodated in holds without ventilation.

A New Zealander wrote that what he witnessed during the first few days of the campaign was 'like nothing so much as a scene from the Inferno'. It was such a scene aboard the animal transport ship *Lutzow*, which took hundreds of seriously wounded men to Egypt; the only medical officer aboard was a veterinary officer who did valiant work in treating as many soldiers as he could possibly handle.

In Alexandria, hospital staff were appalled at what they discovered when they boarded the ships. Many men were filthy and bloody, just as they had left the battlefield days before; their wounds were gangrenous and septic, their bandages unchanged; on ships where there had been insufficient or no medical staff, there were soldiers with broken limbs still unset. Perhaps 300 men were taken off the ships dead, and others died soon after. In Egypt both hospital accommodation and staff were pitifully inadequate; buildings were requisitioned and hundreds of British women volunteered to act as nurses.

When the senior administrative officers were able to get off the *Arcadian* and join Birrell in organizing a proper transport and treatment system, the horror lessened – but by then many men had died hopelessly. For a few weeks conditions for the wounded were as bad as for those soldiers found by

Florence Nightingale sixty years before at Scutari – not far from the Golden Horn of Constantinople, which these soldiers of 1915 hoped to reach.

Sergeant John Hollis of the Royal Field Artillery had been acutely ill with fever in hospital in the Citadel, in Cairo, and was told that he was being discharged to make room for wounded from Gallipoli. Hollis was feeling weak and resented his discharge until he staggered down the stairs and came across the first arrivals from the peninsula. The sight was so horrific that he straightened his back and marched out; he reckoned that what he was suffering was nothing compared with that of these men.

At Helles more suffering was about to take place. Hunter-Weston ordered that 'every man will die at his post rather than retire'. But he was being over-dramatic; the Turks were too weak to consider an assault, and instead withdrew to form their new line in front of Krithia and the hill of Achi Baba, which Hamilton wanted so desperately to capture. Under Hunter-Weston's orders the first battle of Krithia began at 8 a.m. on 28 April, by which date the Anglo-French force had almost lost its advantage in numbers. Nevertheless, an hour later it seemed that the British would capture Krithia almost without casualties as the Turks retreated before them. At 11 a.m. the British were actually on the slope of Achi Baba. But a short hour later the British centre was disorganized and the left, on the Aegean coast, was held up by opposition in the precipitous ravines. Then the British line wavered and broke under a determined charge by about 120 Turks. Hamilton and his aides watched this incident from *Queen Elizabeth* and Hamilton described it:

> . . . At a trot they came on . . . their bayonets glittering and their officer 10 yards in front waving his sword. Crash! and the *Q.E.* let fly a shrapnel [shell], range 1,200 yards, a lovely shot; we followed it through the air with our eyes.

Range and fuse – perfect! The huge projectile exploded fifty yards from the Turkish right and vomited its contents of 10,000 bullets [more likely 24,000 shrapnel balls] clean across the stretch whereon the Turkish company was making its last effort. When the dust and smoke cleared away nothing stirred on the whole of that piece of ground.

Hamilton did now take a direct hand by sending ashore one of his aides, Colonel C.F. Aspinall, to collect the scattered British soldiers and coax or coerce them up the cliffs to their original position. This action helped to steady the front.

On the right the French wing of the attack had run into the only organized Turkish resistance. Hunter-Weston's vague orders, which had arrived late at battalion level, were resulting in the inevitable penalty – lack of purpose and cohesion. The General steadily lost control over his units and the course of the battle and ordered a withdrawal – though one of his detachments had actually entered Krithia.

By nightfall everybody knew the battle was lost. Hunter-Weston had committed 14,000 men and lost 3,000 killed or wounded. It could not be said that the Turks had actually won the battle; the victory had come to them through Allied default. Their morale went up enormously as they reazlied that the British had withdrawn, and as their own reinforcements began to trickle in – and the first shells from batteries in Asia began to fall among the British and French lines on Helles.

In the agonizing period between dawn on 25 April and sunset on 28 April the army had lost 150 officers and 2,500 men killed, another 250 officers and 6,000 men wounded. Nearly all the rest were exhausted, and the first signs of sickness were beginning to appear. Yet, on 27 April, Hamilton reported to Kitchener: 'Thanks to the weather and the wonderfully fine spirit of our troops all continues to go well.'

There can be no denying his extraordinary spirit, but to claim that all was going well was not merely an overstatement, it was an untruth. Hamilton dared not tell Kitchener the truth; he was too frightened of the great man. Hesitantly, he asked if he could have the 42nd Territorial Division – from East Lancashire – 'just in case'. He added placatingly: 'You may be sure, I shall not call up a man unless I really need him.'

Kitchener knew that Hamilton really needed reinforcements because he had received a sober account of the campaign from the realistic Admiral Guépratte. Being firm with the obstructive Maxwell, Kitchener ordered him to release the 42nd to Hamilton.

On the night of 30 April Hamilton, on his way to the *Arcadian* – having transferred from *Queen Elizabeth* – met a big batch of wounded:

> I spoke to them, and although some were terribly mutilated and disfigured, and although a few others were clearly dying, one and all kept a stiff upper lip – and all were, or managed to appear – more than content – happy! This scene brought tears into my eyes. The supreme courage of our soldiers! Were it not so, war would be unbearable.

The poet mastered the general in this diary entry. Soldiers of the time were noted for their stoicism, but Hamilton goes too far. A dying man can appear content because by then he lacks the strength to appear anything else. Also, many men were under the influence of morphia when Hamilton saw them and could well have appeared 'content'. Again, the faces of some wounded men, near to death, lose all tension and can even form the faintest of smiles. Was this the happy appearance Hamilton noted? Certainly a few of those still fit and well could be happy, but these were men who had not seen the full horrors. Writing home on 5 May, Chaplain O. Creighton of the 29th Division admitted as much.

The strange thing, I find, is that I am really extremely happy, though . . . I have not had anything bad to shake me. There is more goodness and true unselfishness about on this bloodstained peninsula than there is at a race-meeting, for instance, and that seems the only thing after all that matters. It is no excuse for war, but it makes it quite possible to be happy in it.

Before Hamilton could initiate contentment and happiness for other soldiers, the Turks struck at Helles. Von Sanders had not wanted to make such an attack, but as a hireling he could hardly ignore Enver's insistent command to 'drive the invaders into the sea'. Accordingly, on the night of 1 May, he sent waves of bayonet-brandishing Turks to their deaths in frontal assaults against the British and French lines. The British command had shown no great intelligence in attack but the soldiers' doggedness in defence was superb, and several thousand Turks fell dead in heaps before the Allied trenches.

At two points the Turks broke through the British line and occupied some trenches, but the Royal Scots and the Royal Fusiliers came in to block the breach. In savage hand-to-hand fighting they retook the trenches and held them. The most serious crisis occurred on the right, where French African troops – Senegalese – broke and ran under the Turkish artillery. Two battalions of the Royal Naval Division were hurried into the gap and were supported by all other soldiers who could grab a rifle. In yet more violent fighting the line was re-established. As military practice demanded, the British then launched a counter-attack – although the troops were so exhausted that they could barely stand. Good targets in broad daylight, they suffered heavily before being forced to withdraw in the evening. General d'Amade was distraught with his 2,000 casualties, but Hunter-Weston's 29th Division had suffered more significantly, having lost many experienced officers, including five battalion commanders.

The Turks' blood sacrifice had not ended. On the night of 3 May they were back again with wild assaults on the French lines, ending them only with daylight. The barking French 75s – field guns with a reputation almost as devastating as their shells – made the night an Allied victory when they caught Turkish reinforcement battalions in the open. Even so, it was clear next morning that the British and French troops could stand little more.

But stand they had to, for a massive counter-attack was planned. The object was to capture Krithia. Confident that Anzac would hold and impressed by the fighting spirit of the Australians and New Zealanders, Hamilton asked Birdwood for a brigade of each from Anzac. With these men, the first 42nd Division brigade from Egypt, twenty Australian field-guns and their crews which had just arrived, and some Sikhs and Gurkhas, he built up a force of 25,000 men for Hunter-Weston. The Commander-in-Chief wanted to attack before dawn on 6 May, as 'it would be good tactics to cross the danger zone by night and overthrow the enemy in the grey dawn'.

Hunter-Weston opposed this idea; he said that without enough trained officers an advance in the dark was unwise. Hamilton did not insist on his 'good tactics' and, as on other occasions, he bowed his own more imaginative judgement to that of a subordinate. A few days later, when Hunter-Weston's approach had been proved wrong and when he could devise no course other than to repeat it, the Commander-in-Chief lacked either the perception or the strength to overrule him.

Secure from 'interference', Hunter-Weston was left alone to plan a frontal assault in daylight. The orders he issued were crude in terms of military finesse, as well as vague and late – some units received them several hours *after* the assault began. In no case did any commander, from brigadier to platoon commander, have adequate time to study what was required of him. Some did not know that they were involved in a major attack, while others reached their jumping-off positions in the dark, and barely knew in which direction they faced.

If Hunter-Weston had actually wanted to be beaten he could hardly have improved on his plans. His attack was timed for 11 a.m., by which time the Turks would be breakfasted, rested and organized. He did not know the position of the Turkish trenches, the shell supply was seriously short, and he was attacking on a narrow front – three miles – without any feint, deception, oblique or flank attack to make things more difficult for the Turks.

The exhausted British went into action behind the fire of their field-guns and howitzers, but at the end of the day little progress had been made.

On this day Hamilton received from the War Office a reply to his plea for more ammunition to be sent immediately. It read:

Until you can submit an account of the amount you have in hand to enable us to work out the rate of expenditure, it is difficult to decide about further supplies of ammunition.

More encouragingly, General Bailloud, commander of an additional French division, had arrived. Though aged seventy, he was an infinitely better leader than d'Amade. Hamilton had acted more decisively than usual in getting rid of d'Amade, complaining to Kitchener that the Frenchman had sent pessimistic and inaccurate messages and that he needed constant reassurance. His successor, General Henri Gouraud, was much more competent. He assumed command of the whole French Corp on 14 May.

On the night of May 6, Hamilton wrote:

We are now on our last legs. The beautiful Battalions of the 25th April are wasted skeletons now; shadows of what they had been. The thought of the river of blood against which I painfully made my way when I met these multitudes of wounded coming down to the shore was unnerving. But every Commander has to fight these pitiful sensations. . . . To over-drive the willingest troops any General ever had under his command is a sin – but we go on fighting tomorow.

The fighting was yet another attack planned by Hunter-Weston for the following day, 7 May. It was on precisely the same pattern as that which had already failed, though this time it would begin at 10 a.m. Again his men pushed stubbornly into the attack, taking a few yards here and there. Properly exploited, some of these local gains may have led to a wider victory, but Hunter-Weston did not study them. He knew only that little progress had been made.

So for a third day Hunter-Weston ordered an assault – this time for 10.15 a.m., 8 May. The Turks, most of their machine-guns still intact, appreciated the routine nature of the assaults, and being more or less stationary and sheltered they were less troubled by the hot sun than the British. Hunter-Weston's third attack was more limited, and the most siginficant attack would be by four battalions of New Zealanders – the Otago, Wellington, Auckland and Canterbury battalions. But they were weak in numbers – 2,493 officers and men – after the Anzac fighting, and they were being sent in against a position held by nine Turkish battalions. The 29th Division and the French had separate objectives, though they were so imprecise that even battalion commanders knew only that they were charging enemy trenches. Some apologized to their officers for being unable to give them better information.

Hamilton came ashore with his staff to observe the action, which foundered by lunchtime. Not that there was any lunch for the attacking troops, except perhaps for the French, who did not leave the protection of their own trenches. The gallant New Zealanders and British were back in their lines by 3.30 p.m., sadly depleted and totally exhausted. Colonel F.E.

Johnston, commanding the badly mauled New Zealand Brigade, protested to Hunter-Weston about his order to repeat the frontal attack yet again, but was told it would go ahead.

Hamilton, doing some thinking on his own account, faced a critical decision. Some of his advisers held that the force had done all it could. But Hamilton reasoned that if he did not go on with the action he would be admitting failure in the very first stage of his plan.

Having discovered to his surprise that three brigades, including the Australians, were still in reserve, Hamilton made a command decision. His order: The entire Allied line, with the Australians, would fix bayonets and storm Krithia at 5.30 p.m., after the artillery had battered the defences – to the guns' last round if necessary. The Australians had a special role – to take the exposed Krithia Spur, a daunting prospect for even the best troops.

And they were good troops – 2,568 men of the 2nd Australian Brigade under Brigadier-General W. McKay. The brigade consisted of four Victorian battalions – 5th (Lieutenant-Colonel Wanliss), 6th (Lieutenant-Colonel McNicol), 7th Lieutenant-Colonel Gartside) and 8th (Lieutenant-Colonel Bolton).

While Brigadier-General McKay and his staff were hurriedly writing orders for the brigade, General Paris of the Royal Naval Division telephoned to say that the Commander-in-Chief wanted the line to go forward with as much display as possible, in order to encourage the hesitant French. 'Have you any bands with you?' Paris asked.

McKay said he had none: the idea of bands in the front line trenches might well have astonished him.

'Well, have you any colours?'

The Australians had no flags with them either; they were well aware that waving flags only drew heavy fire.

'You have bayonets at any rate,' said Paris, and he told McKay that Hamilton wished for as much use of the bayonet as possible. This exchange, if nothing else, showed McKay that Paris and Hamilton were out of touch with the realities of modern war.

The Australian soldiers had been preparing their evening meal, and the order to move up for an immediate advance was a surprise. But they obeyed quickly and competently and within minutes – or so it seemed to some of them – they were in action. Despite the shells that fell on them, the Turks were ready for the infantry assault, and their own shrapnel balls and rifle and machine-gun bullets were as thick as hail. In terms of sheer gallantry, the Australian attack was inspiring, and several observers wrote about it. 'They were not men but gods, demons infuriated,' a British officer said.

Where there was no officer, an NCO or a private led the others on in a display of valour that is indescribable, though a young wounded officer of the 29th Division attempted an assessment when he told Hamilton that 'it was worth ten years of tennis' to see the Australians and New Zealanders go in.

In their astonishing uphill charge the Australians took and held 1,000 yards of enemy territory – the only significant advance in three days of battle. They lost more than one man in three killed or wounded in this achievement. In hard figures the brigade went out 2,900 strong and lost 1,056, including sixteen officers killed and thirty-two wounded. In the 6th Battalion only one of the original combatant officers was left.

Having lost 6,000 men in all that night, Hamilton and Hunter-Weston gave up the fight. So ended the second battle of Krithia.

John Masefield viviedly describes the ferocity of the battle:*

Gathering themselves together, brave men dash out to break the wire and are killed; others take their places and

* *Gallipoli*, Macmillan, 1916.

are killed; others step out with too great a pride even to stop, and pull up the supports of the wires and fall dead on top of them. Then machine guns open on the survivors and kill all in thirty seconds. . . . The supports come up . . . those who are not killed lie down among the flowers and scrape little heaps of earth with their hands . . . many are blown to pieces or hit in the back as they scrape. . . . A man peering from his place in the flowers may make out that the man next to him is dead, and that the man beyond is praying, the man beyond him cursing, and the man beyond him out of his mind from nerves or thirst.

As darkness fell, the battlefield for half a mile beyond the foremost line was filled with the cries of the wounded calling for stretcher-bearers. Their task of getting all these hurt men to the dressing stations during darkness was almost impossible. The official Australian historian, C.E.W. Bean, describes the patience of the wounded as astonishing:

As they lay craving water above all things, some soldier, carrying a supply to the front line, poured a little in a mess-tin, explaining that the rest was needed 'for the boys up there'. One after another the wounded and the dying merely moistened their lips with it. . . . Those at the front line were equally patient, though asking continually if the stretcher-bearers were near. 'You won't see them tonight – they're rarer than gold,' replied one thoughtless youngster. 'You might let us think we will,' was the faint retort.

Many of the stretcher-bearers had been continually carrying British and Australian wounded since noon the day before, and they were staggering drunkenly from exhaustion.

Chaplain Creighton was on hand when the 'ghastly mass of casualties' was brought in during the next twenty-four hours. 'They came in all day. Terrible stomach wounds and head wounds. The Australians, who were the vast majority, were wonderfully plucky. . . . They don't seem to understand fear and even the wounded were only anxious to get better and have another go. But what a terrible waste it all seemed of such magnificent men. . . .'

The Australians saw it as a waste on other grounds as well, for they were quick to realize that the advance made at such a cost during daylight hours could have been accomplished after dark almost without loss. They became bitterly critical of the leadership.

On the evening of 8 May, Hamilton wrote to Kitchener:

The result of the operation has been failure, as my object remains unachieved. The fortifications and their machine-guns were too scientific [they were not] and too strongly held to be rushed, although I had every available man on duty. Our troops have done all that flesh and blood can do against semi-permanent works [they were not] and they are not able to carry them. More and more munitions will be needed to do so. I fear that this is a very unpalatable conclusion, but I can see no way out of it. . . . I should be glad if you would give me your views as to the future operations that will be necessary.

He followed this on 10 May with his own intentions for the future of the campaign:

The only sound procedure is to hammer away until the enemy gets demoralised. . . . Everyone is in good spirits and full of confidence.

This may have applied to everybody aboard the *Arcadian*; it was certainly a false statement of the men's feelings. Young men had grown old within a few weeks, and they were haggard and unsmiling. They had buried many comrades and seen others carried away with shattered bodies. Short of almost everything, they were being baked by a sun which daily grew hotter, and all round was the smell of pestilence. Whether at Anzac or Helles they were constantly harassed by deadly snipers. What Hamilton took for 'good spirits and full confidence' was nothing more than the soldier's relief at being left alive. This relief can masquerade as 'good spirits', but it does not deceive a regimental officer. These men would fight, but the earlier notion of the great adventure had been buried with the dead.

Hamilton was more realistic in his private description of the Plymouth Battalion of the Royal Naval Division, which he saw as it returned from the front line:

. . . They had come to the end of their tether. Not only physical exhaustion but moral exhaustion. They could not raise a smile in the whole battalion. The faces of officers and men had a crushed, utterly finished expression. As each company front formed [into a line] the knees of the rank and file seemed to give way. Down they fell and motionless remained. . . . They have not the invincible carelessness or temperamental springiness of the old lot [the old, regular army].

While the generals at Gallipoli pitted their men in assaults increasingly unlikely to succeed – a fact as obvious and demonstrable then as by hind-sight – a first-rate row was building up in London. Kitchener, to get the ammunition he had promised Hamilton, ordered Sir John French to send 25,000 shells to Gallipoli at once. This was only a quarter of what French had used in a futile offensive at Festubert, but he was already angry with the Prime Minister for having publicly denied a shortage of ammunition, and Kitchener's request stung him to his usual choleric fury. Through friends he leaked Kitchener's order and the shell shortage to the Press, to David Lloyd George, Kitchener's implacable enemy on the Shell Committee, and to the leaders of the Conservative opposition, Arthur Balfour and Bonar Law. The news broke publicly on 14 May. Revolted by plots and counter-plots, Kitchener recorded, 'I am deadly sick of this system of intrigue. . . . I am out to fight the Germans, not Sir John French.'

The intercommand fighting and its results on the conduct of the war would not have surprised some of the soldiers who were its victims. A Lancashire soldier, Private Charles Watkins of the 6th Battalion Lancashire Fusiliers, wrote:

> . . . I am astonished that none of us had been given the least guidance from higher authority of what to expect or what to do. Presumably we were to land and the rest was up to the Almighty to sort out. This lack of planning, lack of direction, became for me all too evident as the campaign developed.

Private Watkins expected too much; 'higher authority' had little information to pass on about what to expect or do. But at about the time of the second battle of Krithia, it was again thinking of naval action.

7

'The Unfortunate State of Affairs'

After the abortive second battle of Krithia, and in view of the stalemate at Anzac, on 14 May the War Council – not yet the Dardanelles Committee – considered three options. They were: To abandon the peninsula; to send Hamilton strong reinforcements and go for a rapid breakthrough; or to send light reinforcements and wear down Turkish resistance by steady pressure.

In retrospect the third option was unrealistic, but it must have seemed practical at the time. Any decision was difficult, though all those senior officers who were pressing for action and still more action on the Western Front would have emphatically recommended abandonment of Gallipoli. It was not so easy as that. An evacuation was expected to involve heavy losses; also it would proclaim failure and this could not only throw the Balkan States into the German Camp but encourage Muslim uprisings against the British and French throughout the Islamic world. On top of all this, Kitchener had received a message from the Russians (12 May) saying that they desperately needed the Britith so defeat the Turks at the Dardanelles. Having lost heavily in Galicia, the Russians wanted the British and French to tie down as many Turks as possible. The Russians naively believed that only some temporary setback had delayed the British from decisively defeating the Turks at Gallipoli.

As for strong reinforcements, in Kitchener's view because of the chance of a German invasion not another man could be spared from England. The possibility of an invasion of England was the creation of his own anxiety; no serious Intelligence estimate forecast such an invasion. For an invasion even to begin the Germans needed to take and hold several Channel ports – and this they signally could not do.

Nevertheless, Hamilton was asked to revise his request for reinforcements – upwards. He was to base his estimate on the assumption that adequate forces were available. Far from making the situation easy for Hamilton, this instruction created a dilemma. He needed really strong reinforcements but did not want to be greedy. A request for a lot of troops would embarrass Kitchener, who had to cope with the more pressing demands of the Western Front. In any case, Hamilton would find it difficult to accommodate large numbers of reinforcements. The ground was already overcrowded, and the addition of even another four divisions – roughly 60,000 men at that time – would cramp manoeuvre.

Hamilton was hampered by lack of good Intelligence about the Russians, Greeks and Bulgarians. Sector commanders were often kept in the dark about larger strategical matters, rather as if each theatre of war had no connection with any other theatre. Hamilton (17 May) reported to Kitchener that if a Russian corps were to land at the Bosphorus, or if Greece or Bulgaria declared war against Turkey, he could take the Dardanelles with two extra divisions; otherwise he needed four.

Hamilton was veering away from the idea of rolling up the Turks from the toe of the peninsula. He would go only far enough to capture the heights of Achi Baba, so as to make the Helles beaches safer. Then, in a surprise attack from Anzac, he would cut off the lower leg of the peninsula. He would thus capture or kill many Turks, hold a lot of territory and secure the Narrows for the fleet. The vision was appealing.

Kitchener replied with a discouraging cable, promising him one division and saying: 'From the standpoint of an early solution of our difficulties your views are not encouraging. The question whether we can long support two fields of operations draining on our resources requires grave consideration. I know that I can rely on you to do your utmost to bring the unfortunate state of affairs in the Dardanelles to as early a conclusion as possible, so that any consideration of a withdrawal, with all its dangers in the East, may be prevented from entering the field of possible solutions.'

This was Kitchener at his wordy worst. He was threatening his Commander-in-Chief Mediterranean Force as a headmaster might threaten a schoolboy for not doing his best to pass an examination. And Hamilton that same day responded as a scolded schoolboy. 'Although I have made requests for certain additional troops, I am sure that you will realise that does not imply that I am not doing all I possibly can with the force at my disposal, and every day sees some improvement in our position.'

True, there was *some* improvement: The lines at Helles and Anzac were stronger and morale was rising; the enterprising Australians and New Zealanders were unnerving the Turks by raiding. But against this was the Intelligence that another Turkish corps had reached the peninsula.

Excellent supports were also arriving at Anzac. On 12 May, Birdwood received the best reinforcing troops he was ever to get – 1,500 men of the Australian Light Horse and New Zealand Mounted Rifles, with more on the way. These young men, nearly all from the country districts, were fit, intelligent, daring and proud. Resentful though they were of being deprived of their horses – which would have been useless at Anzac – they nevertheless became excellent infantrymen. Their blooding took place only two days after their arrival.

Sixty-five troopers of the 2nd Light Horse from Queensland, under Captain D.M. Graham, were sent over the parapet to fill in some communication trenches from which the Turks were firing. Within minutes forty-six were killed or wounded; the dead included Captain Graham.

Because of the shorter front line and the compressed lines of communication, the slaughter at Anzac was worse – and more obviously worse – than at Helles. The Australians and New Zealanders held their ground heroically and here and there pushed the Turks a little farther back, but the cost was appalling. The conditions for just existing were bad enough, without any fighting.

Kemal, in command on this sector, threw his men at the Anzac line in a kind of command frenzy; he was like a man in a rage picking up cup after cup and throwing them at a brick wall. And like cup after cup the Turkish platoons and companies and battalions smashed under Anzac bullets and bayonets – possibly 14,000 of them by 4 May. It is hard to know whether to call the Turkish charges fanatical or heroic; even some Turkish historians concede that fanaticism was a stronger force than heroism.

Under incessant strain the Anzacs grew tense. Colonel G.F. Braund of the Australian 2nd Battalion, the Colonel of the Deal Battalion of Marines, and the Adjutant of the Portsmouth Battalion, were all shot dead by nervous sentries when they did not quickly enough respond to challenges. The Marines thrown in to make up the great losses among Australians and New Zealanders also lost heavily. They were 'nearly useless', Birdwood said. 'They are special children of Winston Churchill, immature boys with no proper training. . . .'

Immature, untrained boys the Marines certainly were, but they were not useless and they did not let Birdwood down, as he had feared. They learned quickly and held firm while Birdwood and his commanders reorganized the Anzacs, and quite soon, in bloody and costly battle, they won the admiration of the Australians.

Any movement by day was difficult because the many Turkish snipers dominated the lower Anzac lines. Gradually both sides gained command of certain mounds and hills, the Anzacs with an advantage here, the Turks there. Overall, the front was so interlocked that each side held the other tightly in check. The taking of any one position put the whole defence system of either side in danger, hence the ferocious fighting to hold ground. At Anzac there was no such thing as a 'tactical withdrawal', as there was on the Western Front. To withdraw here was to fall over the brink of a precipice. By digging saps forward and then joining the heads of the saps, the Australians created a new front line even closer to the Turks.

Along the narrow ridge, at places which became famous as Quinn's Post, Courtney's Post and Steele's Post, the Turks and Australians were in places only five yards apart. At this intimate distance the tension was unbearable, for a quick rush could swamp an opposing trench. Any man foolhardy enough to stand for a quick look was shot dead in a second. The Turks could easily lob grenades, but the Australians could not move out of range because no other defensible position existed.

So great was the strain at Quinn's Post that the garrison was relieved every forty-eight hours. The word 'post' might in other theatres of war indicate a place held by a section (ten men) or a platoon of thirty. Courtney's, Quinn's and Steele's* were mostly held by two companies each – perhaps 200 men – and at times by a battalion, so great was the Turkish threat.

---

* They were named after officers who distinguished themselves in their defence – Lieutenant Colonel R.E. Courtney, 14th Battalion, Major H. Quinn, 15th Battalion and Lieutenant Steele. All were killed at Anzac.

At one point on the ridge was a shallow saddle which could never be occupied because it was exposed to the rifles and machine-guns of both sides. It is said that one day a Turkish soldier who had apparently lost his way reached this spot, from where he looked into the crowded, frenetically busy Monash Valley. The Australians who saw him were so surprised that for once their aim was poor – and the Turk, running madly, apparently survived the fusillade which followed him. It is unlikely that any other man of either side reached that particular spot and lived.

As they settled in with that extraordinary adaptability for which they became famous, the Anzacs mastered the Turkish snipers. Under Birdwood's insistence, the officers on the spot evolved anti-sniper teams of two men; one would put a hat on a stick and move it along the trench top while he observed from arm's length. When a Turkish sniper shot at the hat, the Australian sniper would try to fire at the flash. Either he or his decoy spotter would sooner or later pick up the enemy sniper's hide and kill him. As these teams became expert, so the sniping menace declined, though on 14 May Birdwood had his skull grazed by a bullet and the next day Major-General Sir W.T. Bridges, commanding the Australian division, was mortally wounded in Monash Valley.

Later in the campaign there was grudging admiration by the Anzacs for 'Johnny Turk'. It was not evident during the first month. The Australians and New Zealanders hated the Turks as barbarous, screaming savages who never took prisoners, bayoneting any captives. Part of the Anzac hatred was that which arises from the exhausted impotence to retaliate. Through what amounted to criminal negligence, the War Office had sent Hamilton's men to war without hand-grenades, mortars and trench periscopes. Trench warfare, the planners decided, would not develop at Gallipoli. The thinking apparently went like this: Trench warfare is happening in France because the ground is mostly flat and troops cannot advance over it without being mowed down, therefore they dig; but Gallipoli is broken and precipitous, troops can advance, so trenches will not be necessary.

At Hamilton's request the War Office promised to send twenty mortars, but on 12 May told him that only ten could be spared. The entire output for the UK between January and March 1915 was seventy-five.

The Anzacs in positions close to the Turks were constantly under attack by enemy grenades of the 'cricket ball' variety. Having no grenades of their own, the Anzacs could only catch and throw back the grenades or smother them with sandbag or greatcoat before they burst in the crowded trenches. Either way death was always only a second or two away. When they were throwing from a range of five yards or so, as at Quinn's, the Turks learned to hold their grenades for a few seconds after igniting them, so that they blew up in the hands of the catching Australians.

Sometimes the rain of grenades was intolerable, especially when they caused loss of sleep. On the night of 13–14 May a big Queenslander, Driver David Browning, with pieces of Turkish grenade iron in both sides of his face, decided that something had to be done about the Turks. He went to the rear and returned with an armful of the new jam-tin bombs being made on the beach. He knew nothing about bombs, but he lit the fuses and threw one bomb after another rapidly into the Turkish trenches at the point which had been tormenting the men in Quinn's. The Turkish bombers were either killed or they got the message, and they threw no more grenades that night.

Only a soldier who has lived among putrefying flesh in a hot sun, with the intermingled stink of excrement and urine, of body odour and cordite, can know what it was like at Anzac front. Whatever the Australians had been before, in this environment they became rough, hard, foul-mouthed and immensely casual in dress and behaviour. It took a much respected officer to draw a salute at Anzac. Major-General H.B. Walker, who commanded the Australian division after Bridges, was a tough, hard man, and forthright, but he met his match in an Australian he encountered in Shrapnel Gully. The man was smoking a cigarette and gave Walker only a passing glance.

'Don't you know who I am?' Walker asked with stern emphasis.

'No,' the soldier said, unimpressed by the famous Walker jutting chin and flashing eyes.

'Well, take a good look at me,' Walker said, and put his shoulders with their badges of rank under the soldier's eyes. 'What now?'

The soldier took a good look and shrugged. 'Well, judging by your crossed swords and battle-axes, you're either a butcher or a pioneer.'

The Australians could not be induced to conform to normal British military discipline, and the less rigid British commanders, such as Birdwood himself, gave up trying. Much has been made of the Australians' 'love' of 'Birdie', but it was nothing more than the tolerance they granted any 'decent enough bloke'. Birdwood and the Australians came from opposite ends of understanding, and all they had in common was a form of English language, limited and crude in the case of many of the Australians, stilted and artificially affable in Birdwood. But he genuinely liked the Australians, and while he might have wished for more British-type military discipline, he recognized their quality as fighters and active-service soldiers.

One of his men, with typical Anzac ingenuity, invented the periscope rifle, which a soldier could place on the trench parapet and aim by means of a double-mirror telescope. The inventor, Lance-Corporal W.C. Beech, of the 2nd Battalion, was spotted at work by Major T. Blamey, who had Beech brought to Headquarters to demonstrate his rifle; then he was given charge of a 'factory' on the beach. When tested, Beech's rifle was found to be deadly up to 300 yards, and its efficacy transformed the situation at Quinn's Post. The post was more than half surrounded and wholly overlooked, but the periscope rifle gave the Australians so much advantage that the local Turkish commander ordered his men not to show his heads above the parapet.

By mid-May the Turks already regarded Anzac as a greater menace than Helles. It was less than five miles from the great supply depot at Kilia Bay and only a few hundred yards from positions on the main ridge, from where the Narrows could be observed and fired on. Three Turkish divisions outnumbered the Anzacs in the astonishingly small bridgehead. In May it was roughly triangular shaped, with a base of one and a half miles on the coast and its apex at Quinn's Post, 1,000 yards from the sea. It covered less than 400 acres – two-thirds of a square mile. Tenacity held the position rather than force of arms.

In a normal region of war a rest area might be twenty miles behind the lines. At Anzac the one rest area was a gully less than 800 yards from the Turkish front line. Enemy fire could not reach it, but every noise of battle did so and the men were still required to work They had to fight and dig and tunnel, build roads, disembark stores and carry food and water to the front line and wounded away from it, though at Anzac practically everywhere was the front line. It was just that certain parts were more dangerous and exposed than others.

Artillery support was grotesquely inadequate. The principal guns were 18-pounders and artillery officers were constantly looking for suitable places at which to place their guns, but by the middle of May only twenty were in position. Birdwood had two Indian mountain batteries, one New Zealand battery of 4.5-inch howitzers and two old 6-inch howitzers landed by the Navy. The Turks had about fifty guns, and with many miles of ground had no problem in finding good places at which to station them. Had they been well supplied with shells they could have caused havoc in the crowded Anzac lines.

British Intelligence, never particularly effective at Gallipoli, was frustrated by the aimless shuffling of Turkish units. Reinforcements came not from regular depots but from other regiments, thus unintentionally defeating the efforts of British Intelligence officers to gauge the Turkish strength. In fact, by 16 May the Turks had about 40,000 troops in position at Anzac, and they were working up to a major attack whose objective was to push the 12,500 Australians and New Zealanders into the sea.

18 May puzzled and worried the defenders – it was too quiet. The incessant rifle fire had stopped; this could mean that the Turks were regrouping or perhaps were issuing ammunition and supplies. Naval aeroplanes reported that the Turks were concentrating and that reinforcements were reaching Ak Bashi Bay. In fact the Turkish Army was moving to the orders of Enver for a general assault. The plan was simple: Break the centre of the Anzac line, then crumple up the separated portions and massacre the Anzacs on the beaches.

The Anzacs slept fitfully. At 3 a.m. the entire garrison stood to arms, peering into the gloom as it slowly gave way to daybreak. At 3.20, the first Turks were seen in Wire Valley and soon after several columns came over 400 Plateau. In general, the Turks had to cover 200 yards of flat, scrubby ground. Forming into two rows, they came on steadily, looking in the dim light rather like cardboard cut-outs on a rifle range. The Australian bullets hit them just as easily. The Australians sat or stood on their own parapets so that they could aim more precisely and the Turks went down in hundreds, with individual Australians killing thirty or more Turks. Men came up from the gullies to try and 'buy' a place in the firing line with some food luxury or other desirable item. 'Come on down and give us a go, Bill,' a soldier would plead, 'I'm a miles better shot than you.' Some of these reckless Australians were shot from their perches.

At Quinn's the Turks mounted five fierce attacks, and at the Nek, at Pope's Hill and on Bolton's Ridge they stubbornly pressed on towards the Australian rifle muzzles. At Courtney's a party of bomb-throwing Turks captured a small part of the post, but were killed or ejected by the heroism of Lance-Corporal Albert Jacka, 14th Battalion. He won the Victoria Cross.

By 5 a.m the Turkish attack had collapsed, but at various points local commanders tried to revive it. The Turks hardly got out of their trenches before being hit. Before noon the great battle was over, and the weary but exultant Australians counted 3,000 Turkish dead in front of their trenches. The shocked Turks suffered 10,000 casualties in all to the Anzacs' 600, including one hundred killed. In repulsing the Turks, the Australians fired 948,000 bullets from their rifles and machine-guns.

Now was the time for a spirited counter-attack, mainly with the 2,500 Australian reserve troops, who had not been involved in the battle. The disparity in numbers would not have permitted a complete breakthrough, but good plateau land could have been taken. Any senior British or Australian officer had only to look over the parapet at the bloody carnage to know that the Turks must for a few hours be in a state of desperate confusion. But no plans had been made in advance, and now orders were slow in arriving. It was 2 p.m. before General Godley ordered a company of the Wellington Mounted Rifles to raid enemy trenches at the Nek. The Turks, steadied by surviving officers, checked this small assault. At 2.15 Birdwood received an order from GHQ; he was to counter-attack as soon as the Turkish assaults had been repulsed. But that had taken place three hours before, and now it was too late and a great chance had been missed. Virtually all orders arrived too late during the Gallipoli campaign.

On that warm evening the Australians faced a worse threat from the dead Turks than from the living. Within a few days their corpses would present a dangerous sanitary problem. In any other terrain the troops could have retreated twenty yards;

at Anzac a pullback of only a few feet was impossible. Birdwood told Hamilton he wanted to arrange a truce while dead and wounded were removed. Hamilton was reluctant. On no account was Birdwood or his staff to initiate such a truce, but they could accept one if proposed by the Turks. Hamilton should have known by then that corpses did not bother the Turks; they often let them rot rather than bury them and they were unperturbed about having them in the trenches. Nor were they much concerned about bringing in wounded men from no-man's land, even when they cried out for help.

By the following night Colonel R. Owen, temporarily commanding the 1st Australian Brigade, could no longer tolerate the conditions on his front, and the suffering of the wounded Turks appalled him. Unaware of Hamilton's order, Owen hoisted a Red Cross flag, which was at once shot down. This angered the Australians, but before they could open fire a Turkish messenger with a white flag ran across to apologize for the incident. Within minutes several Red Crescent (the Muslim Red Cross equivalent) flags shot up from the Turkish trenches and stretcher-bearers climbed out. Australians advanced to meet them, and both sides dug graves.

A Turkish soldier picked up an Australian grenade and was making off with it when an Australian called out. A Turkish officer chased the thief, grabbed the grenade and kicked the culprit. Then with a bow and many apologies he handed over the bomb. The soldiers' paper, *Peninsula Press*, observed that 'the burial proceeded easily, thanks to the correct attitude of the Turkish officers'.

Birdwood brought the unofficial truce to an end in case the Turks made a sneak attack, but a message was sent that a normal truce could be arranged if a staff officer would report to Birdwood's headquarters. This and another meeting resulted in an armistice agreed by Hamilton and von Sanders, between 7.30 a.m. and 4.30 p.m. on 24 May. In these nine hours at least 3,000 Turkish dead were buried.

Aubrey Herbert, author and Member of Parliament, was an interpreter at Gallipoli, and at the time of the truce was much in demand. At one place he saw about 4,000 dead, with two wounded men crying in 'that multitude of silence'. The dead filled acres of ground, with entire companies annihilated by machine-gun fire as they ran forward; their heads were doubled under them with the impetus of their rush. The Turkish captain with Herbert said, 'At this spectacle even the most gentle must feel savage and the most savage must weep.'

From the 'Defence of Anzac', as the action is known in British military history, the Turks learned that only heavy artillery and a vast quantity of high-explosive shells could drive the Anzacs out, and they never again tried on the same scale. Equally they had learned that there was little chance of the Anzacs breaking through the Turkish positions. They had had an opportunity but had not taken it.

The British commanders learnt that a small number of good troops could hold the Turks. This important fact might have been more imaginatively explored with a new approach to tactics.

Before the battle of Anzac Birdwood had suggested breaking out of his bridgehead, pointing out to Hamilton that he had a chance to crack the Turkish lines, which were weakest on his own extreme left flank. If he could use General Cox's brigade of Indian troops, used to hill climbing, he could take the heights of Koja Chemen Tepe, anchor his line on this feature and have a view towards the Straits. Then, with Achi Baba in the south captured, a 'really large force' could be landed at Anzac. With these troops Birdwood would take high ground dominating Kilia Bay. 'With luck' – Birdwood's words – the Turkish communications along the peninsula would be cut.

Since Hamilton's original plan had been to cut the peninsula across from Anzac, he liked Birdwood's idea, especially as the battles for Krithia had done nothing to gain control of the Narrows. He wrote to Birdwood on 18 May:

More and more it seems to me that when we have once got Achi Baba we may not find it advisable to press on further from the south. Then, if my half-formed ideas mature as I think possible, the main push and decisive movement will be made from the base you are so gallantly holding. I want you, and especially your regimental officers and men, who have not and cannot possibly have a wide view of the war chessboard in their ken, to realise the full importance of the work they are making good at the hourly risk of their lives. To them it must sometimes seem a very inadequate reward to hold a few miles of worthless scrubby mountain, but it is not so; and the maintenance of the position at Sari Bair may prove to be the fulcrum for the lever that will topple over Germany and the pride of the Germans.

This letter shows Hamilton's interest in the overview; he was thinking outside Gallipoli and the Dardanelles. It is possible that he was too concerned with the strategic importance of his mission and thus too little concerned with his own tactics.

While Hamilton's 'half-formed ideas' were maturing, the New Zealand Mounted Rifles were probing the left of northern flank to find a way of reaching the main ridge near Chunuk Bair. Major P.J. Overton of the Canterbury Mounted Rifles led some particularly daring patrols into the fastnesses of the dried-out watercourses of Sazli Beit Dere and Chailak Dere.

Birdwood evolved a plan which he sent to GHQ on 30 May, and which formed the basis of a much larger operation in August. Birdwood reckoned he could succeed in these operations with 22,000 men – and he needed only the Indian Brigade to have this number. Later he would occupy Gun Ridge, for which he would need one fresh additional division. Unfortunately, about the time Birdwood was sending in his report, the Turks began to strengthen their right and it was clear to officers who were often on patrol in the ravines, including the observant Overton, that it was already too late for an Anzac attack. Once again the interval between concept and execution was too long.

The ferocious battle of Anzac had an interesting side effect. As Bean observes, from the morning of 19 May onwards 'the attitude of the Anzac troops towards the individual Turks was rather that of opponents in a friendly game'. The Australians had seen at close quarters the carnage their small-arms fire had inflicted on the Turks, and they were sorry for them. These generally inarticulate men, so afraid of appearing sentimental, seemed to realize that they and the Turks had at least one thing in common – they were both victims of the schemes of politicians and of the insensitivity of generals.

On 30 May Hamilton was writing with apparent sensitivity:

There are poets and writers who see naught in war but carrion, filth, savagery and horror. The heroism of the rank and file makes no appeal. They refuse war the credit of being the only exercise in devotion on the large scale existing in this world. The superb moral victory over death leaves them cold. . . . To me this is no valley of death – it is a valley brim full of life at its highest power . . . a radiant force of camaraderie in action.

That the moral victory over death had been won by dying seems to have escaped Hamilton. Within a few days he would have other valleys brim full of life in death.

In Britain the scheming was still going on, the necessary prelude to the next bloodbath on the peninsula. Perhaps the most significant event was a public speech by Winston Churchill at Dundee on 5 June. Despite his demotion and near disgrace, Churchill still had his teeth firmly into the bone of contention. Calling for the seizure of Constantinople with a victory 'such as this war has not yet seen', he spelled out the advantages:

> There was never a great subsidiary operation of war in which a more complete harmony of strategic, political and economic advantages has combined, or which stood in truer relation to the main decision, which is the central theatre. Through the Narrows of the Dardanelles and across the ridges of the Gallipoli peninsula lie some of the shortest paths to a triumphant peace.

Quite apart from the debatable nature of his assertion, it seemed that even now Churchill was unaware of what 'over the ridges' meant in human terms. He was always strong on concepts, weak on casualties.

8

'Singularly Brainless and Suicidal Warfare'

On the Helles front, at the end of the second battle of Krithia on 8 May, the Allies held a line of about two and three-quarter miles, a third of it French, stretching from the Aegean coast to the Dardanelles. On average the distance between front line and base – the landing beaches of W and V – was three miles. It was as if the Allies held the tip of a long finger pointing downwards. Much of the area was under observation by the Turks on Achi Baba, from where they could direct their guns. From Allied general to corporal the cry was, 'if only we could take Achi Baba'.

It has always been a military maxim to 'take the high ground', but in the case of Achi Baba the maxim became mania. By the first week in May the Navy had much more valuable observation by kit balloon and aeroplane than any possible view from Achi Baba. Since this hill was the Turks' main observation platform it would have been helpful for the British to deprive them of it, but its capture was not imperative. The truth is that Kitchener, Hamilton, de Robeck and Hunter-Weston had an unhealthy obsession about this fatal hill and it lured them as moths to a flame.

The British forces consisted of the 29th Division, two

brigades of the 42nd Division, the 19th Infantry Brigade and five battalions of the Royal Naval Division. Something must be said about this last formation. Largely Churchill's idea, the RND was formed of seamen and marines for whom no sea jobs were available. These men were naturally more at home afloat and most became soldiers with great reluctance. They were formed into battalions named after great naval commanders, Nelson, Collingwood, Hawke, Hood, Anson. Trying to remain as naval as possible, the RND had petty officers instead of sergeants and leading seamen for corporals. No attempts were made to conform to army parlance; thus men absent without leave were 'adrift' and sick men attended not the regimental aid post but 'sick bay'. Anchors were stencilled on gun limbers and other equipment and, most startling of all to the other soldiers, the RND men were allowed to grow beards. Generally older than their army comrades, the RND troops consequently found conditions at Gallipoli harder and more exhausting, but their discipline was good and their trenches were often cleaner and in better trim than those of the soldiers.

The French had two divisions of African troops. By one of those extraordinary faults of administration so typical of the Gallipoli campaign, the British had no Corps HQ staff at Helles. General Headquarters, remote from events on the island of Imbros, commanded in principle, but in practice the Helles operations were masterminded by Major-General Hunter-Weston, who, as Henry Nevinson wrote, 'certainly never spared his troops'.

Whatever Hunter-Weston's failings he could not be faulted for energy and optimism. The day after the second battle of Krithia he produced an order for his division, instructing his subordinates to maintain 'a ceaseless initiative' as well as unending offensive and continual trench work. He wanted reconnaissance right up to the enemy lines, night advances and steady nibbling away of no-man's land. His last sentence: 'If another offensive in the immediate future is prepared along these lines Sir Ian Hamilton feels sure that the capture of the Achi Baba position will be certainly and speedily achieved.'

At that moment Hunter-Weston had no right to be ascribing such optimism to his chief, though his own buoyancy was to lead Hamilton into other gambles. The troops knew very well that things could hardly be more wrong but in the 29th Division Hunter-Weston and Hamilton were blessed with men of exceptional courage and stoicism. For seventeen days and nights they had fought without relief, losing more than half their officers and about half the rank and file. In a special order Hamilton announced: 'They have been illuminating the pages of history with their blood. . . . I tender to Major-General Hunter-Weston and to his division my profoundest sympathy with their losses and my warmest congratulations on their achievement.'

The achievement was mediocre, though through no fault of the men. After the battle they quickly recovered their spirits, helped by the perfect weather, reasonable food – at this time – and bathing in the sea.

Not all deaths occurred in action or at the hands of the enemy, as Private W.J. Crawford of the 6th Highland Light Infantry discovered. He had been sent in the early morning on an errand from the front to battalion HQ in the rear, and passed a clump of stunted trees with a sentry on duty at what appeared to be an entrance to the wood. After he had walked about 150 yards past the sentry he was surprised to hear a rifle volley from the wood. A few hours later as he returned to the front he came to the sentry still on duty, but this time there was also a small board nailed to a nearby tree. On it was a typed announcement that a private soldier of a regular battalion had been tried by a Field General Court Martial for deserting his post in the face of the enemy, for the second time. Having been found guilty he was sentenced to be shot and the sentence had been duly carried out that morning.

One man who took seriously Hunter-Weston's insistence on

local offensive action was Major-General H.V. Cox commanding the Indian Brigade, who captured a troublesome Turkish spot on the extreme left. It was as neat an operation as any at Gallipoli. Under cover of naval bombardment, on the night of 12 May a double company of I/6th Gurkhas (Lieutenant-Colonel C.G. Bruce) crept along the shore to the foot of a bluff (later known as Gurkha Bluff) at the north end of Y Beach, where they scaled the cliff and dug themselves in without opposition. At 4 a.m. another double company crept along the beach to extend the captured position to the right.

Turks in the intervening nullah, fearful at finding themselves outflanked, retired. An hour later the rest of the Gurkha battalion, supported by Sikhs, advanced in the open to occupy a new line. Without loss, the Gurkhas had gained more than 500 yards where progress had been considered impossible. To a point, the lesson was observed by Hunter-Weston; he told his brigadiers to steal ground by night advance and without fighting, so that the British line could be advanced closer to the Turkish line – hopefully to within 200 yards – before the next major assault. It did not occur to him that the major assault itself might succeed by night.

On 24 May the War Office promoted him to Lieutenant-General, to command the new VIII Corps, made up of all the British units at Helles. The Corps rapidly grew in strength, though it still lacked an adequate HQ staff.

On the right of the line, General Gouraud had taken over from the recalled d'Amade and found the troops still badly shaken by their losses in the second battle of Krithia. The French colonial troops faced formidable Turkish lines. Fearful of any creeping advance along the Dardanelles shore, the Turks had two lines of trenches supported by four small but powerful redoubts on Kereves Spur – known to the French as Fortin Le Gouez, La Rognon, the Haricot and the Quadrilateral. Almost everywhere the French were fearfully vulnerable to the Turkish guns on the Asiatic shore, which could fire on the French right and the entire back area. Twice on 21 June the French stormed and captured Haricot, but lost so many officers – thirty of them, as well as 2,500 men – that the African troops could not hold it. The action had been badly conceived. Gouraud's front was only 650 yards, giving him all the benefits of a concentrated artillery attack, but if the French soldiers broke through – as they did – they at once came within easy range of the Truks on either flank. On 31 May, in a more intelligent surprise attack, the French captured Fortin Le Gouez with little loss.

Gouraud was as obsessed with Achi Baba as were his British colleagues. Its capture, he had told GHQ on 20 May, was a military necessity, but any future attack would need to be prepared with all the care of a trench attack in France. Such attacks in France had been consistently disastrous, but Gouraud offered nothing more imaginative. As with the earlier battles for Krithia, he favoured an all-out assault, with the line pivoting on the French right and swinging like a door from the left. With Achi Baba taken, he suggested, every available man should be moved to Anzac for a straight thrust across the peninsula to Maidos. The idea made sense – provided that any breach in the Turkish defences was quickly exploited.

At this moment Hamilton could count on fairly high morale, as the Turkish defeat at Anzac had put most officers and men in good heart. Hamilton himself was worried as he had received Intelligence reports that the Turks opposing him amounted to 100,000. He telegraphed Kitchener on 17 May: 'The movement of a quarter of a million men [a gross exaggeration] against us seems to be well under way . . . and the positions we hold are not such as to enable me to envisage with soldierly equanimity the probability of such large forces being massed against my troops without let or hindrance.'

This prolixity brought a direct answer on 3 June: 'Are you convinced that with immediate reinforcements . . . you could force the position [of Achi Baba and the Kilid Bahr plateau] and thus finish the Dardanelles operations?'

While Kitchener had been mulling over this question, Hamilton was preparing a general attack – though the plans were, in fact, those of Hunter-Weston and Gouraud. Since Kitchener's question had been overtaken by events, Hamilton replied: 'Tomorrow I am fighting a general action. I feel sure you will wish me to defer my answer till I see the result.'

He was referring to his third attack of Krithia. With this battle on 4 June the contest at Helles entered the stage of trench-fighting on the European pattern, which Gouraud wanted. The British trench line at this date faced the enemy's at an average distance of about 200 yards along most of its front, and the trenches of both Allies and Turks ran clear across the peninsula.

The plans, though wrongly conceived, were thorough and clear, and 30,000 men were to be used, 20,000 of them in the first fighting. Intelligence had no idea of the Turkish force opposite, but it amounted to at least 25,000 men and possibly 28,000, plus sixty-four field- and mountain-guns and twenty-two guns and howitzers of medium and heavy calibre.

The Allied infantry assault was timed for noon on 4 June, with certain preliminaries. On paper it appeared like this:

8 a.m. to 10.30 a.m.	Bombardment of strong points. Final registration by field batteries.
11.05 to 11.20	Bombardment of enemy front line.
11.20 to 11.30	All guns cease fire, except those on enemy's line of approach. Infantry will cheer and show fixed bayonets above trenches to induce the enemy to man his parapets.
11.30 to noon	Intensive bombardment of enemy front line.

| 12 noon | Batteries increase their range. Infantry, 1st wave, assault 1st objective. |
| 12.15 p.m. | Infantry, 2nd wave, assault 2nd objective. |

Parts of the plan brought wry smiles from the officers and ribald comment from the men. For instance, units were informed that the best way of clearing an enemy trench was by squads of bombers. Most of the British troops had never seen a bomb. In the 42nd Division the allotment was eight to a platoon, mostly of the jam-tin variety. As the Australians at Anzac already knew, the Turks had a much superior bomb, in large quantities.

The artillery bombardment was heavy, and the dust and smoke gave the British the impression of great destruction. How could anybody be left alive in the Turkish front trenches? The answer was simple: The British 18-pounders were provided only with shrapnel shells, designed to burst in the air and shower down their steel balls. But the Turkish trenches had head cover and the riflemen fired from loopholes, so that the shrapnel caused few casualties. The 11,000 rounds of 18-pounder shrapnel shell fired that day were mostly wasted. The heavier guns firing high-explosive shells had only 1,240 rounds among them. Shrapnel is ideal against troops in the open, but only high explosive can destroy trenches.

At midday the whole line of British and French infantry advanced in an onslaught that succeeded beyond expectation. On much of the front they captured three successive lines of Turkish trenches, and many senior officer spectators believed that in some sectors the Turkish defence system was so thoroughly penetrated that the ground beyond was open. But within a few hours the Turks repelled the French in a counter-attack and reoccupied their trenches on a dominant ridge. From this height they could fire directly along the trenches taken by the Royal Naval Division in the hollow of Kanli Dere. Inevitably the right of this division was thrown back, suffering heavily in the open. The Collingwood battalion, having moved off splendidly, was caught by this heavy flanking fire and within minutes ceased to exist. The men of the Howe and Hood battalions also marched into heavy fire. The result was that within forty-five minutes sixty out of seventy officers were casualties and more than 1,000 of 1,900 men; the shaken survivors retreated to their old front line.

In the centre the Lancashire Territorials held out, but their flank was hanging loose and Hamilton eventually ordered them to withdraw. The 29th Division clung valiantly to a salient south-west of Krithia, but was driven back from this advanced position. In this battle about another 4,000 British soldiers became casualties. The Turks, alarmed at losing their front line for a time, soon extended their whole trench system into a virtually impregnable gridiron of trenches, of formidable depth and breadth.

It is possible that the repulse of 4 June forced Hamilton to rethink his policy of 'hammering away' at the Turkish trenches. At Anzac an opening still existed – indeed, it had been open right from the beginning. The Turks had not fortified the heights on the northern flank leading to Koja Chemen Tepe, known as Hill 971, in the belief that they were impassable. The summit of 971 overlooked the Turkish land *and* sea communications, and it was possible that by capturing it the British could cut the Turkish Army's lines of communication. Almost certainly, von Sanders would have to withdraw whole divisions. As Hamilton noted, he had a chance to strike a major blow 'unexpectedly against some key Turkish position not prepared for defence'. Braithwaite opposed the plan as over-adventurous, but Birdwood thought he could carry it through with an additional division and brigade.

On 7 June, the Dardanelles Committee met for the first time, under Asquith's chairmanship, to consider what action to take at Gallipoli. The members had two papers to consider, one each by Kitchener and Churchill. Kitchener rejected all thoughts of evacuating Gallipoli – to do so would have been to admit that he had erred in going there in the first place – but doubted that even with much stronger forces Hamilton could achieve success. He proposed to replace Hamilton's losses and allow him to move ahead gradually – a wait-and-see attitude.

Churchill wanted Hamilton to be given enough reinforcements to bring about a decisive victory. He made some pointed comparisons. Gallipoli might not be going well, but it had better prospects than the Western Front. Here, in two months, the Allies had suffered 320,000 casualties in taking eight square miles of territory. Furthermore, the Germans had lost only 100,000 men. It made sense, Churchill reasoned, for the Allies to remain on the defensive in France and Belgium throughout 1915 while mounting a powerful thrust at the Dardanelles. Kitchener and others – French as well as British – while not perhaps supporting the idea of a main campaign at Gallipoli, certainly wanted Western Front offensives postponed until 1916. But the Commander-in-Chief, Joffre, and the British military leaders in France, wanted to retain top priority for the Western Front.

Impressed by Churchill's arguments – or perhaps glad of the opportunity to have a scheme for which he could blame Churchill if everything went wrong – Kitchener came around and proposed to send Hamilton the reinforcements he needed so that another major offensive could be mounted in the second week of July. Thus, Hamilton heard from Kitchener that three New Army divisions were available to him. This was spectacularly good news, since it implied that the Dardanelles Committee had renewed its trust in him. Losing no time, Hamilton outlined his northern scheme to Birdwood – who had already thought of it – and to Hunter-Weston and Gouraud on 11 June. To Hamilton's satisfaction, 'everyone was keen and sanguine'.

Gouraud was yet another general who had wanted to land in Besika Bay and advance on Chanak. As he said in a report on 19 May, this would clear the Straits and allow the fleet through, but 100,000 men would be required. Hamilton, with nothing like 100,000 men, could do no more than 'take note' of the French leader's proposals. Now, hearing that three more British divisions were on their way to Gallipoli, Gouraud produced a quite different plan on 13 June. He recommended a landing north of Bulair which he rightly noted could threaten Constantinople itself. A valiant as well as an intelligent man, Gouraud was seriously wounded on 30 June and was taken back to France, so he could not press his Bulair plan. The French command now devolved on General Bailloud, described bluntly by Hankey as 'the most confirmed pessimist . . . should be superseded.' But Bailloud was not entirely stupid: He urged his government to insist that Hamilton divert two of his three new diversions for an attack in Asia. In this he was following Gouraud. Again Hamilton declined, on the grounds that a landing in Asia would be too difficult and dangerous unless the Allies could first weaken the garrison there by forcing the Turks to send reinforcements to the peninsula.

Rather belatedly, Kitchener was now convinced that assaulting prepared positions was a futile waste, so he sent Hamilton a message: 'The only way to make a real success of an attack is by surprise. . . . When the surprise ceases to be operative, in so far that the advance is checked and the enemy begins to collect from all sides to oppose the attackers, then perseverance becomes merely a useless waste of life.'

The significant fact is that this message was sent verbally through Lieutenant-General Sir Frederick Stopford, who was to command the new Corps now assembling. Stopford committed Kitchener's words to memory – but took absolutely no heed of them when it fell to him to achieve surprise and so prevent a useless waste of life.

Hamilton, irritated by Kitchener's patronizing advice, told

Stopford that Kitchener had not only anticipated his own plans for the new campaign but had 'dived right down into the muddle of twentieth century war and finds lying at the bottom of it the only original idea of war in the year I' [that is, the idea of surprise in attack].

Before the new great offensive got under way, Hamilton authorized two more attempts to 'hammer away' at Achi Baba. The Australian official historian, Bean, says that Hamilton's approval of these assaults 'is harder to understand than any other act of his leadership'. Indeed, his approval shows complete lack of judgement, and one wonders if the dysentery from which he was suffering had made him incapable of real decision. 'It fills me with a desperate longing to lie down and do nothing but rest,' he wrote on 13 July.

If any thought at all lay behind the great attacks, it was inspired by a report that after months of passive duty troops tended to become reluctant to leave the trenches to attack; hence, so this report concluded, it was necessary to keep attacking. The idea of maintaining both activity and fighting spirit by constant raiding had not yet gained ground.

On 28 June Hunter-Weston advanced the 29th Division for 1,000 yards along the Aegean sea coast at Gully Spur. At the same time, a brigade of the 52nd Division, next to the 29th, with its right edge anchored on the centre of the British line, made a wheeling movement to retain contact with the 29th. The shell supply was deficient for such a large general movement, and the artillery commander concentrated his bombardment on the 29th Division's front.

Here some enemy trenches were taken, but elsewhere the operation failed – yet Hamilton was to write that, 'We had the Turks beaten then . . . we felt victory in the air. . .'. Hunter-Weston also claimed a victory. The 4,000 British casualties were not aware of any victory, and in the dreadful summer heat the survivors were near prostration with exhaustion and thirst. Some became demented. Padre

Creighton of the 88th Brigade observed much of this action, and wrote in his diary:

> Only about 1,300 of the brigade came back, the brigadier and two colonels killed and some 1,700 men knocked out, practically nothing gained and almost a whole brigade put out of action. These things seem to happen every battle. The amount of unnecessary lives simply thrown away is appalling.

The generals assessed the gain of a little ground as 'victory', but such a gain meant nothing unless a path had been opened or the Turks flung into retreat. Though suffering many casualties – something like 16,000 between 28 June and 5 July – the Turks mounted counter-attack after counter-attack. The staff at GHQ and at VIII Corps HQ interpreted these furious assaults as Turkish desperation and were consequently pleased. The divisional generals, closer to the action, were caustically critical and even bitter. Hunter-Weston had told the Brigade-Major of the 156th Scottish Brigade that he was glad of the opportunity of 'blooding the pups'. He had blooded them well and truly – the brigade lost 1,353 men, nearly half its total strength. The divisional commander, Major-General C.G.A. Egerton was profoundly angered when he heard of this Hunter-Weston observation. Later, when he took Hamilton around the division on an inspection tour, he introduced each unit as 'the remains' of the particular battalion. Hamilton endured this for a time but finally rebuked Egerton. There is no record that he rebuked Hunter-Weston and his equally enthusiastic hammerer and chief General Staff Officer, Brigadier H.E. Street. Hunter-Weston urged Hamilton to send Egerton away. Even here Hamilton could not make a decision for himself but passed the matter to Kitchener, describing Egerton as 'highly strung'. Rather later Egerton himself settled the matter by collapsing from strain and being evacuated – but not before

Hunter-Weston had paid him a supreme insult, described later in this chapter.

What it felt like to be at the receiving end of a Turkish counter-attack is well described in a previoulsy unpublished account by Lieutenant Greville Cripps, originally of the 9th Somerset Light Infantry but sent as a reinforcement to the Royal Dublin Fusiliers. On the evening of 4 July, Cripps was in the front line and uneasy about signs of an impending Turkish attack against his position, which was weakly held with little support possible from the rear:

Sure enough at just before sunrise, I saw the tops of many ladders protruding from the Turkish trenches and soon over they came in their hundreds, led by a man with a large crescent flag and all shouting to Allah. My dozen or so men panicked, dropped their rifles, picks and shovels and bolted down the communications trench leaving me alone between the two sandbag barricades.

I lit one of the ridiculous jam-tin bombs which I hurled out towards the advancing Turks, when to my horror one Turk climbed on top of the further barricade and another had shoved his rifle through the loophole in the steel plate. All I could do was to dive into the sort of alcove where the steel plate was and attempt a back-handed throw of another jam-tin bomb. This bomb hit one of the top sand-bags and bounced back to me, say some 3–4 yards behind and all I could do was to present my rear end to receive a very unpleasant spattering of pieces of the jam-tin in my back side, legs and lower back. However I managed to light another jam-tin bomb and this was most successful, knocking out the Turk standing on top of the barricade and wounding the Turk firing madly through the loophole in the steel plate a few inches from my head.

Quickly I managed to shove out this Turkish rifle from

the loophole in the steel plate and seizing a rifle and with a full box of ammunition in my reach, I fired a very rapid 15 or more rounds a minute into masses of Turks completely filling this 90/120 yards of dead straight trench. My aimed bullets did frightful slaughter; at this mighty short range, every bullet must have dug into more than one Turk. Soon the rifle got so damned hot that I had to seize another until this second rifle also became far too hot and then with even a third rifle I carried on until there seemed nothing standing to hit by which time the dead and wounded Turks in that very deep wide and straight original Turkish fire trench must have numbered between 100 and 200. While I was so busy firing and handing out such drastic killing at such short range, I recall that I was shouting and yelling like a madman.

Then foolishly I looked over the top, even climbed out to collect some of the Turkish black cricket ball bombs, when Lt Young came along with some men, and I started to snipe at some Turks I could see, only to get a Turkish bullet hit my rifle, and break up, leaving a piece stuck in my forehead and a small fragment in the wall lining of my tummy. The rest of this bullet wounded one of the Dublin Tommies who had come along with Lt Young.

I then handed over this corner to Lt Young and managed to get down to the Nullah to see the MO, so that he could do something about all the jam-tin in my rear quarters and after being somewhat patched up, I returned to the famous corner junction just as the Turks attacked again. Three of these Turks managed to drop down flat by the parapet of the now partly built circular trench we had been digging.

Seizing a rifle, I shoved in 5 rounds, jumped on top of the barricade and had these three very scared and sheepishly looking Turks at 3–4 yards range, lying prone. I hit number one and his head was a mere shambles and then fired quickly at numbers two and three, hitting both but as they seemed still alive, I gave each another shot, but then of the very many Turkish bullets whistling around me one went straight through my upper right arm, right and cleanly through the single bone, also damaging my artery and the main nerve.

It was like being hit with a sledge hammer but what was in a way worse was that I was knocked off the top of the parapet, head over heels and landed with the rifle on top of me.

On another occasion Cripps wrote: 'I got so keen on sniping that I was at it every spare moment and had some narrow squeaks myself. One morning a Turkish sniper had first shot at me and put his bullet right through the peak of my cap, its exit being through the back band; the bullet must have parted my hair. Another day I was firing through a sand-bag loophole when a Turkish bullet cut the side of the bag nearest my left ear, filling my eyes and ear full of sand and almost deafening me. Unfortunately, I came in for a lot of criticism as I naturally drew attention to our trench; I once got a definite order from the major to stop sniping. The Tommies, so I heard, had given me the name of the "Mad Mullah".'*

Another 'professional' sniper was Private Charles Watkins of the 6th Battalion Lancashire Fusiliers. One of the best soldier-chroniclers of the human side of war, Watkins tells the story† of two 'Aussie blokes' who visited his Helles trench one day when he was on sniping duty. Australian infantry was not engaged at Helles after the May attack, but

---

* At Delville Wood, on the Somme in 1916, Cripps was awarded the Military Cross in what he called a 'beastly do'. Though recommended, he received no award at Gallipoli.
† In his privately printed book *Lost Endeavour*, 1971, and reproduced with his permission.

some of their artillery was supporting the British, and Watkins' visitors were artillery sergeants:

Huge chaps – about 6' 4″ and broad with it – they were seeking an Artillery observation post as far forward as possible for the next offensive of ours. That's how they came to be in front of our front line and chatting with me. One was a Staff Sergeant and did all the talking and the other, a Corporal, just listened and didn't say a lot. The Staff Sergeant grew intrigued with my job and wanted to have a go himself but I told him the score and that if you didn't know the trick, you'd be a dead duck before you could look round. This seemed to peeve him – 'didn't want any Pommie to tell him all about shooting'. 'Back in Austry-lia he could shoot the toe-nail off a 'possum's left foot'. He was a genial smiling bloke of about 35 to 40 with a huge fair moustache, and pleasant enough to talk to, so I tried to kid him into talking about life 'down-under'. I didn't want any trouble round this steel plate.

But he still ached to have a go and finally got real mad. As we say in the Army he 'shoved his stripes under my nose' and told me to hand him the rifle, 'and that's an order,' he says. So I handed it over, deeming it best to say no more, and stood alongside him pissing myself with anxiety while he took a long and careful sight. Then there was a 'plop' and when the Corporal and I picked him up he was as dead as ever a man can be. Then the Corporal cussed and swore – said, 'I'll get the bastard who did that to my pal' and in spite of my protests, poked the rifle through the hole himself. I hollered for our Sergeant, who came quick. But not quick enough and the Corporal, badly wounded, was later carted off by the stretcher-bearers. The body of the Staff Sergeant was carried to our front trench and we sent word back to his Battery as to what had happened.

Some two hours later, three friends of the dead Staff

Sergeant came to carry his body away. As I'd finished my two hours' sniping duty, and feeling a bit responsible for the whole business, I offered to make the fourth man and between us we carted him away with the laudable intention of carrying him to an improvised cemetery that had just been started, about a mile away. It was a very hot afternoon and after some 200 yards or so over this rough and broken country, one of the Aussies who had been the Staff Sergeant's closest friend back home, decided 'one place is as good as another once you're gorn,' so in a tuck of the ground sheltered from rifle fire we laid our burden down and scratched out a shallow grave. A good hour's sweating work it was, too, and punctuated all the time by homely Aussie expressions of grief and regret, and maledictions on the hot sun that scorched our labouring bodies. Alongside us, and indifferent to the proceedings, the cause of all our labours lay stiffly, his wide-open eyes coldly watching us with the baleful malevolence of the dead. Whenever I looked at him I seemed to detect in those immobile marble eyes, a frightening malignity. . . .

In between his labours of digging, the dead man's pal continued with his lamentations. 'How I'm going to face old Jack's Mum back in Sydney, I just don't know. Her last words to me, Tommy, afore we left, were "Keep an eye on him, won't you. He's a bit headstrong. Promise me you'll keep an eye on him."' He gave a deep sigh and rested from his digging for a time, squatting on his haunches and regarding his dead pal. 'You always was a cocky bastard, wasn't you, Jack?' he said kindly, and wagged his head reproachfully.

It was a macabre scene – this bare-headed, big, live Aussie – his sun-browned torso glistening with sweat, squatting alongside his indifferent dead pal and carrying on a reminiscent monologue of old times together. 'Remember that sheep farmer, Jack, who tried to gyp us of the week's pay he owed us for shearing, and the way you held him upside down to empty his pockets. And then the way you chucked him into the sheep-dip trough after. I thought I'd 'a died laughing.' Chuckling reminiscences like this went on for a few minutes – and I sat and watched 'em – an interested spectator of these two Aussies, the live and the dead, in comradely communion. Somehow, death doesn't seem to have the same dreadful finality among the irreligious soldiery as it does with their more religious brethren. It's more as if one of their gang had been posted away on detached duty. Maybe it's this attitude that enables them to survive, while still keeping their sanity, the daily harvest of the grim Reaper. Or maybe it is that in the blind ignorance of the teachings of religion itself, they've stumbled accidentally on the real truth of the matter.

Then I blurted out what I considered to be my share of responsibility for this tragedy. But the dead man's pal laughed this aside. 'You don't think, do you Tommy, that an Austry-lian boy is going to let any Pommie bastard stop him doing what he wants to do.' Switching suddenly to serious and solemn vein, 'Well, I guess we'd better do old Jack the honours,' and we laid him in his shallow grave.

Then the Aussie unstrapped his wide-brimmed feathered slouch hat from the top of his pack, straightened out some of the creases and knocked a cloud of dust off it before solemnly donning it, stood alongside the grave for a few seconds, then just as solemnly doffed it. The proprieties of interment thus duly observed and completed to his satisfaction, he said, 'I suppose someone should say a bit of a prayer. Any of you blokes know any – I've forgotten all mine.' There was a shuffle of denial from the other two Aussies, so I volunteered the Lord's Prayer, wondering at the time how many others from this place had gone to meet Him, 'which art in Heaven', and armed with no more letters of introduction than this brief prayer. Then we filled in the space above the dead Aussie, and yet another hump appeared on this sacred ground of lost endeavour.

The other two Aussies were mostly silent, and didn't say much except for an occasional interjection of the soldier's favourite obituary, 'Poor bastard.'

The dead man's pal raised the point of marking the grave with something – 'a bit of a cross or something.' I thought of all the other 'little bits of crosses' scattered all over the Peninsula in all sorts of odd places – little wooden crosses, crudely fashioned from pieces of biscuit box wood, and with their identities scrawled in indelible pencil that the rains had by now smeared into indecipherable smudges, and said, 'Does it matter much?'

But this great big hunk of sunburnt Australian manhood was genuinely and sentimentally shocked. 'Does it matter much? There's a little lady back in Sydney, Tommy, I've got to face when I get back. How can I tell her her boy's in an unmarked grave?' He seemed appalled at my callousness. One of the other Aussies begged a bit of wood from a cook-house some distance away and returned in triumph, and with our bayonets we cut some sticks of wood and with the aid of a spare bootlace, fashioned a rough cross and pegged out our dead man's claim to immortality. With much licking of the stub of an indelible pencil he recorded the name of the dead Staff Sergeant and stood back to admire his handiwork. 'That's better, old-timer. Now I can tell yer Ma you're all tucked up nice and comfy. How many 'l's in killed, Tommy?' I told him; also, told him how to spell 'action'. As regards the date, we hazarded a guess, but the Aussie thought accuracy was of first importance, and after canvassing the opinion of a few chaps idly watching, we split the difference and settled for July 10th, 1915. Even now, the Aussie wasn't completely satisfied. He'd still got some more of the stub of the pencil left and the urge for registering immortality was strong upon him. 'Shouldn't there be some other words after the name, Tommy? A sort of good wish?'

'Requiescat in pace,' I suggested.

'Come again, Tommy?' said the Aussie, puzzled. 'What's them letters they put after a bloke's name when he's dead?'

'R.I.P.?'

'Yes, that's it, Tommy. What's it mean?'

'Oh, about the same, I guess.'

So Staff Sergeant Ballantyne, through an unfortuante error in calligraphy, became Staff Sergeant Ballantyne-RIP. One of the Aussies had some fags and we sat around a bit and smoked. Oh! blessed and mighty rare weed – how it mellowed us. Discussions ranged about the future life of Staff Sergeant Ballantyne-RIP. 'Wonder what it's like up there,' said the talkative Aussie, waving an arm vaguely skywards.

'Rum sort of place, from all I gather,' one of the others said. 'Sitting round all day singing bleeding hymns and playing harps. Praising God and all that mush.'

'What do you think, Tommy?' the talkative one asked me.

Startled, I had to admit that I didn't know much about it, but Sunday School teaching memories seemed to corroborate the description already given. 'Much about like your mate says,' I opined.

The Aussie appeared troubled. 'No sheilas?' he asked.

'Sheilas?'

'Girls. Bints,' the Aussie explained impatiently. 'Ain't there none there? And what about booze and fags? Ain't there none there, too?'

I said I didn't know, but I thought not. Memories of childhood Band of Hope Temperance Meetings were still strongly with me, with drink as the Devil's Handmaiden.

The Aussie was pensive for a bit, then gave a long low chuckle. 'No sheilas, no booze, no fags. Cor! I can just see old Jack's face when he finds out.' Then he corrected his unseemly merriment and said piously, 'Poor old Jack. And as nice a bloke as ever you could wish to meet.'

Many other 'nice blokes' were destined for the same fate as Staff Sergeant Ballantyne, since Hunter-Weston was proposing a fresh attack on 12 July. He intended to use the Royal Naval Division, either unaware or heedless of the division's dreadful condition; after two months of combat the surviving officers and men were exhausted and ill to the point of near-prostration. Only urgent appeals and warnings by senior medical officers persuaded Hunter-Weston to use the 52nd Division instead. These men were wearing the thick khaki serge in which they had left England – in the stifling, blistering heat of a Turkish July day.

Corps HQ ordered that all maps, sketches and diagrams of Turkish trenches were to be destroyed before the attack. The instruction was faithfully carried out – and vital new trench diagrams made from an aerial photograph taken two days before went up in smoke before the frontline officers ever saw them. The order was ludicrous because the Turks already knew their own trenches; if anything needed to be destroyed it was diagrams of the *British* trenches.

As usual, the plan of attack was brutally simple. At 7.45 a.m., with the sun already high, the British bombardment lifted and four lines of British and French infantry went into the attack. As usual, the men's courage was extraordinary and, as usual their losses were immense. In less than thirty minutes the 1/4th Royal Scots Fusiliers lost all but one of their officers and half their rank and file. The 1/4th King's Own Scottish Borderers, in a fruitless advance, lost more than sixty per cent of its numbers. Yet at 4.50 p.m., as planned, Hunter-Weston ordered in the second part of the attack, the 157th Brigade (of Highland regiments) with the same dismal results. By nightfall all was in confusion. Hunter-Weston's response next day was to ignore medical opinion and bring up the Royal Naval

Division, and to tell Hamilton that he and the French commander planned the capture of the original objectives with a fresh attack. Hamilton approved – adding, 'Provided our troops have the go in them, now is the time.'

He knew as well as anybody else that the men did *not* have the go in them; when ordered they nearly always got up and went forward, but this was discipline, not dash. Battalions of the Royal Naval Division and of the Royal Marine Light Infantry went into the slaughter, many of the men falling dead or wounded as they tried to make secure an exposed line under withering fire.

At 5.30 p.m., with the battle still raging, Hunter-Weston delivered his insult to Major-General Egerton by recalling him to Corps HQ and placing Major-General Shaw in temporary command of the 52nd. Shaw, just arrived on the peninsula, had no knowledge of the ground, the battle situation or the troops. Still fuming over Egerton's implied insults about his leadership, Hunter-Weston had chosen this means of disciplining him. Fortunately for everybody, the Turks did not counter-attack that night while Shaw tried vainly to come to grips with the responsibility unfairly thrown upon him. Egerton returned to his command next morning. Later he would say that the battle of 12–13 July was 'positively wicked in conception and wasteful in execution'. It is easy to understand how angry he felt; his division had landed at Helles on 6 June with 10,900 officers and men; by the evening of 13 July, it numbered 6,500.

From hospital, on 19 July, Gouraud wrote to his own Minister of War, Millerand. In his unequivocal fashion he said that the French Corps could be destroyed by the troublesome guns in Asia. They had to be silenced by a land attack, preferably at Besika Bay. Millerand was so impressed that he appealed to Kitchener to consider a landing in Asia. Kitchener's request to Hamilton for his views is Churchillian in its loaded phraseology:

The French state that the fire from the Asiatic side allows them no rest. They propose secondary operations on the Asiatic side to deal with enemy artillery, and suggest employment of 20,000 British assisted by French 75 monitors [the invaluable .75 calibre gun mounted on a floating platform]. *Would the main scheme of our operation be jeopardised by thus detaching a considerable force which may find itself employed with hostile forces of unknown strength?* [My italics.]

The question did not merely invite Hamilton to say yes, it almost demanded that he do so. Hamilton obliged. 'I am sure you will agree that a diversion, if and when necessary, must be made at my own time, not at Bailloud's, to whom I have not yet confided my plans.'

This allowed Kitchener to write to Millerand: 'You will understand how difficult it is to impose upon a commander-in-chief an operation which does not fit in with his own most carefully prepared plan.'

This was hypocrisy. Months earlier Kitchener had imposed operations on Hamilton by forbidding a landing in Asia and by limiting the number of men under his command.

On 20 July Hunter-Weston collapsed from sunstroke and, it is said, from strain. Invalided home on 25 July, he left his Helles army too exhausted and depressed to show any reaction to his departure. The British official historian, in a transparent effort to say something complimentary to Hamilton, states:

There is good reason for saying that these losses [7,700 British and 4,600 French in the three battles of 21 June, 28 June and 12–13 July] were justified by the cumulative results obtained even though the main objective, the capture of Achi Baba – was never achieved. . . . Once again . . . Sir Ian Hamilton had created a situation where an immediate resumption of the attack with fresh troops and an abundance of ammunition might have opened the road to victory.

These comments must be among the most pathetic in the literature of the Gallipoli campaign. There were no 'cumulative' results. The truth is that once again Hamilton had allowed Hunter-Weston to create casualties and nothing but casualties. The official historian's comment is, moreover, incorrect. He was writing in 1932, by which time he well knew that despite their enormous losses the Turks quickly reinforced the Helles sector with their Second Army. Given Hunter-Weston's tactics, there never was a road to victory from Helles.

Ellis Ashmead-Bartlett, correspondent for the *Daily Telegraph* and a critic of Hamilton's tactics at Gallipoli, understood the futility of Hamilton's tactics at Helles, but was constantly handicapped by military censorship. On 15 July, on the HQ island of Imbros, Ashmead-Bartlett wrote a cynical entry in his diary:

I completed what I could put together about the latest 'big victory' in front of Achi Baba. I do not know what value these accounts will be to the Press as Sir Ian Hamilton apparently now acts as his own correspondent and sends in cables a long time ahead of ours. It is almost impossible to know what to write, but I could put together an official bulletin which would apply to all these attacks out here. 'After a concentrated bombardment our infantry advanced against the demoralised enemy and speedily captured four lines of trenches. We were on the verge of taking Achi Baba when unfortunately something (generally the French) gave way on our right, leaving us with an exposed flank. Our centre then had to retire, suffering heavy casualties. On our left something else gave way, and the enemy was unfortunately able to reoccupy his old positions. We are now back on the same line from which we started this morning. The enemy's counter-attacks were most gallantly repulsed with enormous losses. At least ten thousand of his dead are lying in front of our lines and it is reported that thirty thousand wounded have been evacuated to Constantinople. Our troops are much elated by their success, and declare themselves ready to attack again at any time. We have made a distinct advance of at least five yards in some places.'

Thus we carry on at this hopeless game, ignoring all the strategical possibilities in the situation by persisting in these murderous frontal attacks on impregnable positions, losing tens of thousands of our best and bravest men without achieving any result or carrying us any nearer to our goal, while only a few miles away at Bulair lies the key to Gallipoli, to the Narrows, and to Constantinople.

On 24 July Ashmead-Bartlett again bitterly expressed himself:

I met Colonel Leslie Wilson, who commands the Hawke Battalion of the Naval Division. . . . His denunciations of certain generals beat anything I have heard up to date. He told me that they were trying to get rid of him, but are afraid because he is an MP, with too many influential friends. His tale of muddle, mismanagement, and useless slaughter is an appalling one. He criticised particularly the hardships inflicted on the elder men, the Marine Reserves, many of whom are over fifty, and who never expected to serve on land. He maintains that they have been dragged out here under false pretence, to be slaughtered in front of Achi Baba. He related to me what happened in regard to a trench of absolutely no importance, which lay in front of the ground occupied by his battalion. He was ordered to take it, but pointed out that it could not be held, even if captured. Time and time again he protested, but finally received a definite order which had to be obeyed. He took it without much trouble and then got bombed out, exactly as he had predicted, losing three good officers and eighty men. Finally, he retired with only six survivors. A Marine battalion then replaced his, and were ordered to capture it, which they did, but were turned out again. He said that the orders issued to the 29th Division were seldom intelligible and always had to be changed, modified, or ignored. They could never get a definite objective for an attack, as the orders always ended up with 'Go as far as you can and entrench'. He described the battle of June 4th as 'a cold-blooded massacre.' . . . He criticised with equal severity the cruel fate of the wounded, many hundreds of whom perish miserably without any effort being made to arrange an armistice and bring them in. I agree with him on this point. The Turks suggested an armistice to bury the dead at Anzac, so why should not others be arranged to bring in the wounded lying between the lines? No secrets would be given away. The ground has been fought over time and time again and is perfectly well known on both sides. Yet no attempt is made, except by volunteers creeping out at night, to bring in these hundreds who are left to perish of their wounds, tormented by heat, flies, and thirst, till death comes as a merciful release.

The torments of those men wounded and still on duty were bad enough, with heat, thirst, exhaustion, depression and shock. Conditions were abominable. The men could get little sleep by night because the line was thinly held and everybody had to do sentry duty, so they tried to sleep during the day. This was no easy matter 'what with the sun and the flies', as Lieutenant Cripps wrote. 'I well remember seeing one poor Tommy asleep in the trench with his mouth wide open and crammed full of flies. I had to wake him up and I do not know how many he swallowed but he was spitting out squashed flies for some time.'

Condemnation of the Helles campaign was implicit in much that the men of Gallipoli wrote. It became more explicit when the historians came to study it. What John North wrote in 1936 – in his book *Gallipoli* – remains unequalled in concise comprehensiveness. 'To the last Helles conformed to a singularly brainless and suicidal type of warfare.'

9

Anzac: The Breakout That Nearly Succeeded

By June the resilient Winston Churchill was recovering lost ground, and in meetings of the Dardanelles Committee he pushed through acceptance of Hamilton's request for more divisions. The Allies had no chance of breaking the statlemate in France, he said, and small-scale now-and-then reinforcements to Gallipoli would always enable the Turks to match the British strength. A really massive build-up was necessary.

Hamilton was relieved to be getting the reinforcements but General Sir Henry Wilson, one of Hamilton's most implacable opponents and a leading member of the 'Kill Germans school', was outraged. 'It is simply incredible,' he told Lord Riddell. 'This makes nine divisions at the Dardanelles and twenty-two here [in France and Flanders] and not a single Boche facing the nine. How they will laugh in Berlin!'

Berlin had reason to laugh on 15 June, when, at Givenchy, France, the British lost nearly fifty per cent of their strength in a frontal offensive against the German line. This gave weight to Churchill's pronouncement that 'Constantinople is the prize, and the only prize which lies within reach this year. It can certainly be won without unreasonable expense, and within a comparatively short time. But we must act now, and on a scale which makes speedy success certain.'

Churchill wanted to make a tour of inspection of the Dardanelles, but Kitchener, suspicious about what Churchill might do – or more dangerously, lead others to do – insisted that Colonel Hankey accompany him. Kitchener also informed Hamilton that Churchill must in no way be allowed to interfere with military operations. With his wings so clipped Churchill refused to make the trip, so Hankey went off by himself as the Prime Minister's representative. In his first report at the end of July he stressed the difficulties of the exhausted and under-strength units; they were weak from disease and under constant enemy observation and shell-fire.

During July the men were being weakened more by dysenteric diarrhoea than by battle fatigue. With the green 'corpse flies' swarming over everything, the 'Gallipoli Trots' – as the Anzacs called their hideous ailment – spread rapidly. When they were off duty men slept beside some foul latrine pit – if they were lucky enough to have a sufficiently long period without griping pains to go to sleep. Many a soldier spent entire nights perched in misery on one pole placed across a hole while he leant forward against a support pole. Thus suspended within a foul stench, he tried to sleep a little.

But Hamilton demanded of these men a great new attack. He had belatedly learned his lesson, and in a letter to Kitchener on 2 July said, 'To attack all along the line is perfect nonsense – madness!' The nub of his offensive was a breakout by the Australians and New Zealanders from their Anzac beach-head. First they would feint at Lone Pine, and then converge on Sari Bair Ridge. Since this advance would necessarily expose their flank, Hamilton arranged for a complementary attack after an easy landing at Suvla Bay, the troops sweeping the Turks from the hills and joining with the Anzacs. A mock attack would be made at Bulair and a diversionary attack at Helles, to prevent reinforcements from reaching the vital central Anzac sector.

By linking Suvla Bay and Anzac, Hamilton would have an immeasurably larger area from which to operate – it still covered only 400 acres at the end of July – and if he attained all his objectives he must be in a position to cut the peninsula in two. On paper the plan was good, though Hamilton's staff on Imbros Island had no understanding of the incredibly difficult country the Anzacs had to move across. More surprisingly, Birdwood's staff, living at Anzac, appeared to have not much more understanding.

The Anzac and Suvla offensives were designed to proceed concurrently, but they were so separated geographically and by differences in the quality of leadership, the standard of troops engaged and in fighting conditions, that they must be considered separately. (Suvla follows in the next chapter.)

Decisive action was certainly necessary, for at both Helles and Anzac the tensions, the climate and the unbearable closeness of the enemy were taking their toll. At Helles on 13 July, Joseph Murray of the Hood battalion of the Royal Naval Division wrote in his diary:

This miserable piece of scrubland has been paid for over and over again; this continual nibbling is getting us absolutely nowhere and is costing us the youth of Britain. . . . With a handful of half-starved, sick and battle-weary men whose courage alone enables them to walk to and from the firing line, we go on trying to defeat an army deeply entrenched in a natural fortress. It is pitiful to see men, not long ago strong and healthy, now with drawn faces and staring eyes, struggling towards the firing line. . . . They are walking corpses – the ghosts of Gallipoli.

Whatever the conditions were like at Helles, they were twice as bad at Anzac, where the Australians and New

Zealanders lived in continual danger of being pushed off the cliffs. Australian miners suggested the use of a powerful pump and hose to sluice the Turks out of their front line trenches and tunnels on the Anzac front. It was a bright idea and a workable one, but Hamilton turned it down; the unconventional notion of a hose as a weapon of war was beyond him.

But tunnelling was commonplace, and many grim but unrecorded fights went on in the darkness under the front line. Each side strove to get underneath the other. Not long before the August offensive, New Zealand engineers dug some deep mines near Quinn's Post, under the Turkish tunnels. A crack developed in the roof and the Australians could hear the Turks talking and laughing. When the talking ceased abruptly the Australians realized that their candlelight had been seen. They pretended to withdraw from the tunnel but working in darkness and disciplined silence, they packed the tunnel with high explosive. Then they exploded their big mine. The official historian records that after this there was no sound of any human being, but from under the debris came the ticking of a watch.

Death came to some men within a day or two of their arrival in the line; others had many narrow escapes and came through unscathed. Private Walter Gifford, aged 18, of the Australian 10th Battalion survived several near misses. He writes about three of them: 'I was in the front line at Anzac having shot for shot with a sniper when our Lieutenant Tarrant came along. "You can't shoot straight," he said. He took my rifle and stood up and then fell straight back into my arms, dead – shot through the head. On another occasion a mate of mine who had just come into quite a lot of money, was detailed to go on the water party. He was playing cards in the dugout so I went in his place for the water. When I came back I found a shell had landed in the dugout and killed them all. From there I went to Quinn's Post for two weeks on sapping duties. As the two shifts were changing over we sat and chatted for a while. We didn't know that the Turks were sapping from the other side of the hill until they blew the trench we were about to work.'

The Turkish snipers, though numerous and deadly and with the advantage of higher ground, by no means dominated the battlefield. Some Australians and New Zealanders, accustomed to rifles from boyhood, survived and prospered as snipers; some were credited with as many as sixty or seventy probable victims. One of the best-known snipers was 'Hitchie' of the 11th Battalion, from Western Australia – No 443 Postal Corporal H.V. Hitch. He was officially the 11th Battalion postmaster, but he was also a dead shot. He lived in a little dugout behind Battalion HQ and from there he distributed mail – on the infrequent occasions when mail arrived. Mostly Hitchie was engaged in the agreeable pursuit of sniping. A remarkable figure on Gallipoli, he had a dark-tanned face surrounded by a great growth of beard, dressed in shorts and carrying a captured Turkish bandolier and a German Mauser rifle. As the battalion historian commented: 'Hitchie looked more like one of the Faithful than a son of the Golden West.' He was asked again and again to 'go and get' certain Turkish snipers, and he seldom went in vain. He would sometimes be away for more than a day, and was several times arrested as a spy and had to be vouched for by somebody from his own battalion. He was always profanely annoyed that a good Australian should be taken for a Turk.

Hamilton's great attack was to begin on 6 August, a night without a moon. Two closely co-ordinated attacks from Anzac would occupy the high ground from Kiretch Tepe (650 feet) to Koja Chemen Tepe (Hill 971).

While the Anzac actions were in progress, the 10th and 11th Divisions would land near Nibrunesi Point, Suvla, during the night of 6–7 August; by daylight they would hold Lala Baba, Suvla Point, Chocolate and W Hills and Tekke

Tepe (900 feet). At dawn on the 7th two brigades of the 10th would move smartly for the Anafarta Gap, from where they would threaten the right rear of the Turkish line.

The Suvla Bay area was known to be lightly defended, so there was every expectation of surprise, and the British troops had to cover only four miles of open plain to capture the surrounding hills. If they could occupy them within twenty-four hours – a quite reasonable expectation with competent leadership – the Turks opposing Birdwood's Anzac Corps would have their right flank turned; Birdwood would then find it relatively easy to occupy Koja Chemen Tepe, the really vital point of the Sari Bair hills, by dawn on 7 August. During these operations VIII Corps, at Helles, would commence a containing offensive to stop von Sanders from moving men from the south to reinforce the threatened areas in the north.

Hamilton had even more troops than he had ever dared to ask for. At Anzac were the Anzac Corps of 40,000 men, principally the 1st Australian Division, the New Zealand and Australian Division, and 29th Infantry Brigade; at Suvla, IX Corps made up of the 10th, 11th, 13th (also used at Anzac) 53rd and 54th Divisions. At Helles remained the 29th, 42nd, 52nd and Royal Naval Divisions.

Had Liman von Sanders been in Hamilton's place he might well have made similar plans. The concept had every appearance of a carefully thought-out battle plan, avoiding at last – for the most part – the bloody frontal assaults which had marred the operation to date. Birdwood was counting on a flank assault to achieve what the frontal assaults were conspicuously failing to do. Credit for the plan – and blame – goes to Colonel A. Skeen, Birdwood's Chief-of-staff, who spent months working on it. The two assaulting columns were leaving by the left side of Anzac, to make separate detours to the rear of the Turkish position and above it. The plan promised much – but it demanded that all movements conform to a complicated and rigid timetable. It also ignored the poor health of the men. In the worst state of all was the Australian 4th Brigade (Brigadier-General J. Monash) weakened by three months' combat, sleeplessness and dysentery. Yet this brigade was to make the attack on Koja Chemen Tepe – involving a climb of more than six hours through some of the most savage country in the world. The Anzacs were paying the penalty of their own spirit; they had shown that they would 'be there when the whips were cracking' and now the impossible was expected of them as a commonplace. But the belief that a worn-out brigade could remain a viable fighting unit after a six-hour night march through this country was fantastic.

On August 5 Hamilton issued an order of the day – a 'pompous proclamation' in Ashmead-Bartlett's opinion:

SOLDIERS OF THE OLD ARMY AND THE NEW. Some of you have already won imperishable renown at our first landing, or have since built up our foot-holds upon the Peninsula, yard by yard, with deeds of heroism and endurance. Others have arrived just in time to take part in our next great fight against Germany and Turkey, the would-be oppressors of the rest of the human race.

You, veterans, are about to add fresh lustre to your arms. Happen what may, so much at least is certain.

And to you, soldiers of the new formations, you are privileged indeed to have the chance vouchsafed you of playing a decisive part in events which may herald the birth of a new and happier world. You stand for the great cause of freedom. In the hour of trial remember this and the faith that is in you will bring you victoriously through.

Ashmead-Bartlett commented to his diary on 6 August: 'The passage which says: "The faith which is in you will carry you through," is quite lost on British soldiers. They have no time to think of faith. All they want is ammunition, competent officers, plenty of food, and, on this particular enterprise, water. [This] alone can carry them through, not faith.'

One of the few really competent leaders was General H.B. Walker of the Australian 1st Division. He outspokenly opposed the so-called feint at Lone Pine, and he was supported by his staff. To Walker, the one general at Gallipoli who thought first of his men, the attack was madness. No-man's-land at the Pine was one hundred yards wide, flat, bare and fatally open. Because of this natural advantage the Turks considered it one of the strongest parts of their whole line, and they made it even stronger with barbed wire, covered trenches, deep communicating trenches and interlocking machine-gun fields of fire, and with reserves nearby in a protected valley. Before Walker agreed to the Lone Pine attack he had several violent arguments with Birdwood, and he won changes that gave his men a better chance. Events were to show that Walker had not exaggerated the risk, but perhaps even he under-estimated the fighting quality of his men.

The battle opened at Helles at 2.30 p.m. on 6 August. Almost at once VIII Corps' acting commander, Brigadier-General H.E. Street, exceeded his orders. Instructed to carry out a holding attack, he fell for the fatal lure of Achi Baba and attempted to capture it and Krithia. It was a foolish action, and Street lost 2,000 of the 4,000 committed. The Corps commander replacing Hunter-Weston, Lieutenant-General F.J. Davies, had reached Imbros on 5 August and did not assume command until the first battle was over.

The Anzac attack on Lone Pine was to commence at 5.30 p.m. – though the Turks nearly upset this programme by making fierce attacks early that morning. They were repulsed, though the fighting left the Australians even more exhausted. But the 1st Brigade moved into position for the attack on Lone Pine with, as Bean records, 'an excitement which put new vitality into the troops'. The 3rd Brigade had distinguished itself at the landing on 25 April, and the 2nd in the charge of Helles, so the 1st was spoiling for victory.

Under covering fire from the other brigades, the 1st went into the attack precisely on schedule, charging in three lines. After crossing no-man's land, the Australians found the enemy barbed wire flattened by the earlier artillery fire, but instead of the expected trench they came across a continous sandy mound forming the roof of a heavily protected covered gallery. The Turks fired through loopholes. Some Australians stayed at the front line and gradually tore holes in it, while others raced even further into enemy territory to gain entry through sally-ports and rear entrances. With reckless gallantry men leapt into open spaces and let themselves down, feet first, through holes in the head cover. In several places Australians soon lay dead four and five deep, sometimes with Turks similarly heaped a few paces from them.

In the labyrinth of tunnels and trenches it was difficult for the Australians to know whether they were facing friend or foe. A party with Major L.J. Morshead was held up at a corner by some unseen group beyond it. One man went forward to scout, but returned moments later: 'They are Turks, all right,' he said, 'and they got me in the stomach.' He spoke quietly for a few minutes before he sat down and died in agony.

Captain Lloyd of the 4th Battalion reached a break in the Turkish defences caused by a shell and jumped in on a number of Turks, who scattered to either side. Watching both ways at once as the Turks attempted to take aim at him. Lloyd shot several enemy; then, his magazine empty, he dropped and feigned death. The Turks were almost instantly into the trench, passing over Lloyd and even handling his rifle. Twenty minutes later somebody turned the captain face upwards and he found himself looking at an Australian of the 3rd Battalion. The position had passed into Australian hands.

One particular episode of the Lone Pine fighting on

9 August is worth recounting to illustrate the ferocity of the battle. Lieutenant F.H. Tubb became responsible for a post at the barricaded entrance to a trench; he had just ten men, eight on the parapet and two corporals, Webb and Wright, whom he told to stay on the floor of the trench to catch and throw back enemy bombs or smother them with Turkish greatcoats lying about the trench. Some Turks rushed the trench but were shot or bayoneted; Tubb and his men killed all who came up the trench or attempted to creep over the open ground. Using his revolver, Tubb exposed himself on e parapet and his men followed his example. 'Good boy!' he shouted to one soldier who, by kneeling on the parapet, shot a Turk.

In the trench the men who were catching bombs were living dangerously. And they died game, as Australians say. Wright failed to catch a bomb which burst in his face and killed him; Webb had both his hands blown away but walked from Lone Pine, only to die from loss of blood not far away. Then the Turks landed several bombs in the trench simultaneously; four Australians were killed or wounded and a fifth was knocked over. Tubb was himself bloodily wounded in the arm and head but went on fighting, supported now only by Corporal Dunstan and Corporal Burton. Some Turks managed to set off a great explosive charge, which blew up the barricade and knocked down the three defenders. Turks rushed the post, but Tubb, fighting fiercely, drove them off while Dunstan and Burton rebuilt the barrier. Then a bomb killed Burton and temporarily blinded Dunstan. Tubb shouted for some more men and held the post against all that the Turks could do. He, Dunstan and Burton were awarded the VC, three of seven awarded in this one battle.

Acts of startling gallantry and soldierly inventiveness abound in this fierce fighting. At one point Captain W.T. McDonald, 4th Battalion, though bayoneted, went forward to an angle in a trench and fired at the enemy. He then ordered his men, who were farther back, to throw him bombs already lighted, which he caught, blew on the fuse and threw farther. While he held his ground the men built a trench barricade behind him. When it was several feet high McDonald ran back over it. He won no decoration for this feat, though it had been well witnessed. In many places a few witnesses of outstanding bravery remained alive.

In one corner of Lone Pine eight Turks and six Australians were found dead, lying as they had bayoneted one another. The bottoms of the trenches were so thick with dead and dying that Australians and Turks alike trampled upon bodies, without discrimination of race.*

Despite the loss of Australian life, the attack on Lone Pine was successful. In stark contrast, on the morning of 7 August, 600 men of the Australian 3rd Light Horse Brigade, fighting as infantry, made a charge as futile and as costly as that of another 600 men in the Crimea sixty years earlier. For a combination of sheer blind courage – and sheer blind stupidity – it stands alone in the Gallipoli campaign. Just before dawn the 150 men who were to make the first charge filed into trenches at Russell's Top; they were to attack across the Nek and hopefully take the smooth, round knoll called Baby 700, uphill from Lone Pine.

The idea was to draw the Turkish forces to the head of

---

* The losses of the Australian battalions:

	Casualties	
	Officers	Others
1st Bn (went in with 21 officers, 799 others)	7	333
2nd Bn (went in with 22 officers, 560 others)	21	409
3rd Bn (went in with 23 officers, 736 others)	15	490
4th Bn (went in with 20 officers, 722 others)	12	459
7th Bn (went in with 14 officers, 680 others)	12	342
12th Bn (went in with 24 officers, 998 others)	4	164

Many wounds were not reported.

Monash Valley and away from the New Zealand infantry during the critical hour when they were approaching the summit of the ridge. The task was gigantically beyond such a small force as the 3rd Light Horse Brigade, and suicidal if certain other positions had not already been captured. The Light Horse troopers were required to begin their charge along a narrowing hillcrest between steep gullies. The hill they were heading for was protected by forty trenches and connecting saps, and by flanking machine-guns. The troopers, inexperienced in this form of battle, were excited about the prospect of a fight in the open, and several men too ill to take part managed to hide their sickness from the medical officer.

In shorts and shirts because of the heat, the troopers – from Victoria and Western Australia – carried 200 rounds of ammunition, but had been ordered not to load their rifles or charge (fill) the rifle magazine. They were to trust to the bayonet alone. It must be assumed that this order was designed to obviate any slowing down of the charge while men paused to fire and reload their rifles. It makes no sense otherwise. Not that loaded rifles with a bullet in the breach would have made much difference in the face of the overwhelming resistance.

Because the naval barrage had cut out seven minutes earlier than planned, the Australian officers dared not start the charge in case the shelling was resumed and their men ran into it. The seven-minute lapse was fatal. The Turks pulled themselves together, lined their trenches two deep, held their rifles to their shoulders and waited for the charge.

'Go!' ordered Lieutenant-Colonel White, and he led the first wave of 150 Light Horsemen as they leapt over their parapet. They were hit by sheets of bullets fired at no more than sixty yards' range. Hardly a man got more than ten paces; in thirty seconds the line was annihilated. Two minutes later the second wave of men, knowing that they must be hit, went forward into the steel rain. And they fell beneath it.

Under Major Todd, a third line – of the 10th Light Horse Regiment – was now in the jumping-off trench. Todd told the regimental commander, Colonel Brazier, that success was impossible. Brazier hurried to Brigade HQ, close by, for orders. Here he found Colonel J.M. Antill, the Brigade-Major, who had heard that an Australian signal flag was waving from one end of the Turkish line. 'Your regiment must go in at once to support any of our men who have reached the Turkish trenches,' he said.

At 4.45, the troopers went over the top and they too fell. The commander of the fourth line, Major J.B. Scott, protested to Brazier that the attack was futile and impossible. Brazier again took the matter to Antill, who again ordered an advance. Brazier then referred to the brigade commander, Brigadier-General F.G. Hughes, who told him to continue the attack but by a different direction. While they discussed the matter the fourth line attacked, with much the same result. In the fifteen minutes that the charge lasted the brigade lost 435 men, including twenty officers and 232 men killed. It was as concentrated a slaughter as any on the British side during the campaign, and C.E.W. Bean says that on no other occasion during the entire war did Australians have to face such concentrated small-arms fire.

His assessment of the action needs no amendment. 'For sheer bravery, devoted loyalty and that self-discipline which seldom failed in Australian soldiers the attacks stand alone in their annals of their country. Not once during the deadly fighting did the troops display the least sign of hesitation in performing what they believed to be their duty. . . . With the exception of the attempt near Abdel Rahman the following day no other experience in 1915 was so powerful to create the disillusionment which superceded the first fine fervour of Australian soldiers.'

Bean blames Birdwood and his Chief-of-Staff, Skeen, for not knowing the strength of the position they expected men to attack. He also accuses Antill of negligence in not informing himself about the impossibility of the assault on the Nek. Thirdly, he attributes much of the heavy loss to the blunder in timing over the preliminary bombardment.

The attack, it will be remembered, had begun early in the morning. As the sun rose and the heat became intense, the suffering of the wounded Australians was acute. A few managed to slide back and fall into their trenches, a few others were brought in by mates taking dreadful risks. Sometimes a wounded trooper called out or raised an arm or groped, often uselessly, for his water bottle. Gradually movement subsided on that dreadful ridge, which today is as desolate a piece of land as any in the world; it never was worth the blood which the sun dried in pools on its coarse soil.

Elsewhere on the ridge other Light Horse units were also engaged in bloody attacks. Charging from Quinn's Post, the first wave of the 2nd Regiment in just one minute lost every man except one killed or wounded. Major G.H. Bourne had the sense to order the second line not to advance.

Bean does not go far enough in apportioning the blame for the total failure and heavy losses at the Nek and elsewhere lower down the range. A contributory factor was the failure of leadership in the night march on the Sari Bair Heights – Hill Q, Abdel Rahman, Chunuk Bair and Koja Chemen Tepe. This march began directly Turkish attention was concentrated on Lone Pine. Two columns of troops under Brigadier-General Johnston and Major-General Cox set out at 7.30 p.m. to seize the Sari Bair ridge. Ashmead Bartlett has set out the terms of this incredibly difficult undertaking: 'It was launched against positions the like of which had never been attacked before under modern conditions of warfare. The men were expected to climb mountains during the night over unexplored ground, so tortuous, broken and scrubby that, had the advance taken place during peace manoeuvres it would have been an extremely arduous task for troops to reach the summit . . . in the prescribed time.'

The Left Assaulting Column, as it was called, was made up of the Australian 4th Brigade under Brigadier-General John Monash, and the Indian 29th Brigade under Major-General Cox. Monash was over fifty years old, naturally cautious and now exhausted. A superb administrator and planner, he was the wrong man to lead a brigade on such a daunting task – he was to take Abdel Rahman and from there Koja Chemen Tepe. Major C.J.L. Allanson, commanding the 1/6th Gurkhas, met Monash early on the morning of 7 August and found him 'running about saying "I thought I could command men, I thought I could command men,"' He was, Allanson thought, 'temporarily out of his head.' The 4th Brigade was then stationary – Monash had convinced General Cox, much against his will and battle-sense, that his men were in no position to go forward.

The New Zealanders, in a superb feat of arms, were high on the ridges as early as 1 a.m. that morning. The Otago Battalion, under a forceful commander, Major Frank Statham, had done well, and by 4.30 a.m. was in a saddle on the way to Chunuk Bair. It was vital for the success of the Australians' attacks lower down that the New Zealanders take Chunuk Bair and thus, in effect, threaten the Turks from the rear. Little opposition was coming from Chunuk Bair and, in fact, New Zealanders outnumbered Turks by ten to one at that moment. But the New Zealanders' commander, Brigadier F.E. Johnston, gave the order for the men to eat their breakfast. It was one of the most expensive breakfasts in military history; by the time the men had finished eating, Turkish reinforcements were swarming over Chunuk Bair, despatched there by Mustafa Kemal, from less than a mile away. Johnston told Godley that after consultation with his battalion commanders he did not think it 'prudent' to attack. Godley, in response, ordered Johnston to attack at once. But it was then 9 a.m., and another ninety minutes elapsed before Johnston got his men forward. It was too late – New Zealanders and Gurkhas with whom they had joined were being hit, and Johnston ordered them to dig in. Godley had no choice but to concur. More forcefully, General Cox called for reinforcements to make the drive on Chunuk Bair, but the crazy maze of ravines defeated his efforts and only the 7th Gloucesters finally reached the New Zealanders.

Early on 8 August, the Wellington Battalion, led by the spirited and stubborn Lieutenant-Colonel Malone, captured Chunuk Bair summit, in one of the most determined feats of the campaign. The Official History is almost lyrical in its description of this moment. 'The men were in high spirits. Away on their right the growing daylight was showing up the paths and tracks in rear of the enemy's lines at Anzac, now at last outflanked. Straight to their front were the shining waters of the narrows – the goal of the expedition. Victory seemed very near.'

But victory was illusory. The Turks had abandoned Chunuk Bair – for a reason still unknown – but they held Battleship Hill and Hill Q.

Meanwyile Allanson's Gurkhas had reached a position far in advance of other troops. After waiting in vain for support, Allanson attacked Hill Q on his own. After a fierce fight he established his men one hundred feet below the crest and dug in. But at 2 p.m. General Godley, for no good reason, suspended operations until the following day.

A conference was called at New Zealand Brigade HQ on the afternoon of 8 August to decide on the route to be taken by Brigadier-General A.H. Baldwin's 38th Brigade, which was fresh into the action. North describes this conference as 'the most critical ever held throughout the Gallipoli campaign'. Godley did not attend this meeting, but promised to send a staff officer; he failed to do so. He had suggested that Baldwin's column should move along Rhododendron

Spur – a sensible idea that would have taken the men forward without difficulty – but was not present to enforce his wishes. Indeed, Godley abandoned the battlefield when his officers so badly needed his help, and boarded a destroyer. From here, through a telescope, he saw the 6th Gurkhas in their remarkable assault on Q. Had Godley been ashore he might have pushed the Gurkhas the support they so badly needed; plenty of support was available in the masses of unused soldiery in the ravines below Q.

On the summit the New Zealanders were heavily shelled by the desperate Turks and driven off, though they clung to the upper slopes. Late in the afternoon the New Zealander officers saw a British warship open fire in their defence and they were delighted – until the shrapnel exploded above them. Among the dead was the gallant Malone, the spirit of Chunuk Bair.

A battalion of 760 had started the attack in the morning; by dusk only seventy were unhit. The Gloucesters had lost every officer and sergeant and more than 350 men; the 8th Welsh Fusiliers seventeen officers and 400 men. Chunuk Bair was a scene of carnage. Meanwhile, Monash's 4th Brigade had been badly mauled on the 8th, and had lost its cohesion. But for its well-handled machine-gun sections, it would have suffered even more severely. It was effectively out of the action that night.

Godley renewed the attack on the 9th, limiting his objective to the main ridge from Chunuk Bair to Hill Q. Johnston was to assault the former and Cox the latter, while in between Brigadier-General Baldwin was to attack with his brigade. As night fell Baldwin advanced along an unreconnoitred path, so that long halts and delays followed. Then the track ended in a precipice, so the whole body had to counter-march. While this part of the advance was all confusion, Johnston's forward troops met the Turks in battle. Because Baldwin's troops did not appear, Johnston and Cox abandoned their attack. Allanson's reinforcements had gone astray, so again he attacked on his own and actually gained the top, a tremendous achievement which Allanson describes in his diary: 'The roar of the artillery preparation was enormous: the hill was almost leaping underneath. I recognised that if we flew up the hill the moment it stopped we ought to get to the top. . . . I said that the moment they [his men] saw me go forward carrying a red artillery flag everyone was to start. I had my watch out, 5.15. I never saw such artillery preparation; the trenches were being torn to pieces; the accuracy was marvellous and we were only just below. 5.18 it had not stopped, and I wondered if my watch was wrong. 5.20 silence: I waited three minutes to be certain, great as the risk was. Then off we dashed all hand in hand, a most perfect advance and a wonderful sight. I did not know at that time that Godley was on a torpedo-boat destroyer and every telescope was on us. I left Cornish with fifty men to hold the line in case we were pushed back and to watch me if I signalled for reinforcements. [He also left at battalion HQ the medical officer, Captain E.S. Phipson.] At the top we met the Turks. Le Marchand was down, a bayonet through the heart. I got one through the leg, and then, for about ten minutes, we fought hand to hand, we bit and fisted, and used rifles and pistols as clubs; blood was flying about like spray from a hairwash bottle. And then the Turks turned and fled, and I felt a very proud man; the key to the whole peninsula was ours, our losses had not been so very great for such a result. Below I saw the Straits, motors and wheeled transport, on the roads leading [south] to Achi Baba.

'As I looked round I saw that we were not being supported, and thought I could help best by going after those who had retreated in front of us [the Turks]. We dashed down towards Maidos, but had only got about 300 feet down when I saw a flash in the bay, and suddenly our own Navy put six 12-in monitor shells into us, and all was terrible confusion. It was a deplorable disaster; we were obviously mistaken for Turks and we had to get back. It was an appalling sight: The first hit a Gurkha in the face; the place was a mass of blood and limbs and screams, and we all flew back to the summit and our old position just below. I remained on the crest with our 15 men. It was a wonderful view; below were the Straits. . . . A message came up to say that Cornish had been very badly hit and had gone. . . . I saw that the advance at Suvla Bay had failed, though I could not detect more than one or two thousand Turks against them. . . . Victory was slipping from our grasp and all in my neighbourhood from want of dash, and at Suvla from want of appreciation of how little there was in front of them.'

During that afternoon the Turks counter-attacked the Gurkhas five times and died in hundreds, never reaching closer than fifteen yards of Allanson's line. Ordered back to make a report, Allanson, weak and faint from loss of blood, found the nullahs on the way back 'too horrible', full of dead and dying Maoris, Australians, Sikhs, Gurkhas and British soldiers, blood and bloody clothes, and of the two-day smell of the dead.

He left the Gurkhas under the nominal command of Captain Phipson, though the military command rested on Subahdar-Major Gambirsing Pun. Phipson, who had climbed to the battle line, discussed the situation with Gambirsing Pun and then set off to find some other troops to help the Gurkhas hold their vital position. 'I sought out what appeared to be the nearest, a unit of Kitchener's army. I found them comfortably disposed in a small glade, surrounded by trees about half way down the main nullah, having a hearty meal from steaming field kettles. . . . I explained the situation to the CO who, in answer to my earnest requests for reinforcements firmly and indignantly refused. . . . He could not think of disturbing his lads who had not had a square meal since breakfast that morning at Suvla.' [No rations or water had reached the Gurkhas for days.]

In his capacity as acting CO Phipson tried written messages to the troops on his flanks – the South Wales Borderers, the 9th Worcesters and the South Lancashires. All replied that they had retired or were about to retire.

Nevertheless, the Gurkhas had *some* support. Somewhere close to them Major G.R. Mott, a marksman, of the 6th South Lancashires spent four hours firing continuously at the enemy. When the barrel of his rifle became white hot another was passed to him with fresh ammunition. Mott was always reluctant to put a figure on the number of Turks he hit – he was firing at ranges between 150 and 180 yards – but members of his company said that his aim was so good that it was not necessary for anybody else to join him on the firing line.

It can now be seen that the Turks had won the battle for the ridges by 8 August – or rather that the British had lost it – but the New Zealanders on Chunuk Bair held out until relieved after nightfall on the 9th by the 6th Loyal North Lancashires and the 5th Wiltshires. Nearby were Warwicks and Royal Irish Rifles, as well as the indomitable Gurkhas.

The condition of every man on the ridge was pitiful. Many had been fighting and moving for four days without sleep; all were thirsty, dazed and sun-shocked, and many were wounded. Held together by army disipline, most hardly knew where they were.* Few men had full equipment and the shallow trenches and ground around them was strewn with debris and bodies.

Mustafa Kemal regarded the British on Chunuk Bair as a cancer victim might regard a malignant growth. Given just a little time the British would steadily reinforce and strengthen the Chunuk Bair outpost and from it would dominate the peninsula. Kemal had already lost over 13,000 men since

---

* Over several years I have found several survivors of the Chunuk Bair battle; not one has given me a coherent description of the terrain on the ridge or of the view from there. One comment in particular is poignant. 'All I can remember are bits of bodies. I don't know if the ground itself was green or brown or purple – just bits of bodies.'

6 August, but he ordered an assault at first light on the 10th. Every man he could muster would form part of a tidal wave of humanity to sweep the British off the ridge. It was a command decision of paramount importance, and Kemal stuck to it despite the protests of his staff, who were fearful of the penalty of failure. Kemal has said that he made a short speech. 'Soldiers! There is no doubt that we shall defeat the enemy opposing us. But don't hurry, let me get in front first. When you see me wave my whip all of you rush forward together.'

They did. In the breaking light they swarmed over the skyline in a massed bayonet attack. The 1,000 British of the garrison at Chunuk Bair and the nearby pinnacle disappeared from view and from life. Elsewhere, British soldiers, caught completely by surprise in their exhaustion, were without their rifles and could only run. Ten New Zealand machine-gun crews in flanking position cut down hundreds of Turks, and gun crews on the warships threw salvo after salvo of shrapnel into the mass. But it was as irresistible as lava. Down the seaward slope it went, rolling onto the small plateau at The Farm and leaving 1,000 men dead or dying after savage fighting. Dead Turks lay everywhere – perhaps 5,000 of them – but Kemal had done what he intended – removed the cancer from Gallipoli's throat.

Hamilton wrote of the Turkish attack, 'It was a series of struggles in which Generals fought in the ranks and men dropped their scientific weapons and caught one another by the throat. So desperate a battle cannot be described. The Turks came on again and again, fighting magnificently, calling upon the name of God. Our men stood to it, and maintained, by many a deed of daring, the old traditions of their race. There was no flinching. They died in the ranks where they stood.'

The only British troops left on the upper ridge – that is north of the original Anzac lines – were the 1/6th Gurkhas. Capt. Phipson found it difficult to persuade Gambirsing that a general withdrawal had been ordered. Convinced at last, the

Subahdar-Major destroyed anything which might help the Turks, then made a disciplined retreat without losing a man – and six hours after everybody else had left. Phipson was full of praise for the Subahdar-Major. 'To retire 900 feet down a rocky declivity, intersected by deep and narrow gullies, many of them choked with bodies, and the infinitely difficult job of carrying the wounded . . . presented little difficulty to Gambirsing Pun, whose knowledge and competence seemed complete and undefeatable.'

Bean did not believe the Navy was responsible for shelling the Gurkhas, and blamed a British artillery battery, whose crew could not have known that soldiers running at that particular spot were friends. The Navy denied that the bombardment was theirs, but Allanson was an experienced officer and he knew the explosion and characteristics peculiar to any type of shell. He had no doubt, writing about the incident forty-eight hours later, that his unit was hit by naval 12-in shells; the Turks had no 12-in artillery at this point on the front. In any case, they would not have fired just one salvo and then stopped. The Navy was accustomed to firing at such opportunist targets, and its officers had never before seen British troops running in the direction the Gurkhas were taking. The incident was tragically unfortunate but understandable. In one way Allanson himself was responsible; he should not have led his Gurkhas in a charge downhill 'towards Maidos'.

'Most of us thought that the shells came from HMS *Euryalus*,' wrote Captain Phipson,* 'a most familiar and encouraging sight at anchor in the bay. But Allanson thought, and perhaps correctly, that they came from a monitor's 12-inch guns. . . . The blast was so tremendous that although protected by the ridge, I was blown backwards, heels over head out of the trench. . . . I shall never forget that sight of

---

* In *The Gallipolian*, the Journal of the Gallipoli Association, in June 1970.

the casualties after the naval shelling. They looked as if they had been sprayed with canary-yellow colour-wash – the effect of the Lyddite used in the high explosive shells of 1915.'

Some writers on naval history deny that the Navy shelled the Gurkhas, while others do not mention the incident. Commander K.G.B. Dewar, serving on the War Staff in 1915, is much more honest. 'The naval bombardment reopened. Heavy shell burst among the Gurkhas, causing numerous casualties. . . . Corbett [the official naval historian of the First World War] does not mention this regrettable incident. The Military Historian states that the Navy and shore artillery subsequently declared that the shelling was done by the Turks. There is, however, no doubt that it was a continuance of the naval bombardment.'

In the Sari Bair action the 1/6th Gurkhas lost all its British officers as casualties, two-thirds of its Gurkha officers and more than half its other ranks.

The attempt to break out from Anzac was justified and it is misleading to call it, as some historians do, a fiasco. This word has connotations of inevitability, as if the plan never had a chance. Events proved that on the night of 8 August the British had their 'best chance of the campaign at Anzac', as Bean calls it. 'The vital objective, the actual crest at Chunuk Bair, was for several days within Birdwood's reach, and for a few hours actually in his hands,' he writes in a tone of tempered reproach. 'The opportunity passed, never to return.'

The spirit of the men was great enough to meet the demands placed upon them by the overoptimistic schemes of Birdwood and Skeen, and their fortitude was such that they could endure the hardships and master the tough Turks. But the soldiers depended on leadership that, at senior level, betrayed them. Monash of the 4th Brigade was inadequate, Hughes was ineffectual, Antill was tragically rigid, Johnston had none of the qualities needed, and Godley had failed to attend a vital preliminary conference though its decisions affected him; so weak was his presence that few officers knew he was commanding the attack on the ridge.

Birdwood, who prided himself on his closeness to the Anzacs, did not understand that their attitude to him changed after the battles of early August. Bean recognized this change – 'The effect on intelligent men was a bitter conviction that they were being uselessly sacrificed.' But Birdwood went on talking to the troops in his avuncular manner: 'I expect you boys are eager to have another go at the Turk with the bayonet, eh?' As the boys saw it, they had had enough goes with the bayonet to achieve victory – if the leadership had been right.

Birdwood sometimes showed powers of leadership, but he did not exercise them during the battles of 6 to 10 August. The battles were fought perhaps 3,000 yards from his HQ, but Birdwood and his staff had the completely mistaken idea that they were progressing to plan. As late as the afternoon of 9 August, the staff officers were confident of progress on the hills. It was almost as if, convinced of the viability of the master plan, they were blind and deaf to contrary evidence, and they isolated themselves in their HQ valley. Staff officers should have been sent out in all directions, and it would not have been inappropriate for Birdwood himself to go to the scene of the action. In places he would have found scenes of dangerous *inaction* with communications dreadfully disrupted.

Allanson wrote after the battle of Chunuk Bair: 'All my ambitions to be a successful soldier have gone; knowing all I know now, I feel the responsibility, the murderous responsibility, that rests on the shoulders of an inefficient soldier or one who has passed his prime to command.' He went no further than this, but it is clear that he was not referring to himself but to some of the generals at Gallipoli and indirectly to the 12,000 British and Empire casualties between 6 and 10 August.

Aubrey Herbert's diary describes the scene on 10 August.

'The wounded lie in the sand rows upon rows, their faces caked with blood and sand; one murmurs for water; no shelter from the sun; many of them in saps with men passing all the time scattering more dust on them. There is hardly any possibility of transporting them. The fire zones are desperate, and the saps are blocked with ammunition transport and mules, also whinnying for water, carrying food. . . . Some unwounded men almost mad from thirst, cursing.'

Herbert admired, more than anything in the war, the spirit of sixty-three New Zealanders he met somewhere on the left flank of Anzac. They were the last survivors of a battalion and their spirit was 'unconquered and unconquerable'. He was sorry that the New Zealanders rarely received the same recognition as the Australians in the Press – indeed many of their deeds were unrecorded, or were attributed to the Australians. The New Zealanders, said Herbert in his diary, 'had a silent pride that put these things into proper perspective'.

10

Suvla: 'Such Generalship Defies Definition'

General J.F.C. Fuller considered the battles of Sari Bair and Suvla Bay so important that he included accounts of them in his three-volume *The Decisive Battles of the Western World*, written between 1954 and 1957. Sari Bair, he says, was 'a battle of valour run waste, and of muddle exceeded only by the landing at Suvla Bay'.

The muddle was infinitely worse at Suvla, and with much less reason. Twenty-two British battalions, comprising 20,000 fresh soldiers, landed on the shores of Suvla Bay on 7 August, 1915. They were required to reach low hills from two to five miles inland – at that time not occupied by the Turks. And they had only to defeat a Turkish force of 1,500 men. The British failed. These are the bare facts of the Suvla operation. The reasons why such a ripe plum as Suvla could not be plucked provide several lessons in the perils of inept leadership.

C.E.W. Bean has said that the Suvla failure affected the fate of the Australian and New Zealand forces more profoundly than any other episode of the Gallipoli campaign. Present throughout the campaign, Bean understood, as some later historians have not, that the breakout from Anzac was the main part of Hamilton's August offensive, and that Suvla was a paramount supporting offensive. Bean hoped that the reasons for the Suvla failure would be 'laid bare by future historians, probing unflinchingly for causes'. To the end of his long life, Bean believed that the only compensation for the amount of blood spilled would be the truth.

The first truth is that when a corps was being assembled for the Suvla operation, Kitchener saddled Hamilton with 'the most abject collection of generals ever congregated in one spot'.*

The most abject of all was the corps commander, Lieutenant-General Sir Frederick Stopford, the officer who carried Kitchener's instructions to Hamilton about the importance of speed and surprise. Hamilton had asked for an experienced corps commander from France, and mentioned Lieutenant-General Sir Henry Rawlinson or Major-General Sir Julian Byng. Kitchener refused to ask Sir John French to spare them. He pointed out that both these officers were junior in rank to Lieutenant-General Sir Bryan Mahon, who had trained the 10th Division and was taking it to Gallipoli. He was unwilling to invite Mahon to serve under a corps commander junior to himself. Hamilton regarded Mahon as 'quite hopeless', but since Mahon was coming to Gallipoli anyway, it was necessary – considering the etiquette of the time – that the corps commander be senior to him. Only two men could be considered – Ewart or Stopford. Hamilton dismissed Ewart with almost Kitchener-like curtness; he was too big and stout a man for trench warfare. This was a specious objection as trench warfare was not considered at Suvla. In any case, Hamilton considered that Ewart had a poor relationship with his men. By elimination, Stopford was left – a general whose closeness to his men could not be assessed since he had never commanded troops in battle.

Hamilton had told Kitchener on 15 June that the

* The opinion of A.J. Smithers, in his biography of Sir John Monash.

commander of the proposed IX Corps at Suvla would need a good stiff constitution, and a month later he added to the requirements, 'power of digestion, sleeping and nerve power . . . compared with these qualifications most others are secondary.' Stopford was so feeble that he was unable to lift his own despatch case into the train when he set off for Gallipoli. He had served as an ADC in Egypt and the Sudan in the 1880s, and had been military secretary to the brave and bovine General Buller early in the Boer War. In retirement since 1909 and brought back into service because of the war, Stopford was only sixty-one but was in poor health – and he was sent to a climate which taxed the fittest man.

Hamilton knew Stopford's limitations, yet he gave him a free hand to plan and control the Suvla operations; it was like giving a blank, signed cheque to a bankrupt and asking him to invest your money as he saw fit.

When Stopford first reached the peninsula he was given command of VIII Corps at Suvla for a few days, so that he could get some experience of Gallipoli conditions and of war. So extreme was Hamilton's insistence on secrecy about the August offensive that even Stopford was kept in the dark until 22 July, when Hamilton crossed from Imbros to Helles to explain the plan. He impressed upon Stopford that Chocolate and W Hills 'should be captured by a major, forceful assault before daylight', on 7 August, and urged him to show bold and vigorous leadership. Stopford accepted the plan, but General Mahon, when he was told, criticized it as too intricate and convinced Stopford that this was so. GHQ failed to keep stressing to Stopford that his troops must take and hold W Hills, the most important feature on the Suvla front.

Birdwood escorted Stopford to vantage points on the cliffs at Anzac, and pointed out to him the country over which he was expected to advance after the Suvla landing. After studying the ground for a time, Stopford said, 'I like this better than I thought I should.'

'Of course you do,' Birdwood said. 'And you will get through if you take my advice. There are no continuous trenches – only short lengths. If you land on a broad front, with every unit going forward at once you will take every existing trench. On the whole of that front we think there are no more than a thousand men of the Turkish gendarmerie. Land, as I did, just before dawn. With the moon just right the men can't lose their way.'

Stopford again seemed to like the idea, but said that his men had done no night work. Birdwood, ever encouraging, said, 'Nor had mine – and you have a week to practice them on the islands, where there is country very similar to Suvla. Give them plenty of night practice and make sure every officer knows his objective, and you can't fail.'

Stopford's pessimistic Chief-of-Staff, Brigadier-General H.L. Reed, VC, said gloomily, 'What about the preliminary bombardment? We never attack without it in France.'

'In France, yes,' Birdwood said, 'but here, no. What have you to bombard? Your one great chance lies in surprise, which any bombardment would destroy.'

Stopford decided that he knew better than Birdwood and did not use his plan. Birdwood also did his best to help Stopford secure surprise. He gave strict orders that no attack or even a demonstration was to be made from Anzac in the Suvla direction. He wanted the Turks to think that the British were completely ignoring Suvla, and that any breaking out they might contemplate would come from the Helles end.

But Suvla was ignored so completely that reconnaissance of the area was cursory and incompetent. Yet the British had been at Gallipoli for three months, and night scouting parties could have been sent out to gather detailed information. Able scouting officers abounded, among the New Zealanders particularly.

Hamilton issued final orders to Stopford on 29 July:

> Your primary objective will be to secure Suvla Bay. . . .
> *Should . . . you find it possible* to achieve this object with
> only a portion of your force, your next step will be to give
> such direct assistance as in your power to the General
> Officer commanding Anzac in his attack on Hill 305
> (known to the Anzac commanders as Hill 971). . . . He
> directs your special attention to the fact that Chocolate
> Hills and Green Hills are known to contain guns which can
> bring fire to bear on the flank and rear of an attack on Hill
> 305. . . . *If, therefore, it is possible*, without prejudice to the
> attainment of your primary objective, to gain possession of
> these hills at an early period of your attack, it will greatly
> facilitate the capture and retention of Hill 305. (My italics.)

The insistence that the landing was *the* objective is seen by
some historians, notably General Fuller, as the greatest error of
all at Suvla. It was certainly a basic cause of the disaster,
because 'secure Suvla Bay' indicated to Stopford that Hamilton
expected him above all to make a good landing. In fact, this
was only a beginning, a means to an end. The landing itself
called for little more than good administration by the naval and
military staffs. Once ashore, generalship was needed. But
Stopford knew little about field generalship and did not land
with his troops, as he could have done in perfect safety.

Von Sanders had been trying to divine Hamilton's
intentions, and he suspected that a landing could be made at
Suvla as part of an operation to capture the Sari Bair heights.
But he constantly worried about a landing at Bulair, which he
considered vulnerable, and he was almost as concerned about
the safety of Gaba Tepe. Ready for almost any eventuality, he
had three divisions at Kum Kale in Asiatic Turkey, three at
Bulair, three on the Anzac front where Essad commanded,
two south of Gaba Tepe, and five at Helles. Under the highly

competent Bavarian officer, Major Willmer, he sent the 'Anafarta Detachment' as a form of strong outpost to Suvla. Willmer had three battalions of infantry, a pioneer company for field engineering, a squadron of cavalry and a labour battalion for digging. This force, which sounds formidable, numbered only 1,500. Willmer believed that he could keep British invaders off Anafarta Spur for perhaps thirty-six hours without reinforcements.

On 3 August, with the battle imminent, Stopford sent Hamilton a message so significant that any alert Commander-in-Chief would have been alarmed and called in his senior staff officers for consultation and immediate action. 'I fear that it is likely that the attainment of security of Suvla Bay will so absorb the force under my command as to render it improbable that I shall be able to give direct assistance to the GOC Anzac in his attack on Hill 305.'

Hamilton better understood the use of English than any other general of his time. He must have known that Stopford was telling him, directly, that he intended to place strict limits on his activities and that he did not propose to co-operate in the Anzac breakout. Indirectly, he was telling Hamilton that he did not understand the purpose of the Suvla operation. Hamilton was apparently unperturbed by the Stopford message. Against naval advice, he even allowed Stopford to induce him to make changes in the landing scheme, with damaging results.

Meanwhile, in all the large army assembling in the islands, and on the peninsula itself, only senior generals and the admirals knew the destinations and objectives. Even at GHQ the majority of the staff were long kept in ignorance that a landing was to be made at Suvla. When Birdwood gave a draft plan to his two divisional generals, Walker and Godley, Hamilton reprimanded him and ordered him to inform the generals, by any pretext, that the plan had been abandoned. Most surprising of all, Brigadier-General Skeen, who had spent months planning the breakout from Anzac, was not told of the Suvla plans. All officers of the New Army divisions arriving at Mudros were ordered to avoid any discussions regarding the *probable* course of the forthcoming operations, even among themselves. This was secrecy at the ludicrous level; at the dangerous level, on the very night of the landing many officers of the 11th Division had never seen a map of the area in which they suddenly found themselves and most had no idea what was expected of them. Yet in current British military doctrine, the officers on the spot were entirely responsible for achieving results. The official historian, often at pains to gloss over some of the worst aspects of the campaign, is forced to concede that 'it is beyond argument that in many instances an all too rigid secrecy was a contributory cause of the initial failure at Suvla.'

When they set off from their camps at Mytilene, Mudros and Imbros, the vast majority of the men had no idea where they were going; some thought they were being taken to Egypt. Few had ever heard of Suvla Bay. Most of the troops were suffering from sickness and pain after a cholera inoculation, and many were in the first throes of diarrhoea or dysentery. Few men could have been conscious of a 'great advantage'. Nor was novelist Compton Mackenzie, who was on Intelligence duty that night at GHQ at Imbros. When he went to bed about four in the morning without receiving a message that the troops had engaged the enemy, there was 'no vestige of hope' left in his mind that the Suvla operation could now succeed. 'The war would go on now . . .' he wrote. 'We should be here indefinitely now. . . .'

At 9.30 p.m. on 6 August, the 32nd and 33rd Brigades of the 11th Division (Major-General F. Hammersley) approached B Beach in pitch darkness to find it undefended. Half an hour later four battalions had landed without a shot being fired. They occupied the heights of Lala Baba and the way was now open to the capture of Hill 10 – but nobody knew its exact position, so no advance was possible. The 34th Brigade (Brigadier-General W.H. Sitwell) entered Suvla Bay, but when fifty feet from the shore near A Beach struck a reef; this so delayed the landing that dawn broke before the bulk of the men could be landed. To compound the confusion, parts of the 10th Division, which should have landed at A beach in readiness to occupy Kiretch Tepe, were landed on C Beach and on a new beach discovered north of A. Orders and counter-orders flew in all directions while Turkish snipers picked off scores of British.

Lieutenant Douglas Figgis,* 5th Royal Irish Fusiliers, part of the 10th Division, wrote that: 'If GHQ had any plan at all it would appear to have been – Put the troops ashore and let them get on with it. How GHQ thought to land the whole of the 11th Division in the dark on a strange shore and, a few hours later, land two brigades of the 10th Division almost on top of them could possibly be successful passes the comprehension. Units became inextricably mixed and my battalion was landed at the wrong beach. This necessitated a march of three miles in full view of the Turks. At the actual landing my battalion lost the senior major, two captains and the adjutant killed and 12 officers wounded.'

With confusion only a few hundred yards away. General Stopford sat in his ship, the sloop *Jonquil*, immensely pleased that his men had got ashore; his Commander-in-Chief sat on Imbros Island and fretted for news. As General Fuller puts it: 'Both generals waited for victory or defeat as if the whole operation was a horse race. Such generalship defies definition. . . .'

Liman von Sanders knew about the Suvla landing at 6 p.m. on 7 August. He understood then that the British objectives had to be Hill 971 and Chunuk Bair, and that Bulair was safe.

---

* Figgis, writing in *The Gallipolian* for Spring 1970, said that the Suvla débâcle had haunted him all his life.

His orders were concise: Every available Turkish soldier on the Asiatic side of the Dardanelles was to march to Chanak and cross to the peninsula; the 8th Division at Krithia was to march north towards Anzac and Suvla and the 7th and 12th Divisions at Bulair were to march south. But none of these supporting troops could be in position before thirty-six hours and some would not arrive for forty-eight hours. It seemed impossible for Major Willmer's tiny force to hold back the invasion. After a day of tension for von Sanders, at 7 p.m. Willmer reported that, although at least one and a half divisions had landed, 'the enemy is advancing timidly'.

The German Colonel H. Kannengiesser wrote, 'Suvla Bay was full of ships. We counted ten transports, six warships and seven hospital ships. On land we saw a confused mass of troops like a disturbed ant-heap. Nowhere was there fighting in progress.'

The Suvla landing was also seen clearly by many of the men of Anzac, high on their ridges. An artillery officer, Captain H.S. Thuillier, saw the beaches and flat plain inland swarming with columns of infantry. 'The columns were marching in various directions but with no signs of attacking lines moving inland. I certainly got the impression that the chance to seize the low hills inland might be missed if no attack was launched . . . supported by the already landed guns.'

Despite reports by Stopford to the contrary, four 18-pounders of the Royal Field Artillery did get ashore the first morning, at a point where casualties were already being collected. Ankle deep in the soft sand, the gunners had the muscle-tearing job of getting guns and limbers with narrow, iron-shod wheels up the steep beach. But before long they were firing in support of an infantry attack. The testing conditions of that day have been vividly described by Gunner G.E. Dale. 'Meanwhile a great brass sun beats relentlessly down from a clear sky, and we learn what the word "thirst" really means. Lips crack and heads go dizzy in the stifling heat. Infantrymen approach begging for water but our bottles are empty. Later the sun is suddenly obscured; we look up in wonder at a small black cloud. There's a roll of thunder and down pours the blessed rain. Parched lips try to catch the drops and we fumble with our canteens, but too late. A few minutes and the vampire sun reappears.'

Twenty-four hours after the landing Hamilton wrote, 'I'd sooner storm a hundred bloody trenches than hang on the end of this wire.' It was the night of 7 August, and no news had reached him since Stopford's early morning report that he had got to 'little beyond the edge of the beach'. This indication of inaction should have sent Hamilton on a fast destroyer to Suvla to put fire into Stopford's belly. Had he gone to Suvla and insisted on an immediate advance, the official historian says, 'the duration of the world war might have been very considerably shortened'. This is an extravagant statement, but it does at least underscore Hamilton's inaction.

At dusk an attack on Chocolate Hill developed and as darkness fell on the 7th the hill was carried, as well as half of Green Hill. On the British left a foothold was gained on Kiretch Tepe. But all the encircling hills remained in Turkish hands – although more than half IX Corps of twenty-two battalions had not been engaged. The Turks had caused the loss of one hundred British officers and 1,600 men, more than the whole of their own force.

The entire military plan had collapsed. Even worse in some ways, so had the naval plan. The unloading of guns, ammunition, water, supplies, carts and transport animals – all were delayed by the general confusion. Water was abundant in the Suvla Bay area, but it could not be found, and many poorly trained men who had drunk their water-bottles dry were suffering badly from thirst in the great heat. Mobs of soldiers collected on the beaches, where Commodore Roger Keyes saw them sucking water through holes they had made in the water hoses with their bayonets.

At 9.30 on the morning of 8 August, Stopford sent a message to the 10th and 11th Divisions, congratulating them on their 'achievements'. Half an hour later he reported to GHQ: 'I consider that Major-General Hammersley and the troops under his command deserve great credit for the results obtained against strenuous oppoisition and great difficulty.'

Taking Stopford's assessment as accurate, Hamilton dutifully gave Hammersley the credit Stopford considered was his due. At 10.30 he cabled Stopford; 'You and your troops have indeed done splendidly. Please tell Hammersley how much we hope from his able and rapid advance.'

The 'strenuous opposition' had come from Willmer's three companies of Gallipoli Gendarmerie (rather like a force of special police) on the Kiretch Tepe Ridge, 1,100 men and five mountain-guns between Baka Baba and W Hill, and two gun batteries on the eastern side of Tekke Tepe ridge. It was a long 'front' for a small force.

The British had not 'done splendidly' for the good reason that practically *nothing* had been done. The word 'rapid' to describe Hammersley's advance was ludicrous; he had advanced nowhere. Apart from an occasional rifle-shot the war was far away. Resting soldiers crowded the sand dunes and many were happily bathing along the shore. Stopford and his Chief-of-Staff, Reed, were still aboard the *Jonquil*, where Colonel Aspinall, despatched from GHQ to get first-hand news, found him.

Aspinall describes the meeting in the Official History, 'Well Aspinall,' Stopford said, 'the men have done splendidly and have been magnificent.'

'But they haven't reached the hills,' replied Aspinall.

'No, but they are ashore,' Stopford said complacently. 'I propose to order a fresh advance tomorrow.'

Aspinall at once sent a radio message to GHQ. 'Just been ashore where I found all quiet. No rifle fire, no artillery fire, and apparently no Turks. IX Corps resting. Feel confident that golden opportunities are being lost and look upon situation as serious.'

Colonel Hankey, who had accompanied Aspinall from Imbros, found dugouts being built. This startled him as it seemed to indicate a complete lack of understanding about the operation. 'You seem to be making yourselves snug,' he remarked to a staff officer. 'We expect to be here a long time,' the officer replied. Then Hankey *knew* something was radically wrong.

Reporting back to his boss, the Prime Minister, Hankey commented on the 'peaceful scene': 'Hardly any shells. No Turks. Very occasional musketry. Bathing parties round the shore. An entire absence of the expected bustle of a great disembarkation. There seems to be no realisation of the overwhelming necessity for a rapid offensive, or the tremendous issues depending on the next few hours.'

While Aspinall was ashore on his inspection, GHQ heard on Imbros that Turkish troops were advancing east of Tekke Tepe. A message was sent urging Stopford to push on. Stopford transmitted this message to his divisional generals – and saw to it that they would do nothing by adding his own qualification: 'In view of want of adequate artillery support I do not want you to attack an entrenched position held in strength.'

His obsession with artillery made no sense because there were no obvious targets for British guns to fire at – no enemy guns, no trenches, no concentrations of enemy troops. And enemy prisoners were saying, with obvious truth, that the British landing was a surprise.

Hamilton decided to go to Suvla, but his destroyer, HMS *Arno*, was having boiler trouble and would not be ready until 4.30 p.m. A major offensive was in progress, but the Commander-in-Chief was stranded because the Navy had not provided him with emergency transport. Rear-Admiral Nicholson was 'sorry for the inconvenience'. The furious

Hamilton told him that convenience or inconvenience was irrelevant; he was preventing a Commander-in-Chief from exercising his functions during battle.

When he finally reached Suvla Hamilton first saw de Robeck, who had radioed while Hamilton was *en route* that he should come to Suvla and see things for himself. Aspinall turned up on the flagship in a fever of impatience because 'chances were being thrown away with both hands'.

He had met a young officer who told him, in tones of great exasperation, 'We are being held up by three men. There is one little man with a white beard, one man in a blue coat, and one boy in shirt-sleeves.'

Roger Keyes, hovering ready to help, rushed Hamilton to the *Jonquil* in his motorboat.

Hamilton found Stopford pleased with himself and obviously happy. He said that 'everything was quite all right and going well.'

'Where are the troops now?' Hamilton asked.

'There along the foot of the hills,' Stopford said and pointed out the line.

'But they held that line more or less yesterday,' Hamilton said.

Stopford explained that the brigadier-generals had been told to gain what ground they could without serious fighting. The men were tired, water was slow in reaching them and the guns were not being landed as quickly as he had hoped. So he had decided to postpone occupation of the ridge, which might lead to 'a regular battle', until next morning.

Hamilton notes in his diary that he was inclined to tell Stopford that a regular battle was exactly what they came for, but he did not say it. In a mild way, he told Stopford that he should have instantly informed GHQ of his inability to obey the order to 'push on rapidly'. Stopford replied that he had made up his mind only within the past hour or so. Anxiously considering the options, Hamilton said, 'We must occupy the heights at once. It is imperative we get Ismail Oglu Tepe and Tekke Tepe *now*.'

Acting as if an order were a basis for discussion, Stopford told his Commander-in-Chief that he agreed with him in principle about the necessity to push on, but many tactical reasons were against it – and he presented all of them, including what seemed to him to be a major obstacle, that the generals ashore said their men were too tired.

It is worth remembering that while this discussion was going on troops at Anzac and Helles who had been in close combat for months and were exhausted to the point of collapse were still fighting. The Suvla troops had been present in a war zone for less than twenty-four hours.

Hamilton hurried ashore to visit Hammersley and his brigadiers; Stopford declined to accompany him – about 400 yards – because his leg was troubling him. Hammersley admitted to Hamilton that all the supply problems, including water, had been solved, but he could not get any of his units moving until the morning. 'There was one huge danger rapidly approaching us,' Hamilton wrote, 'already casting its shadow upon us, which, to me as Commander-in-Chief, outweighed every secondary consideration. We might have the hills at the cost of walking up them today; the Lord only knew what would be the price tomorrow.' Hammersley and his Chief-of-Staff, Colonel Malcolm, said it was impossible to get orders around the division in time to move that night. 'Never in all my long soldiering had I been faced with ideas like these,' Hamilton confided to his diary.

He told Hammersley 'in the most distinct terms', that he wished the 32nd Brigade to advance at once and dig themselves in on the crestline. This order resulted in a search for units and when they were found they were marched and counter-marched in growing confusion. In fact, two battalions of the 32nd Brigade had gone well forward and were established on Scimitar Hill and Abrikjar, both highly desirable objectives. When

Brigade HQ received Hamilton's order that it was to 'dig in on the crestline', the two battalions were recalled. This was a calamity and Scimitar Hill, a vital position, was given up and then had to be bloodily fought for.

In Berlin, that very day, Admiral von Tirpitz, reading the reports as they came in from Constantinople, wrote, 'Heavy fighting has been going on since yesterday at the Dardanelles. . . . The situation is obviously very critical. Should the Dardanelles fall, the world war has been decided against us.'

But he had Liman von Sanders fighting for him, while the British were depending on Frederick Stopford. Von Sanders had also been having trouble from subordinates. Looking down on the horde of invading British, von Sanders was desperately anxious because Willmer had told him late on the 8th that Feizi Bey's troops from Bulair had not arrived. Sending for Feizi to come to him at the gallop, von Sanders demanded to know the reason for the delay. His troops were too exhausted to attack before the morning of 9 August, Feizi said. Von Sanders dismissed him from his post instantly and placed Mustafa Kemal in command of all troops in the Anafarta sector. Dragged to their feet, the exhausted Turks occupied the crest of the ridge. 'The race for Tekke Tepe was lost by rather less than half an hour,' Aspinall wrote.

But there had been no race. The British command had forfeited the event. The soldiers of the 32nd Brigade, knowing nothing of the urgency of their advance, were thrown back in confusion. The 33rd Brigade was stopped on Azmak Dere, where it dug in. Stopford went ashore on the morning of the 9th and Hamilton and his party found him busy with a party of engineers, supervising the building of some shell-proof huts for himself and his staff. 'He was absorbed in the work,' Hamilton recorded, 'and he said that it would be well to make a thorough job of the dug-outs as we should probably be here for a very long time.' George

Brodrick (Viscount Dunsford), Hamilton's aide, wrote at the time that Stopford's staff were 'a lifeless crew . . . with little knowledge . . . and no spirit.'

Even now, Stopford was unable to understand the necessity for thrust, and Hamilton did not further try to enlighten him, merely noting that Stopford was taking the morning's hold-up philosophically. Hamilton, with Brodrick, went ahead more than two and a half miles, and encountered General Mahon. Hamilton had ideas about what Mahon should be doing, but, he records, 'I kept these views to myself until I could see Stopford.' In view of Stopford's inability to act as a corps commander should, Hamilton's reluctance to advise Mahon directly becomes bizarre. At this point, as Brodrick reported to Hamilton, five British battalions were held up by 800 Turks with no machine-guns but could not get on.

Reaching Stopford on his way back to the beach, Hamilton 'begged' him to make 'a push for it'. But the pushing was abortive, and Stopford's men lost Scimitar Hill.

Hamilton had the unusual experience of seeing Roger Keyes, looking dejected that day. He had often seen Keyes 'raging' against delays, incompetence, lack of spirit and broken promises, but Keyes 'simply deprived of the power of speech' was a new experience. Keyes was reacting to the failure of the Suvla generals.

At Anzac that afternoon, Hamilton, Birdwood and Godley put together a message for Stopford. 'After speaking to Birdwood and Godley I think [that the] most important use fresh troops could be put to if not urgently required to reinforce would be the occupation as early as possible of the commanding position running through square 137–119. . . .'

The fresh troops were the 53rd (Welsh Territorial) Division (Major-General J.F. Lindley), but once again Hamilton was leaving a weak subordinate with an escape clause to exploit – 'if not urgently required to reinforce'. As it happened, the

53rd was thrown into a battle to retake Scimitar Hill and assault the Anafarta Spur. The two attacks failed.

What happened to the Herefordshire Battalion of the 53rd Division was typical of the lack of organization. The battalion had been ashore for only a few hours on 9 August, and was at Lala Baba on the coast when the CO, Lieutenant-Colonel Drage, received an order to report to the brigade commander. Drage was told to protect the right flank of the Sherwood Foresters, near Kaslar Chair. 'I don't think you will have much to do or that you will get a dusting,' the Brigadier said. 'Get away as quickly as possible.'

Drage left Brigade HQ knowing nothing of the position of the enemy and without information 'about what our side was trying to do'. He had not been told about the Anzac positions, and found out much later that his battalion was on the extreme right of the Suvla position and could have linked up with the Anzac front. After advancing some distance, Drage lost touch with his two leading companies. 'I was in a quandary and did not know what to do,' he reported. Under Turkish artillery fire the colonel, now wounded, headed for a sheltering bend of the Azmak Dere. At this moment a mounted staff officer galloped up and ordered him to take the battalion back to Lala Baba. But here he was again ordered to report to the Sherwood Foresters the following morning.

Back at Imbros after seeing Birdwood and Godley at Anzac, Hamilton composed a careful letter to Stopford: 'I am in complete sympathy with you in the matter of all of your officers and men being new to this style of warfare and without any leaven of experienced troops on which to form themselves. Still I should be wrong if I did not express my concern at the want of energy and push displayed by the 11th Division. It cannot all be want of experience as 13th Division have shown dash and self-confidence. Turks were almost negligible yesterday once you got ashore. Today there was nothing to stop determined commanders leading such fine men as yours.

Tell me what is wrong with the 11th Division. Is it the Divisional Generals or Brigadiers or both? I have a first-rate Major-General I can send you at once [he was thinking of de Lisle, at Helles] and can also supply two competent brigadiers. You must get a move on or the whole plan of operations is in danger of failing, for if you don't secure the Aja Liman Anafarta Ridge without delay the enemy will. You must use your personal influence to insist on vigorous and sustained action against the weak forces of the Turks in your front and while agreeing to the capture of W Hills and spur . . . it is of vital importance to the whole operation that you promptly secure the ridge without possession of which Suvla Bay is not safe. You must face casualties and remember the Aja Liman Anafarta Ridge is your principal and dominant objective and it must be captured. Every day's delay in its capture will enormously multiply your casualties. I want the name of the Brigadier who sent the message to say his left was retired owing to a strong attack and then subsequently reported that the attack in question was never developed. Keep Birdwood informed as he may be able to help you on your right flank.'

It must be said of Stopford that nothing – neither the Turks nor the promise of victory or the danger of defeat, neither the incompetence of his subordinate generals nor the admonitions of his Commander-in-Chief – pushed him into what he would consider hasty action. In his reply to Hamilton he condescended 'to bear what you say in mind and if I get an opportunity with fresh troops of taking the heights while holding on tight to my right flank I will do so'.

On 9 August Compton Mackenzie confided to his diary: 'There is still no good news of the IX Army Corps. . . . I'm afraid they've ruined the show. It's absolutely damnable. Guy Dawnay [a GHQ officer] was almost weeping when he came back from Suvla today. . . . it's a tragedy. . . .'

By the 11th, Stopford had lost all faith in his new troops, the 53rd Division and 54th (East Anglican Territorial). 'They have no standard to go by,' he told Hamilton glumly. He reported that the 54th Division 'went back at slight provocation and went back a long way . . . lost and under no leadership.' And worse was to come. 'I am sure that the Territorials would not secure the hills with any amount of guns, water and ammunition assuming ordinary opposition, as the attacking spirit was absent; chiefly owing to the want of leadership by the officers.'

If Stopford was able to discern lack of attacking spirit it was indeed lamentablely lacking, so Hamilton and Braithwaite again rushed off to Suvla, where Hamilton 'wrestled' with Stopford for over an hour, while Braithwaite tried to stiffen the resolve of his Chief-of-Staff. 'I found most of the troops strolling about as if it was a holiday,' the anguished Hamilton told Kitchener in a letter that day, the 11th.

The same day Compton Mackenzie recorded that a brigade major of a 'certain' brigade had sent a telegram to the brigadier: 'Two Turkish shrapnel burst over the battalion this morning. Glad to report that battalion kept quite calm and that there were no casualties.' Mackenzie's comment: 'I wonder what they would have said to this telegram at Lancashire Landing!'

Ashmead-Bartlett, as anguished as Hamilton and Mackenzie, wrote the next day, 'We have landed again and dug another graveyard.'

In the middle of his problems Hamilton received (12 August) a cable from Kitchener: 'I am sorry about the 10th and 11th Divisions, in which I had great confidence. Could you not ginger them up? The utmost energy and dash are required for these opeations or they will again revert to trench warfare.'

Sick at heart, Hamilton noted in his diary, '. . . I know he is not capable of understanding how he has cut his own throat, the men's throats and mine, by not sending young and up-to-date generals to run them [the divisions].'

He cabled Kitchener: 'I am acting absolutely as you

indicate by "ginger". I only got back at 11 last night from a further application of that commodity. As a result a fresh attack will be made tomorrow morning by the IXth Corps and 54th Division.'

Stopford constantly baffled Hamilton, but never more so than when he came aboard HMS *Arno* on the 13th. Full of condemnation for his hopeless divisional generals and pessimistic about the chances of an attack that night or next day, Stopford was sublimely confident of success in a week's time – 'or any other time so long as it is not too near us,' as Hamilton wrote bitterly.

On 15 August Stopford stirred himself and ordered Mahon to push forward along the Kiretch Tepe Ridge – but he was twenty-four hours too late. The Irish division fought well and might well have taken the position the day before, but by now the Turks had brought up reinforcements and were in secure positions among the rocks.

Ashmead-Bartlett's comments in his diary were caustic and despairing: 'No one seemed to know where the headquarters of the different divisions and brigades would be found. The troops were hunting for water, the staffs were hunting for their troops and the Turkish snipers were hunting for their prey. . . . Where I had seen one Turk yesterday there seemed to be ten today. . . . Leaving comparatively few in the trenches, large numbers descended into the unburnt scrub, and there, almost immune from artillery fire, awaited our attack. . . . Their snipers crept from bush to bush, from tree to tree, from knoll to knoll, picking off our men . . . and were themselves left almost unmolested.'

Hamilton, now desperate, suggested to Kitchener that Stopford be relieved. Kitchener, in the recent past so particular about seniority, replied, 'This is a young man's war and we must have commanding officers that will take full advantage of opportunities which occur but seldom. If any generals fail do not hesitate to act promptly.' And he notified

Hamilton that Generals Byng, Maude and Fanshawe would be joining him from the Western Front. 'Enchanted' by this news, Hamilton placed Major-General de Lisle in command of IX Corps in place of Stopford.

Stopford had held command of the Suvla Bay operation for nine days – nine days of desperate disaster. In his report to the War Office he explains his failure:

> I feel sure that if we had had even a few Regular troops and adequate Field Artillery support the high ground surrounding the bay would have been gained without much difficulty. The causes of our failure to do so were exhaustion of the men caused by the very hot weather and shortage of water, the inadequacy of artillery support and the employment, in very difficult ground, of young troops without any previous experience, and without any backing of Regular Troops. They were too highly tried and from want of experience suffered unduly and when coming under a heavy shrapnel fire, which they did on several occasions, they would bunch together and stand up instead of spreading out and lying down. The majority of men behaved very gallantly and the officers, though wanting in artillery knowledge and training, led their men right well and suffered heavily in consequence.

Yet Stopford had an easy ride, in that his flanks were secure, with the sea on his left and Birdwood's Corps on his right. Birdwood said that it was impossible to justify Stopford's delay in pushing forward at Suvla. 'Had brigade and battalion commanders been shown their precise objectives in advance – as they could well have been from the decks of destroyers – it should have been no difficult matter to rush forward and seize their allotted positions with little delay.'

Little, if any, attention has been given to two factors which I believe played a major part in sapping Stopford of any fighting will he may have had. One is that from the *Jonquil*, and later from the shore, he could easily see the daunting heights of the Sari Bair range. The sight must have been unnerving to a man poorly briefed about what was expected from him; he knew that his major advance was in that direction, and the prospect overwhelmed him. Had Hamilton stressed to Stopford that he was expected to capture only small hills well away from Sari Bair he might well have been able to pluck up some resolve. But here the second factor came into play. The heat at Gallipoli in August must be experienced to be believed; to make any decision during the hottest hours of the day requires a tremendous effort of will from a fit middle-aged man, and Stopford was not fit. There is a strong tendency in such conditions to take the line of least effort – and this Stopford consistently did.

Major-General de Lisle was a blunt, tough general who had the drive which Stopford lacked. He could get things done but he lacked imagination. It must be said, though, that it is doubtful if any amount of imagination could by now have saved the day at Suvla.

Hamilton virtually apologized to Mahon for bringing in a junior general as corps commander over his head and asked him, gracefully, if he would continue to lead the 10th Division, 'at least for the present', while the battle continued. Mahon's refusal to serve under de Lisle, whom he detested, was inexcusable, and his departure from Kiretch Tepe Ridge while his troops were still fighting bravely and skilfully was disgraceful and tantamount to desertion under fire. He returned after a few days, when his temper had cooled, but soon after left for good.

Prime Minister Asquith regarded the Suvla Bay failure as his worst disappointment of the war, and he wrote to Kitchener on 20 August, 'I have read enough to satisfy me that the generals and staff engaged in the Suvla part of the business ought to be court martialled and dismissed from the Army.'

But worse was to follow.

As Hamilton and de Lisle saw it, the new solution to victory at Suvla was to bring from Helles that much savaged, veteran division, the 29th (Major-General W.R. Marshall). But even this superb formation – surely one of the best in British military history – was not the fighting force it had been in earlier months. Its high standard of discipline, and the quality of its officers and men were no armour against the severely weakening effects of disease.

General de Lisle's plan was to take Kiretch Tepe and Tekke Tepe on 21 August, throwing the 29th Division at Scimitar Hill, the 11th at the Chocolate and W Hills, and a composite Anzac force under Major-General Cox at Hill 60. The 2nd British Mounted Division, of Major-General Peyton, now without their horses, was in reserve. This division was made up of regiments from the country shires, officers from the great landed families and their tenant farmers – the Royal Gloucestershire Hussars, Royal Bucks Hussars, Sherwood Rangers, Warwickshire, Derbyshire and Berkshire Yeomanry, among other units. It was the division's first experience of war and all ranks were 'cheerfully excited'. Fresh and fit, these mostly rural men were ready for anything.

In the early afternoon the last great battle of the campaign – indeed, the greatest of all in terms of numbers – began in a kind of molten, liquid heat. The main attack was locked by 4 p.m., and de Lisle called in Peyton and gave him a Hunter-Weston type of order to 'push through'. The Yeomanry division had been sheltering at Lala Baba, and their route to battle took them across the starkly white Salt Lake, where Turkish shrapnel shells burst above them and sprayed down onto the hard, glaring salt. Five thousand men on that white aiming mark made a good target. The survivors of the ordeal reached Chocolate Hill about 6.30 p.m., when the light was failing rapidly. But the attack was pushed and up infamous Scimitar Hill marched the Yeomen of England. It was the charge of the Australian Light Horsemen at the Nek all over again – just as futile, but on a larger scale. It succeeded in giving the Turks a fright – but the British line advanced not a yard. The cost was great – 5,000 casualties.

Churchill's review of the battle was cogent: 'The British losses, particularly of the Yeomanry and the 29th Division, were heavy and fruitless. On this dark battlefield of fog and flame, Brigadier-General Lord Longford, Brigadier-General Kenna VC, Colonel Sir John Milbanke VC, and other paladins fell. This was the largest action to be fought on the peninsula, and it was destined to be the last.'

The action was nothing more than a forlorn hope assault of the type famous in the British army in earlier centuries. With all else lost, including his reputation, Hamilton launched a pointless frontal attack on commanding heights. General C.E. Callwell calls the plan 'somewhat venturesome', and labels the enterprise 'extremely formidable'. Callwell, writing in 1924, no doubt felt at that time that he had to be euphemistic; the modern historian must call the enteprise 'impossible', and the plan 'suicidal'. Only weeks before, Hamilton had told Kitchener about the absurdity of frontal attacks, yet here he was making one and calling it a 'limited action'.

On 21 August the great Suvla tragedy was effectively finished, though another four months were to pass before the inevitable was accepted.

More than sixty years after his experiences at Suvla, Lieutenant E.D. Wolton of the 1/5th Suffolk Regiment wrote, 'No one who was at Suvla could ever forget the inefficiency with which we were led, the way sheer lack of planning, organisation, orders and of course, water, drained out buoyant enthusiasm. If only the Senior Officers had read their own Field Service Pocket Books on simple principles many of the mistakes would not have been made.'

Ashmead-Bartlett, writing in the third week of August, considered that Stopford had 'committed every error possible in a given time', but doubted if Napoleon himself could have inspired his soldiers to the degree necessary when there was no communication among the jumbled brigades and battalions. The main reason for defeat, in Ashmead-Bartlett's opinion, was that there had been complete failure to learn from the lessons of the landings at Anzac and Helles. The journalist had just met Jack Churchill, a GHQ staff officer, who had told him that the army was in for a winter campaign for certain. And Ashmead-Bartlett wrote in his diary, 'God help the Army if it is left ashore this winter'.

11

Hamilton's Fantasy World and Hill 60

Almost like a marker between the Suvla front and the Anzac front stood the Turkish-held Hill 60, which had become an obsession with Birdwood. He and his staff believed that hidden by the thick scrub on the flat summit were some desirable Turkish trenches. If they could be captured, the British would have a clear view north towards the Turkish lines, the point of junction between the Anzac and Suvla fronts coud be greatly strengthened, and two extra wells would be secured. Birdwood proposed to capture Hill 60 and assoicated minor objectives on 21 August, in conjunction with de Lisle's attack on Scimitar Hill. It would be difficult to say which of the two attacks had the less finesse. But two things are sure. One is that Birdwood's men were more exhausted than de Lisle's. The other is that Birdwood or Godley should have had Hill 60 properly scouted and sketched, to be certain that what they expected to find really did exist. Such a reconnaissance patrol may have cost a few lives, but Birdwood was now risking thousands.

Because of losses from battle earlier in the month and losses from disease more recently, the attacking force had to be scratched together from nine weakened units – those of the 29th Indian Brigade, of the 4th Australian Brigade (again), two regiments of the New Zealand Mounted Rifles – each regiment now down to 200 men each – 5th Connaught Rangers, 10th Hampshires, 4th South Wales Borderers. This composite force, nominally under Godley, was placed under the field command of Major-General Cox.

Because of yet another failure to co-ordinate the artillery barrage with the infantry advance, the first line of 150 Australians (13th Battalion) had almost every man killed or wounded and the second line (14th Battalion) suffered in the same way. The scrub caught alight and many wounded were either burnt to death or were blown up by their own exploding ammunition. Even the wiry Gurkhas of the Indian Brigade made slow progress, and by dark the attackers were only on to the lower slopes, to which they held grimly.

That day Major Allanson and his 6th Gurkhas had been in action. One of their casualties was the redoubtable Subahdar-Major Gambirsing Pun, wounded close to Allanson by a shrapnel ball in the head. When he fell he sent his orderly for the Major. Nearly unconscious, he said to Allanson, 'Sahib, what will you do without me? What will the regiment do? I do not mind death – what is that! But you want me and the regiment wants me, and I cannot be spared.' Allanson wrote of him that night, 'A truly magnificent man, most gallant and fearless, with no thought for anything but the name of the Gurkha and his regiment.'*

In this untidy, twisted battlefield with its many hidden valleys and spiky ridges, strange incidents occurred. Men of the 14th Sikhs, on the night of 21 August, were to take over trenches held by the New Zealand Canterbury Mounted Rifles. As the New Zealanders filed out of their trench in the

---

* The Subahdar-Major recovered from his wound but died four years later, probably from the effects of the wound.

darkness, some Turks filed in at the far end – and the leading Sikhs found themselves looking down on about 300 Turks. Instead of firing, the Turks made surrender signs; while salaaming with their right hands they held their rifles in their left hands. Most had bombs tied to their waist and an officer behind them was ordering them to do something. When the Sikhs and their British officers urged the Turks to give up their arms they refused – with more extravagant salaams. Here and there a Sikh and Turk wrestled for the possession of a rifle 'like any two schoolboys'. About ten Turks surrendered, and the rest were fired on and ran off, leaving some dead and wounded. The British officers assumed that the Turks had been trying to induce the Sikhs to desert, under the mistaken impression that they were brother Muslims.*

During the night Brigadier-General A.H. Russell produced a plan for attacking the hill with fresh troops and convinced Major-General Cox that it would work. Cox asked Godley for the fresh troops. As it happened, in reserve was the 5th Australian Brigade of the 2nd Australian Division, a magnificent brigade of stalwart, fit, keen soldiers which had only recently arrived at Gallipoli. Godley and Birdwood were keeping these men for 'something special' – and what they got was Hill 60. One battalion, the 18th, under Lieutenant-Colonel A.E. Chapman, was marched to the line by night, knowing nothing of what was expected of them. The Brigade-Major, Lieutenant-Colonel C.G. Powles, told Chapman that his men were to attack with bomb and bayonet only. Chapman said his battalion had received no bombs. 'Then you must do the best you can without them', Powles said. The troops were by now under the impression that they were being taken to 'man the trenches', though few were sure what this meant;

* The story is told by Lieutenant-General Sir Reginald Savory, then a young officer of the 14th Sikhs, in *The Gallipolian*, Autumn 1975.

they were so new to war they had not yet seen trenches. Powles led the battalion to its start-line and pointed out Hill 60, about a quarter of a mile away.

The commander of the leading company, Captain S.P. Goodsell, ordered his men to fix bayonets and extend into two lines. And only at that moment did the men from New South Wales know they were about to attack the enemy. As was to be expected, they suffered heavily; within a few hours eleven officers and 372 men were casualties, half of them dead.

The battle for that one hill raged for nine days, and Cox's force suffered 2,500 casualties. The four regiments of the New Zealand Mounted Rifles, which made the most significant advances, were reduced to 365 men all told. One of the dead was Captain W. Grant, who with a friend on 28 August climbed over a low barricade to reach a wounded man said to be lying in front. They found and bandaged several wounded Turks and then, around a bend of a trench, heard voices which Grant's companion thought to be Turkish. After staying still and silent for a while, Grant said, 'We'll just see if that wounded man is here,' and went round the corner. He was at once shot by several Turkish soldiers, and died instantly.

Another chaplain, A. Gillison, a Presbyterian, was preparing to read the burial service over the bodies of some of the men killed in an attack on Hill 60 when he heard a man groaning in the scrub on the ridge. He had been warned against moving in daylight but he went forward and found that the groans came from a wounded man of the Hampshire Regiment, who was helpless and being troubled by ants. The chaplain called Corporal Pittendrigh, a Methodist clergyman serving in the infantry, and a soldier. They crawled forward and reached the wounded man, but had dragged him for only a few feet towards safety when a Turkish sniper severely wounded Gillison and Pittendrigh. The chaplain died the same day and Pittendrigh a week later.

Bridwood got his Turkish trenches – only to discover that

they were not on the summit but on the forward slope of the hill – the side facing the British and therefore the 'wrong' side. The Turks still held the higher northern half of the hill – and they remained there to the end of the campaign. Two and a half thousand men had been killed or wounded for nothing. In his autobiography, Birdwood makes not a single line of reference to the Hill 60 action; it is a significant omission. The official historian is more honest: 'None of the units had ever been so depleted . . . and the men were only able to carry on by sheer force of will. Their spirit was so splendid that the higher commanders . . . believed them capable of greater efforts than were humanly possible. Courage, morale and the excitement of the moment enabled them to fight in flashes, but the prolonged strain at Anzac – the fighting, the heat, the constant debilitating sickness – had made too prodigal a call upon their store of nervous energy. . . .'

That Birdwood misled Hamilton about the results of the Hill 60 action is evident from Hamilton's diary entry on 29 August: 'Hill 60, now ours throughout, commands the Biyuk Anafarta valley with view and fire – a big tactical scoop.' And next day Hamilton records: 'In falling back as well as counter-attacking after we had taken Hill 60, the enemy was exposed to the fire from our trenches. . . . Birdie declares that they have lost 5,000. . . . We have taken several machine-guns and trench mortars as well as some fifty prisoners. Have sent grateful messages to all on the spot.'

Most of this information, fed by Birdwood to Hamilton, was false or grossly exaggerated. Allanson wrote the most realistic comment about Hill 60: 'The whole place is strewn with bodies – Gurkhas, Australians, Connaught Rangers; the smell is appalling, the sights revolting and disgusting.' Hamilton did not see *this* report.

The men of the Field Ambulances attached to the various divisions worked heroically, but there were too few trained men to seek out, rescue and treat the wounded. In this battlefield with its scrub, watercourses and innumerable hillocks, a wounded man could lie undiscovered for days. Having found a casualty the bearers might have to carry him four miles, most of the way under sniper fire.

Sometimes the Field Ambulance men faced life or death decisions. Sergeant John Hargraves, 32nd Field Ambulance, found a man shot through both thighs by one bullet and bleeding quickly to death from tears in both arteries. At that moment a second wounded man appeared, hopping along with a wound in the ankle. Hargraves discovered that two rough tourniquets had been applied to the man hit in the thigh, but the blood still pumped steadily from the wounds. He tried tightening the tourniquets but to no avail. All the time little groups of British soldiers straggled past, retreating towards Suvla. Hargraves helped the other wounded man to hop to a willow thicket, where he found he had a bullet wound right through his anklebone; it had been bleeding for about half an hour, the soldier said, and he was very pale.

Hargraves plugged each hole, padded the ankle and bound it tightly. He had a look at the other man, who was still bleeding and had lost consciousness. It was a race for life. Which man should he attend to? Both men were still bleeding and would die within half an hour. Hargraves reckoned it was hopeless for the tourniquet-man and left him 'passing painlessly from life to death'. The ankle-man's wound was still bleeding through the plugging. Hargraves rolled up a puttee (a soldier's ankle binding) put it under his patient's knee, laced it up and tied it in position with the other puttee. This brought pressure on the artery itself and stopped the loss of blood from the ankle.

'Thanks, mate,' said the man. 'How's the other bloke?'

'He's all right,' Hargraves said; he could see him lying a little way up the hill, still and stiffening. He stopped two regimental stretcher-bearers in the little retreat and got them to take the ankle-man the two miles back to the dressing station.

When British troops next day regained the lost position, Hargraves trudged past the body of the man who had bled to death. The tourniquets were still gripping his lifeless limbs 'and the blood on the handkerchiefs had dried a rich red-brown'.

The Field Ambulance men often saved the life of a wounded soldier, but they could do little to ease the suffering of the many who suffered from dysentery, that loathsome and enfeebling disease. Many soldiers, still on duty, could only crawl on all fours to the latrines, looking like sick animals. All of them, while hunched in pain at the filthy holes, were coated by hordes of flies and many men were hit by bullets, shrapnel or shell splinters, and fell into the filth. Often enough their mates did not have the strength to pull them out of it. Some men died while at the latrines through the loss of blood and intestine.

As at Helles and Anzac, men at Suvla suffered unnecessarily because of poor arrangements for taking them off the peninsula. The authorities in England were slow in providing enough launches and hospital ships – and Hamilton was slow in asking for them. Another difficulty was that in 1915 the British Army had no dentists, and many soldiers suffered real pain from tooth decay and dental damage during the Gallipoli campaign; a few had teeth removed by a mate or, if they were lucky, by a veterinary surgeon or farrier.

More dynamic medical leadership and administration could have averted much suffering. During the first night of the August offensive, Compton Mackenzie was on duty at GHQ when a telegram arrived from Anzac – 'When does the next hospital ship arrive? This one is full.' Mackenzie, seeing the wounded men in his imagination, took the telegram to the tent of the Director of Medical Services, General Birrell. Having awakened the general, Mackenzie read the telegram.

'Tell them General Birrell does not know,' the DMS said irritably. 'Do you mean to tell me that I've been woken up at such an hour to answer a question like that. I've never heard of anything so completely ridiculous in my life.' Under Mackenzie's insistence that he do something, Birrell again protested. 'I feel most strongly that I have been woken up in a totally unnecessary way.' Mackenzie said that he supposed the people at Anzac were also feeling rather strongly. Birrell then grumpily took the telegram to the operations tent, but neither Mackenzie nor anybody else was confident that he would, or could, do anything constructive.

Because of the 'wastage' from wounds and sickness, Hamilton was now asking for another 95,000 men – a tremendous number considering the insatiable appetite of the guns on the Western Front. He was offered a quarter of this number, but when the Scimitar Hill slaughter had finished Hamilton's total losses in the Suvla offensive, including sick, amounted to over 40,000. The offer of 25,000 reinforcements would still leave him below strength.

Hamilton is pictured by some of his contemporaries at this time as 'still optimistic'. In fact, he was living in a fantasy world and what kept him going was the belief – fathered by desperation – that one more determined push would do the trick; he found comfort in Intelligence reports that the Turks were as tired as the British. But *they* were winning. Hamilton had no realistic idea of how low were the spirits of his own men – a fact which even the official history acknowledges. When their Commander-in-Chief visited them the officers and men would produce the obligatory Gallipoli smile and soldierly comment, but all were hoping fervently that Hamilton would not send them yet again into an assault which they knew must fail.

Nevinson observed the way that the soldiers' spirits sank and after visiting the lines near Krithia on 30 August, he wrote: 'A newly arrived draft has usually to join the rest of the battalion in the trenches or firing line at once. The men know nothing of the realities of war and weather. Shells and bullets soon affect them. . . . The sun shines through them like X-rays. Dust fills their eyes and mouths. Flies cover their food and keep them irritated and restless. In the advanced trenches ten to one they get little beyond biscuit and bully beef, with an occasional share in an onion or pot of jam. Diarrhoea begins to affect them. They grow weak and their spirit sinks. In that condition they are called upon to resist or deliver an attack against a tough race of semi-barbarous soldiers famous at trench fighting for generations.'

Further attacks were likely, for the French Minister of War produced an idea by General Maurice Sarrail for a major landing with a powerful French corps in Asiatic Turkey. Sarrail, a popular opponent of Joffre, would lead the expedition and be independent of British command.

Hamilton's instant reaction, as expressed in his diary, was: 'From bankrupt to millionaire in 24 hours. . . . *Deo volente* we are saved; Constantinople is doomed.' The extravagant language was an indication of Hamilton's mercurial spirits. He told Kitchener that under the 'changed conditions' – the Suvla disaster – he was 'not unfavourable' to the French idea. But some people, notably Joffre, were decidedly against the plan, and by being unco-operative Joffre succeeded in taking all impetus out of it. He stalled. He could not fix a date when it would be possible for him to find the French divisions needed – perhaps in mid-October. Everything depended on his Western Front operations, and no new landing could be contemplated until it was clear that equally important results could not be achieved on the Western Front. A further difficulty, Joffre said, was that a minimum of thirteen divisions would be needed for Gallipoli, and France could not spare that number. Even if it could, Sarrail was unfit for such a command.

At least one man present at the meeting – Colonel Hankey – at which Joffre was so obstructive understood that he had effectively prevented a French landing. No matter what, Joffre would see to it that the French troops could not be ready to land before the end of November – and by then the weather would ensure that the operations could not succeed.

In the French mind the whole Dardanelles affair was soon pushed into a secondary place by a wave of public feeding to help Serbia by an invasion of the Balkans, preferably through Salonika. Kitchener now preferred an Asiatic landing – after nearly seven months of opposing it – but he was exasperatedly aware that French interest had evaporated. Pressed to support the Balkans venture, he agreed to supply 75,000 troops. They could only come from Hamilton, who would have to evacuate Suvla Bay. Hamilton and de Robeck fought against this, but the Government was faced with an agonizing choice – Gallipoli or Salonika; they could not maintain the three fronts of France, Gallipoli and Salonika, plus an army in Egypt.

The Americans, still a long way from being involved in the war and therefore still objective, were watching the Dardanelles embroilment with great interest. Some were acutely critical along the lines expressed by a *New York World* editorial writer, on 6 September. He was particularly caustic about 'British madness', and he considered that in failing at the Dardanelles the British had really been lucky. 'England has simply gone mad from fear of Germany. This absurd "German madness" has caused the best of British statesmen to lose sight of Britain's best interests, so causing the British to do that which, if successful, would be the worst possible thing for England's future. Russia is England's great future enemy . . . so England's endeavour to conquer the Dardanelles, to take Constantinople and deliver it to England's greatest rival of the future, is nothing short of political madness.'

On the battlefield, Aubrey Herbert was conscious of another kind of 'madness'. 'Directly we have touched a spade we have ceased to advance,' he wrote in his diary on 24 September. 'We have never achieved anything except with a rush. We shall do nothing more here unless we have an overwhelming force.'

In the midst of the attempts in London and Paris to evolve a grand strategy, news of the beginning of the battle of Loos, on 25 September, reached Gallipoli. Lieutenant R.B. Rathbone of the 6th Loyal North Lancashires wrote about an 'amusing incident' which followed. 'A crackle of musketry was heard from the positions held by the Scottish Horse Brigade on the right of the line. This spread rapidly from right to left and there was a considerable din, augmented in a few minutes by the field batteries. Then after 20 minutes the racket ceased suddenly. The explanation heard . . . is possibly too good a story to be true. . . . The Marquess of Tullibardine, commanding the Scottish Horse Brigade, gave orders that his Brigade would give three cheers for the good news in France. The Turks opposite, fearing an attack opened fire, and the fire was returned. Lord Tullibardine was told that his gesture had cost the country £300,000 worth of ammunition.'

The story *was* true, but for Hamilton, among others, it was no 'amusing incident'. He made this clear in 1936 in a letter to Colonel Sir Henry Darlington, Commanding Officer of 5th Manchester Battalion, 'Our *feu de joie* – or, as our men called it, "the furious joy" – was fired in celebration of the battle of Loos which more than any other single factor lost us the Peninsula. Actually it was rather pathetic that we, of all people, should be pretending – at Home dictation – that this bloody defeat was a victory. The preparation for Loos was the argument used [in Britain and in France] over and over again for holding up our supply of ammunition and issue of trench mortars, a couple of dozen of which would have blown the Anzac Turks clean off the top of the Hill.' More than twenty years after Gallipoli, Hamilton, an old man, was obviously still angry about being starved of ammunition. The battle of Loos cost the French 100,000 casualties and the British 60,000; gains were negligible.

By now the disgraced Stopford, more aggressive against Hamilton than he had ever been against the Turks, had made known his criticisms of the conduct of the Suvla operations, and Kitchener ordered four generals to investigate. Not one of them had ever seen the peninsula and Hamilton was not consulted, but the inquiry concluded that 'the whole series of tasks planned for IX Corps is open to criticism'.

Kitchener reported to the Government that the War Office generals had made 'considerable criticism of Sir Ian Hamilton's leadership'. The Dardanelles Committee also took into account a letter written by the Australian journalist Keith Murdoch which bitterly criticized Hamilton, and a letter from Ashmead-Bartlett addressed to the Prime Minister.

But the most telling evidence against Hamilton came from Captain Guy Dawnay, a young officer on his own staff. With the collusion of other GHQ officers, Colonel Aspinall,* George Lloyd and Captain W.H. Deedes, Dawnay went to London for the express purpose of exposing the mismanagement of the campaign; that is, he was set on having Hamilton recalled. That these officers, who liked Hamilton as a man, could bring themselves to intrigue against him gives a clear measure of their loss of confidence in him. They had convinced themselves that they had a greater duty to their country and to the men of Gallipoli than they had to Hamilton.

That they succeeded in deceiving Hamilton is clear from his diary entry of 2 September: 'Dawnay after dinner left for England. He goes to explain matters first hand to K. Next to my going home myself, or to K. himself coming out here, this is the best I can do. Dawnay is one of the soundest young officers we have, but he is run down physically (like most of us) and jaded. He should benefit by the trip and so should the rumour-mongers at home.'

---

* Aspinall was later to write the official history of the campaign. Interestingly, he does not mention Dawnay, Deedes or Lloyd in the two volumes, and makes no reference to the plot.

The conspirators had convinced Hamilton that somebody should return to England to tell 'the truth', but the truth as they saw it was quite different from the truth Hamilton wanted to be told. He was thinking in terms of the need for more ammunition, artillery and good divisional generals. A friend of the Royal Family and of Asquith, Dawnay had access to everybody. He saw the King, Asquith, Lloyd George, the Conservative leader Bonar Law, Curzon and just about everybody else with influence. For a man of Dawnay's principles this campaign against his chief must have been loathsome.

Many politicians had something to say about Gallipoli, often in public, and their utterances were read with great interest by German and Turkish Intelligence. On 14 October Lord Milner said in the House of Lords, 'When I hear that it would be a terrible thing to abandon our Dardanelles adventure because this would have so bad an effect in Egypt, in India, upon our prestige in the East, I cannot help asking myself whether it will not have a worse effect if we persist in that enterprise and it ends in complete disaster.'

Milner, with Lloyd George, Sir Edward Carson and others, were members of the 'Salonika Circle' and pressed for intervention in the Balkans. Churchill, Asquith, Balfour and Curzon wanted reinforcements for Gallipoli for a 'final push'. Because of the division, the Dardanelles Committee referred the matter to the experts – the War Office and Admiralty staffs. They promptly reported that it was too late to save Serbia so that troops sent to Salonika would be wasted. The best course was to concentrate all might in France and break the Germans. Second best would be a fresh assault at Gallipoli. While Asquith hedged, Kitchener asked Hamilton for an estimate of probable losses if the peninsula were to be evacuated. Hamilton replied that he might lose half his force. In saying this he committed professional suicide. On 14 October the Dardanelles Committee ordered his recall. He had run out of credibility.

Next day Kitchener telegraphed Hamilton that the

Government 'appreciated' his work but had decided to make a change. General Sir Charles Monro, who had been chosen to succeed him, would bring his own Chief-of-Staff so Braithwaite should also return home. Until Monro's arrival Birdwood would be temporarily in command of the Expeditionary Force.

Hamilton was hurt and noted in his diary that Monro 'was born with another sort of mind from me'. He believed that had Monro been sent to the Dardanelles in the first place he would never have consented to go on with the operation. His heart still set on the Dardanelles, Hamilton was determined, when he reached England, to induce Kitchener to go to Gallipoli and run the campaign himself, 'if only he will shake himself free from slippery politics'. Sarrail, he considered, had 'missed the chance of twenty generations'. Finally, he swore that he would 'buttonhole every Minister from McKenna and Lloyd George to Asquith and Bonar Law and grovel at their feet if by so doing I can hold them to the biggest scoop that has ever been open to an Empire.'

In all that Hamilton wrote at the time are the usual signs of a man who had failed putting the blame on others – though it is to his credit that Hamilton did not blame his troops. His leaving affected them adversely. 'The departure of a Commander-in-Chief acts upon an army like sudden heart disease in a man or the collapse of a ship's steering wheel,' Henry Nevinson wrote. 'All is at once bewilderment and uncertainty; a sense of loss and change and failure pervades all ranks.' The men had criticized Hamilton, but his removal made them feel criticized too.

General Monro's mission was not only to take command of the Expeditionary Force, but to report 'fully and frankly' on the situation; to consider the best means of resolving the deadlock and to report from a purely military point of view whether it would be better to evacuate the peninsula or try again to capture it.

Monro was not afraid of Kitchener. He could not be rushed off to Gallipoli as Hamilton had been, and Kitchener was wasting his breath telling him that the Turks would run if they came up against a strong British Commander-in-Chief waving the Union Jack. Monro had what Hamilton lacked – a practical, pragmatic mind. Before he would budge from London he wanted to see every piece of paper available – maps, statistics, casualty returns, reports. Churchill managed to make Monro listen to his opinion. He turned up at the station as Monro and his staff were leaving, threw them a bundle of papers and said sonorously, 'Remember, a withdrawal from Gallipoli would be as great a disaster as Corunna.' [A British retreat in Spain in 1809.]

Monro arrived at Imbros to find analysis prepared by Hamilton's GHQ staff. To be successful, these officers reported, an advance should be made on both sides of the Straits by 250,000 men with plenty of ammunition. As winter was approaching the attack could not be made until spring; to make up for the wastage of troops in the winter-spring interval an army of 400,000 would be necessary.

Kitchener was against evacuation and he hoped Monro would support him. He needed all the support he could get, for on 29 October Joffre travelled to London for a vital conference. Inflexible, stubborn, a devout believer in massive frontal attacks, Joffre wanted England to send 250,000 men to Salonika – 150,000 at least – to help Serbia. He threatened that he might resign if the English did not agree; there could even be a rupture between Britain and France. The British Government agreed – thus putting an end to any chance of heavily reinforcing Gallipoli. Yet at this time Keyes was presenting his detailed plan for a combined naval and military attack on the Narrows.

Under so much pressure, Kitchener cabled to Monro: Please send me as soon as possible your report on the main issue . . . leaving or staying.

Monro had been at Gallipoli less than twenty-four hours, but with Kitchener's whip cracking he visited all three fronts in the course of one day. The ramshackle nature of the occupation startled him – at Anzac he saw the incredible terraces of trenches on the cliff faces, soldiers' uniforms in every state of disarray, equipment and supplies badly stored, and roughly improvised piers. Monro has been much criticized for making an unqualified decision on the basis of a quick trip, but he had an experienced eye and he was seeing more clearly and critcially than was possible for those officers for whom Gallipoli was both home and a way of life. It may have been advisable for him to spend longer at each place but there was no need; on these limited battlefields a professional eye could take in the salient points in an hour.

In a 700-word, well-reasoned report Monro recommended evacuation. Kitchener was dismayed and cabled to ask if the three corps commanders were in favour of withdrawal. When Monro consulted them, Birdwood opposed evacuation and Byng and Davies supported it.

On 3 November the new War Committee decided that before a decision could be made on Monro's recommendation, Kitchener should go to Gallipoli to see the situation for himself. Kitchener's credibility was also running out, and the politicians were glad to have him out of the way for a time. He was now desperate to save the Dardanelles campaign and before he left London he sent his friend Birdwood a top secret message, suggesting a way in which the army could support the Keyes plan. He suggested a landing near the head of the Gulf of Xeros to cut the peninsula's neck. With British ships at both ends of this army line – he was assuming that the Navy would break through the Straits – the Turks would wither on the dead Gallipoli vine. Monro would be given the Salonika command while Birdwood would take over the Gallipoli and use all the best troops for the new operation.

En route to Gallipoli Kitchener sent Birdwood another

cable, and that by now bemused general also heard from Prime Minister Asquith that the Government had not yet decided on evacuation – though Birdwood should make contingency plans.

Kitchener, fighting for a Gallipoli campaign with an intensity he had never shown in Hamilton's time, telegraphed to the Admiralty from Paris asking that Keyes should join him at Marseilles. They would discuss the scheme for a naval attack while on the way to Gallipoli. This telegram was not passed to Keyes, apparently because an Admiralty official decided that he could not reach Marseilles in time to rendezvous with Kitchener. But it seems likely that somebody did not wish Keyes and Kitchener to get together and plan a naval attack, and thus 'lost' the telegram. In Paris, Keyes found unexpected support for holding Gallipoli and the new Minister of Marine, Lacaze – there had been a recent change of Government – even suggested sending six battleships to assist the British attack. When Keyes, after a journey of delays, finally reached Lemnos he found that Kitchener was now in favour of evacuation. He said to Keyes later, 'When you didn't turn up in Marseilles I decided that the naval plan was dead.'

What he said to Birdwood, on being shown the terrain at Anzac, is even more significant. 'Thank God, Birdie, I came to see this for myself. I had no idea of the difficulties you were up against. I think you have all done wonders.' It was a self-indictment, though Kitchener would not have seen it that way. He should have seen the place for himself months before.

In a telegram to Asquith on 15 November, he said, 'The country is much more difficult than I imagined and the Turkish positions are natural fortresses which, if not taken by surprise at first, could be held against very serious attack by larger forces than have been engaged.' These admissions damn him as a Minister of War.

That same day Winston Churchill resigned his office as Chancellor of the Duchy of Lancaster and defended his conception of the Dardanelles Expedition in the House of Commons:

> If there were any operations in the history of the world which, having been begun, it was worth while to carry through with the utmost vigour and fury, with a consistent flow of reinforcements and an utter disregard of life, it was the operations so daringly and brilliantly begun by Sir Ian Hamilton in the immortal landing of 25 April.

In this piece of characteristically Churchillian rhetoric rolling thunderously across the years is embedded a misstatement so great that it destroys the whole of the viewpoint. The operations were not brilliantly begun, and the mistakes made in the beginning prevented the operation from being carried through. As for 'an utter disregard of life', that condition had been met. Churchill went off to France to lead a battalion on the Western Front, a direct form of soldiering for which his talents were better suited.

A week later Kitchener sent his first report and merely echoed Monro's findings; Suvla and Anzac should be evacuated, but the Helles front should be retained 'for the present'. This exclusion was nothing more than a face-saving device. In this message Kitchener for the first and only time admitted culpability in the Suvla debacle. He said he should have let Hamilton have the reinforcements asked for in August, and later he and the Government should have made it possible for the offensive to be resumed there. The operation has been prevented 'by the mistaken policy we have followed, at the dictation of France, at Salonika'.

Asquith was quick to reply: The War Committee favoured total evacuation.

A notable opponent was Colonel Hankey, who submitted a paper in his usual lucid style, arguing that the reasons for holding on to Gallipoli were overwhelming, provided that it could be done. But his reasons did not overwhelm the full British Cabinet of twenty-two members which, on 7 December, finally decided on total evacuation. A factor in the decision was that Bonar Law threatened to resign if Gallipoli were not evacuated; this would have split the Government, leading to complications which made the evacuation of the peninsula a much more attractive proposition.

Nobody asked the opinion of those most intimately affected by a decision to go or stay – the soldiers of Anzac, Helles and Suvla. Sick and exhausted, and in many cases half demented with nervous strain, they had been suffering under another blow – one of the most deadly winters in history.

12

The Blizzard, Lemnos and a Sister's Story

Weather reports had predicted a November of 'glorious weather', but this forecast turned out to be no more accurate than any of the military predictions. During the first three weeks a series of gales badly damaged beach installations and the question of whether to evacuate or not began to seem academic; if the weather continued to be stormy the army would be tied to the peninsula no matter what decisions the generals made. Winter clothing had been landed in large quantities – but had been sent back to Mudros base, Lemnos, only a few days before the blizzard.

A violent thunderstorm on the night of 26 November was followed by a downpour that went on non-stop for twenty-four hours, flooding trenches and dug-outs and soaking the soldiers. Before anything could be dried out an icy northerly hurricane began to blow, bringing with it heavy snow; then followed two nights of bitter frost.

Conditions everywhere were dreadful, but at Anzac many men were able to shelter from the storm in the caves and galleries dug by the busy Australians and New Zealanders. Here even the front-line trenches were protected a little by the hills. Many Australians and Indians had never seen snow, and the episode began with an air of excitement. This did not last long, as rifles jammed and blankets and greatcoats froze solid.

The number of men reporting sick rose alarmingly – the Indian troops in particular were hit by the cold – but deaths from exposure at Anzac were comparatively few. At Helles the trenches were mostly on sloping ground and suffered little from flooding, but here, too, the cold was crippling.

Suvla was worst hit. Most parts of the front were exposed, and in many places the trenches were on flat or low-lying ground or in dry water-courses. Within a few hours these deres or nullahs became raging torrents and British and Turkish soldiers were swept to their deaths, sometmes together, by walls of water. In some trenches men suddenly found themselves fighting for their lives in water up to their chests.

Lieutenant R.B. Rathbone, of the 6th Loyal North Lancashires, with four other officers, was in the middle of a meal – a parcel received from Fortnum and Mason – when the blizzard broke. Within minutes he was ordered to get busy with his platoon on drainage work. 'My men shivered on the brink of the trench, trying ineffectually to shovel out the turbid mud and water. This was useless and calling on them to follow I jumped in and there we were, up to our thighs in icy water, shovelling for all we were worth. . . . At 3 a.m, soaked and unutterably weary, I went to my dugout to find it in ruins and my kit buried beneath the debris. Trudging towards a red glow, I heard a cheery voice, "Would you like a cup of tea, sir?" Here I found warmth, friendliness and good cheer. "Give him a good strong cup – aye, a Lancashire cup."'

Many units of the 29th Division – and the Turks confronting them – were driven out of their trenches. United in abject misery and freezing cold, the soldiers stood about for hours, unable and unwilling to fire a shot. Theoretically it was possible for either side to walk through the opposing lines. Those officers still able to function were afraid that the Turks might recover first and in a surprise attack swamp the helpless British troops. Nevinson says that at least one British general contemplated attacking the Turks, but soon realized that movement was not possible. The fight was knocked out of the men, and for some hours on several parts of the front even sniping ceased. In places Turks and British lit separate fires in full view of each other in an attempt to survive. Once the water froze it was impossible to get back into the trenches.

To soldiers who served throughout the long winters on the Western Front a 'cold snap' of four days might seem just another winter episode. The impact of the Gallipoli freeze lay in its suddenness, its severity, the lack of preparation for winter – even the absence of expectation. Winter on the Western Front did not come as a shock; at Gallipoli it had the force of a major enemy attack. And its effects were as devastating.

Private B.W. Boddy, of the 2/4th Queens Royal West Surrey Regiment, endured the blizzard with two mates in a 'scrape-out', which gave no protection. He lost consciousness and 'came to life' on a bug-ridden ship en route to Malta, where he spent months recovering.

Private C.E.W. Brayley was stretcher-bearing in a biting wind, heading for the frontline trenches. In a letter home, he wrote, 'And when we got there, mud and misery! . . . Men old in a night with exposure, knee-deep in mud and water. We got our case back, poor fellow. Three miles stretcher-bearing such as I have never seen before. We often went over our knees in the Salt Lake. . . . I was in wet clothes for three days. . . . Most of our bearing is done at night and three nights ago we got lost. . . . We ended up on heavy muddy ground and continually got stuck with our loads and more than one bearer fell with a stretcher case on top of him and had to be pulled out. I shall never forget that stretcher-bearing – foaming and sweating as in death throes . . . Gods! The cases we carried and the sundry biscuit-box crosses to be seen with the cold inscription "Died from exposure".'

The 86th Brigade, and especially the 2nd Royal Fusiliers, virtually ceased to exist as a fighting force. The sights were reminiscent of descriptions of the British retreat to Corunna in the winter of 1809 and of the French retreat from Moscow in 1812. All over the Suvla plain demoralized soldiers streamed towards the beaches; many collapsed and froze to death on the way. Every place of shelter was crowded – supply tents, field ambulance posts, animal shelter sheds . . . all were full to overflowing as desperate men congregated for warmth and cover.

Corporal M.E. Gray of the Field Ambulance, attached to the 53rd Division, wrote that 'It was very trying to be in charge of a marquee packed with unconscious men, some badly wounded, and be helpless to do anything useful for them. I was on night duty trying to get some warmth into frozen limbs and bodies. When we saw that one of the boys was breathing his last we would call the medical officer. On more than one occasion I was told, "Don't worry, Corporal, if he came around he would soon die – he has double pneumonia."'

General Maude, one of the divisional commanders from France, showed his worth during the crisis. He got through a morale-boosting message that included the promise that he was sending more coal, coke and rum. Then he appeared at the front himself with three staff officers. Lieutenant Rathbone was astonished to see him faultlessly turned out, his boots mud-splashed but gleaming, his buttons sparkling. 'What a tonic. Nothing could have exceeded his kindness, sympathy and helpfulness. How he managed it the battalion officers never knew as many stores had already been evacuated but that evening Maude sent up braziers, fuel and sheepskin coats. The 53rd was fortunate in its divisional commander.'

The regimental medical teams worked heroically, as did the field kitchens, but it was not even possible to supply all the men with food and drink, let alone treat them.

Poor leadership and inadequate training showed up starkly

in the dreadful conditions, and the Herefordshire Regiment had a particularly harrowing time. Exhausted after intense effort in the rain, snow and cold, the battalion bivouacked miserably in snow-covered sand dunes on the night of 27 November. In the morning many men were unable to get up, while others chafed some circulation back into their limbs. The calamity that followed is told in the diary of Captain Peter Ashton:

Overnight our rations had been sent to us in a lorry. The folk who sent them out, presumably sorry for those unfortunates in the snow, sent with them a double ration of rum. The wagon drivers who brought the stuff . . . had simply dumped it by the side of the road. When morning broke men began wandering about and unhappily found the dump. Instead of telling somebody or even eating the food . . . they broke open the rum jars and started in. The effect on empty stomachs and in that cold was devastating. Filled with a spurious warmth, they lay on the ground and in many cases took off their coats, boots and tunics. Those in the immediate vicinity of the dump were quickly put in the bag, but the majority had filled their mess tins and water bottles and crawled into the bushes to enjoy themselves. We combed the bushes all morning but by the time we found them all a certain number were dead. I found one man in only his shirt and trousers, holding an empty mug in a perfectly stiff arm, quite dead. Coming on top of everything else it was heart-rending. Luckily there were ambulances quite close and we evacuated officers and men in a steady stream. When it was all over there were left Rogers [an officer], 77 other ranks and myself! The battalion had landed in August 750-strong.

The French fared better than the British during the blizzard. Much earlier they had imported large quantities of sheet tin, which they used to make their trenches and dug-outs more weather resistent. Also, by November they were in winter clothing and they were better supplied with coal than were the British. Their casualties were few.

Great damage was caused on the islands and at Anzac and Helles, piers being demolished and many small craft wrecked. But the damage to the men was much worse than the damage to material. In the four days of the blizzard Suvla had 12,000 cases of frostbite and exposure, Anzac 3,000 and Helles 1,000. At Suvla about 220 were drowned or frozen to death. As soon as it was possible to get the suffering men onto ships they were taken to the military hospitals of Egypt or Lemnos.

Lemnos had a vital and too little appreciated role in the Dardanelles campaign. The main base for Gallipoli was Alexandria, 650 miles away, but as the expedition continued to develop, Lemnos – because of its splendid harbour at Mudros – became an extremely important centre. Sixty miles from the peninsula – within distant sight – it was only four hours' sailing time for destroyers and eight hours for trawlers. By September ships were leaving almost daily for the three sectors, usually carrying tinned meat, biscuits or fodder. When large steamers arrived at Mudros the goods most urgently needed were often at the bottom of the holds. Frequently, before ships were unloaded they were summoned to the peninsula or often back to Britain, carrying their undischarged cargo with them. Hamilton always felt the desperate need for somebody with great commercial experience and influence to run his supply services from Lemnos. On 3 July he put this need to the Quartermaster General at the War Office: 'I worry just as much over things behind me as I do over the enemy in front of me. What I want is a really big man there . . . a man I mean who, if he saw the real necessity, would wire for a great English contractor and 300 navvies without bothering or referring the matter to anyone.'

Late in July he got his 'big man' – General Sir Edward Altham, sent to Lemnos to re-organize Lines of Communication business. He reduced the confusion which hampered everything, but he was unable to make the very dull island any more attractive to the soldiers brought there to rest. He cleaned out the malingerers and misfits which are the excess baggage of any army and sent them back to Egypt, but he was never able to get from Hamilton as much authority as he needed – and which Hamilton himself had said he needed. It is possible that Braithwaite was a stumbling block here, as he considered that Altham was poaching on some of his own preserves.

Lemnos was linked to the peninsula, especially Anzac, by a chain of suffering as much as by a chain of supply, whose links were the hospital ships and fleet mine-sweepers which ferried wounded and sick. At Anzac in 'normal' times a hospital ship, such as the *Gascon* or *Sicilia*, lay off the cove day and night and gradually filled with serious cases – the men with red-bordered tickets attached to them. Those with slight wounds or those just moderately ill – they carried white labels – were sent off each night by fleet-sweepers to Lemnos. When the hospital ship was full she sailed for Lemnos, and set ashore at Mudros any light cases before proceeding to Malta or Alexandria with her load, while another hospital ship took up station offshore. This was the simple scheme, but it broke down under the great pressure of wounded and sick, so that by the end of May many serious cases were treated at Lemnos and many light cases went off to Egypt and Malta.

From a command point of view the most important part of Mudros was the SS *Aragon*, hired at the immense cost of £300 a day from the Royal Mail Steam Packet Company as a headquarters for the Lines of Communication staff, and as the General Post Office. She, her staff and crew acquired an evil name for the frequent loss of parcels from home, an unpardonable crime against fighting men. The staff aboard

Aragon were probably not always to blame for parcels 'going astray', but the allegations of indecent luxury aboard the ship were certainly true. Nevinson has said that to anyone coming fresh from the dug-outs, dust storms, monotonous rations and perpetual risks on the peninsula, the *Aragon* was like 'an Enchanted Isle'. It had plenty of varied food, clean cooking, iced drinks, sheets in the bunks, tablecloths for dinner, and baths.

The *Aragon* was moored only a mile or so away from 3rd Australian General Hospital, and Bean records that the sharp contrast between conditions at the hospital, with nurses and patients sleeping on the ground, and the luxury of the ship, 'caused the whole staff to be regarded with bitter and not altogether undeserved dislike'. If one is to believe the reports of the many officers straight from battle who had occasion to visit the *Aragon*, the staff officers on board had nothing but supercilious contempt for the regimental soldiers. One has a mental picture of bored but immaculately dressed officers parading the decks when off duty and peering in a superior way at the curious riff-raff who came aboard. Commander Samson, who risked his life every time he went up in his aeroplane to scout, disliked having to visit the *Aragon*, where he 'had the feeling that he was a beastly nuisance'.

As early as May, the French had a better system of supply than the British because they had abandoned the clumsy scheme of using Alexandria as their main base. They took everything to Mudros, where an efficient management officer with an adequate staff had the authority which Hamilton said he so much wanted in a British Lines-of-Communication chief. The French always knew what ships they had, what they were carrying and where they were on any given day. The mail service was reliable and the supply depots efficiently run. The French officers considered that British supply arrangements were amateurish – and indeed they were. In fairness, the French had a much smaller force to maintain on the peninsula.

Even as late as the end of June 1915, the arrangements for transporting wounded to Lemnos and elsewhere were sometimes grotesquely inadequate. A particular instance, stronly condemned at the time, was the case of the transport *Saturnia*, which appeared in Mudros after the attack of 28 June with about 700 wounded on board. They were crowded haphazardly into every corner and so neglected that their wounds in many cases were putrefying and full of maggots. The ship itself, having been used for horses and mules, was filthy and stinking. Naval surgeons boarded *Saturnia* and one of them, Staff Surgeon Levick of HMS *Bacchante*, operated almost without sleep for four days and nights. For lack of adequate assistance and because of shortage of bandages, dressings and instruments, many died who might have recovered with proper care. Yet this care was available on shore at the military hospitals, had there been an efficient medical services liaison department.

After any action on the peninsula, the wards on Lemnos were hopelessly congested, with the medical staff working themselves to exhaustion in the efforts to cope with the sick and wounded.

One of the nurses at 3rd Australian General Hospital was my mother. Her experiences form part of my narrative and, I think, a unique if small part of the Dardanelles history. I can best relate her story of Lemnos by allowing her to tell it herself.*

I had not even heard of Lemnos when I was sent there as a sister with the 3rd Australian General Hospital. All the way from Egypt I wondered if it would be like the many barren but picturesque white islands the ship passed in the

---

* As a journalist, I 'interviewed' her in April 1950 for an article – 'as told to John Laffin' – to be published on the 36th anniversary of Anzac Day. With some amendment and addition the article is reproduced here.

blue Aegean Sea. And it was. When we anchored in the outer harbour of Mudros we looked onto bare hills clad with rows and rows of white tents, and windmills in the distance. More than 1,000 ships were in the outer and inner harbour – troopships, hospital ships, supply ships and warships with launches scurrying among them. The scene was reminiscent of Sydney Harbour, except that Mudros was not as beautiful.

I could imagine no greater joy than to be working under canvas so close to the gallant men of Anzac. The hospital CO, Colonel Fiaschi, asked me how I liked serving on Lemnos, and when I said it was 'fun' he was surprised. But I meant it. We Australian nurses were very patriotic and anything we were doing we were doing for England. We were all glad to be taking part in the 'great adventure', though none of us was militarily conscious, nor did we have any understanding of the strategy and tactics of the campaign. They were grim and tragic but sometimes inspiring days. At first many surgical cases were brought to Lemnos, but later our main patients were dysentery, paratyphoid, jaundice and trench-feet sufferers, often in great pain and depression.

Sometimes the men arrived via a hospital ship on which they had been cleaned and had their wounds dressed before reaching us in the hospital, but those brought in on the sweepers were filthy, bloodstained and in pain. Some arrived almost completely paralysed, perhaps from being knocked down by a bursting shell and buried with rock and debris. We treated numerous cases of gangrene – the rotting of flesh when a wound was too long untreated. Even slight shell and shrapnel wounds were complicated by much bruising of the surrounding tissue. The seriously sick were often delirious and talked in a disjoined or wild way about incidents on the peninsula. We could do little for some soldiers, except to help them die decently.

Laundry for the dysentery cases was an enormous problem. Soiled linen had to be put aside to be washed when water became available, sometimes a matter of months. When the laundry went putrid it all had to be made into a bonfire.

Our water came from the warships until a condenser was built on the island to convert salt water into fresh. No bread was available, only tough army biscuit. Later our rations improved, but, by grace of the Red Cross, not through official army issue. The Red Cross provided the patients and nurses with powdered soup, with Huntley and Palmer's digestive biscuits and Ideal milk; these issues kept us alive.

Several hospitals with nurses were working apart from ours – the 2nd Australian Stationary Hospital, the 1st and 3rd Irish-Canadian Hospitals and English hospitals. Two Canadian sisters were among the dysentery victims and were buried with the men in the Allied cemetery.

We could find beds for about 1,000 patients, but as we often had more patients than beds many had to sleep on mattresses on the ground, as did the sisters at times. Between the wards and along the sides of the 'streets' in the hospital area the orderlies spent many off-duty hours making models of kangaroos, emus, and maps of Australia from white stones. They were touching reminders of home, which to sick soldiers seemed a long, long way off. It was a long way – 10,000 miles.

In September 1915 the surviving soldiers of the landing on 25 April were brought to Lemnos for two weeks' rest. They came in by night and camped across Sarpi Bay, and we didn't know they were there until the following morning. While they were dispersing from church parade, conducted by Dean Talbot, a tall, bronzed, bearded Anzac came up to me and with a grand salute said, 'Little Sister!' [My mother was only 4 feet 10 inches in height.] It was a soldier I had known in Sydney and I had last seen him in camp at Randwick Racecourse, Sydney. His name was Sergeant Bill Rose and he was posted missing, believed killed, in France in 1917.

'I had to come and find you,' he said. 'I'll go back to camp and have a clean-up and come and see you again later.'

Each evening for a week or so after that I would take four nurses and he four soldiers, and we would meet below the brow of the hill on which our tents were pitched. We had to be very circumspect there. [Fraternizing between the Australian sisters – who were considered to be commissioned rank – and other ranks was not lawful, as it was in the British army.] We laughed and talked and the men flicked mosquitoes off their bare knees, forgetting the war until reminded of it by spasmodic bursts of gunfire from the peninsula. Night duty for me would break up the party.

One night one of my orderlies – good chaps these – whispered mysteriously, 'You're wanted outside.'

It was Bill. With only a few hours' warning the men had been ordered back to the front, certain death for many of them. 'I've run a risk,' said Bill. 'I hope I won't be missed.' And a few minutes later, after a brief farewell in the shadow of a marquee, he had gone. Next morning, as we night nurses were coming off duty, we saw a Highland band playing the troops to the waiting ships, a stirring sight, even a colourful one despite the drab khaki.

One soldier confidently left the ranks, and going up to a group of nurses took one by the hand and said, 'Come walk along with me awhile.' Everyone cheered as she went with him and another band at once struck up 'Goodbye Dolly, I must leave you.' The soldier at last had to break his clasp of the girl and run to catch up with his section.

Lemnos weather became bitterly cold, with blizzards and blinding rain. The wards were dark day and night and outside was the screaming wind, rain and sleet. Walking from ward to ward or to our quarters was an ordeal. We wore big army overcoats and wound puttees around our legs to try to keep warm.

At first we could only imagine what the boys on Gallipoli must be suffering in the cold, but when the trench-feet casualties came in we knew. They suffered excruciating pain. Many of the victims were Englishmen, including little Lancashire men of Kitchener's Army; some were no taller than four feet six inches. They used to cry like children with the pain at night, but during the day they were cheerful. One little man, called Joe, had a pleasant voice and used to sing 'Though your heart may ache a while, never mind', and, 'There'll be sunshine after rain', and other ballads. While he sang, the boys would fall silent and thoughtful.

The wounded men told us of Gallipoli and how men were drowned because their feet were so paralysed by cold they could not escape. Sentries were found at their posts, frozen, and still clutching their rifles. Some, we heard, could only grin at the Turks because their fingers were too frozen to press the trigger. Some of the boys lost both feet, some both hands. And some lost their reason.

The soldiers would tell us that the Turks said, 'When the shells are flying the Indian runs behind a bush. The Englishman, he lies flat on the ground. But the Australian, he stands up, looks around and says, "Now, where the hell did that one go?"' No matter who said it, it sounded true. The Turks called the Australians 'those great white Gurkhas', which was considered a fine compliment as the Gurkhas were such good soldiers. [There is some evidence that the Gurkhas first gave this label to the New Zealanders who made the attack on Chunuk Bair with them.]

As for the amoebic dysentery victims, only they knew what they suffered. We wondered how human frames, so gaunt and grim, could hold on to life so long, as their life drained away. Many recovered, even though there were no sulpha drugs then.

Lemnos was two worlds – the modern one of busy war and the ancient one of tranquillity. The peasants – of Greek extraction – were much as they had been for hundreds of years, slow and unhurried. But even in those distant days there had been hate and killing. The Turks used to raid the islands, slaughter the men and carry off the women. Once the men locked the women in an annexe of the church so that Turks wouldn't find them. But when the men were killed there was nobody to release the women and they died of starvation. Their bones were left there; we saw them in 1915.

The one beautiful thing about Lemnos was the sunset. Sometimes it was like an immense crimson flame over half the sky; at others it was pink and amber. One day when Sister Ruby Dickinson [she died in England during the 1919 influenza epidemic] and I went for a walk to get warm, we came across an Allied cemetery and were amazed to see rows and rows of open graves. They were so neat and even, they could have been cut by machines. We asked the grave-diggers why so many had been dug and they knew no more than we did. It was 'just orders'.

On 11 November, Lord Kitchener [he had arrived from Marseilles the night before], smartly dressed and accompanied by Generals Birdwood and Monro, inspected three of our wards. A crowd of soldiers had gathered outside when he left about five minutes later. Kitchener said, 'I hope you'll soon be well, boys,' saluted, and left. He also inspected the troops in the convalescent and staging camps across Sarpi Bay. Brief though his visit was, it had a great effect on the morale of the troops.

One night we could hear the bombardment on the peninsula, and in the morning found preparations under way to take in 1,000 wounded; not dozens or a few hundred, but 1,000.

There were lighter moments on Lemnos. A soldier once asked me what we sisters had for meals. I told him that we didn't get anything very interesting. He said, 'Listen, don't you go to your mess tonight. I'll get you something interesting.' He returned with a large piece of steak – and steak was as rare on Lemnos as water in the desert. It made a beautiful meal but I never did find out where he got it. [He may have scrounged it from the *Aragon*.]

The camps across Sarpi Bay often invited the sisters to their entertainments, and it was here that we heard some of the rumours of evacuation from Gallipoli, though this didn't seem likely. But one night, while I was on duty, an orderly said, 'They're landing troops on Lemnos in thousands.'

A sister said excitedly, 'Perhaps it's an invasion.'

An orderly we sent to get information came back to tell us that the troops were from Gallipoli; the peninsula *was* being evacuated. It was hard to believe this astounding news, but all that day the men marched in, covered in mud and bowed with equipment. There were no bands this time, as they came back grim and silent from Anzac and Suvla Bay. It was then that we found out the reason for all those empty graves; they were to receive the anticipated dead harvest of the evacuation. There were only three casualties.

The Anzacs left, but before our hospital departed many soldiers came in from Helles. We sisters, about one hundred of us, boarded the hospital ship *Oxfordshire* on 14 January and the ship sailed for Egypt on 21 January. The night after we went aboard the ship a hurricane blew down our tents and huts as if they were paper.

My mother always said that the morale of the men was good. 'They were always glad to get back to the peninsula after leave, as bad as it was, as a matter of conscience –

because their mates were there.' The men she nursed did not criticize their officers or the leadership generally, and as the nurses heard nothing about the conduct of the campaign they had 'no inkling' that it was a failure. The only news of any kind came all the way from Australia.

How many men of Gallipoli wounded themselves to escape from the horrors they were enduring cannot be known, but because Gallipoli was such a congested battlefield the figure would probably not be large. A self-inflicted wound was a serious military offence, so a soldier intent on wounding himself needed seclusion. This was virtually impossible at Anzac and difficult at Helles. Suicide was more likely than mutilation and several veterans have told me that they 'knew of' men who could take no more and had blown out their brains or put a bullet through their heart. Some may have done this at a time of appalling strain when they were not thinking coherently. Coldly deliberate suicide was probably rare, since it was easy enough to get a Turk to do the job; you simply had to stand upright during daylight.

One man to witness and record such a self-inflicted wound is Joseph Murray, a sailor turned soldier of the Hood Battalion. On 5 June, in the front line at Helles, he watched his pal, Tubby, put his thumb over the muzzle of his own rifle and pull the trigger, 'in sheer panic' because he could stand no more. Murray tried to clean up the blood-spurting wound by amputating the stump of the thumb. When his jack-knife failed to do the job he placed the thumb on the rifle butt, put the blade against it and with a sharp tug finished the job Tubby had started. Then he and Tubby agreed on a story which would explain the powder marks on the remains of the thumb – that in the excitement of an attack somebody fired a rifle as Tubby was climbing out of the trench.

My mother did not see a wound suspected of being self-inflicted, but then neither she nor any of the other nurses of her hospital would have bothered to assess or even talk about the chances of a wound having been self-inflicted. But she did, one night, have a problem with a wounded Gurkha; she found him crawling under the bottom of the tent-ward, kukri between his teeth, on the way to finish off some wounded Turks in another ward. She called orderlies to disarm the Gurkha, who was very disappointed at being deprived of his moral right.

Killing a wounded enemy in a hospital ward might have been reprehensible, but in the dreadful conditions prevailing at Gallipoli in the summer of 1915 it became an act of compassion to kill a badly wounded enemy who had no chance of receiving medical help. Lieutenant Greville Cripps, then serving with the Royal Dublin Fusiliers, after repulsing a Turkish attack on his trench on 12 June, found a wounded Turk left behind. 'His thigh was riddled with machine-gun bullets, he had one foot blown away and his skull was opened so that one could see his brain pusling. He was uttering the most awful groans and heaving himself up and down. I realised that it would be a mercy to finish him off, which I did with my revolver.' Later Cripps' conscience bothered him and he wondered if he had 'done correctly'. Most of his comrades would have said that he had. Even more important, so would most of his enemies.

13

'The Shame of it All.'

Contemporary writers called the evacuation a victory, even a significant victory. They said it was a 'triumph over all the odds' and 'a great feat'. I have not come across the view, in as many words, that it was a great feat of arms, but this is the idea which numberous politicians and propagandists tried to convey. And understandably so – since at the height of a war it is unwise publicly to concede defeat. The desire to show the withdrawal as a victory is significant because it is a form of smokescreen thrown up to obscure the brutal truth that Gallipoli was a major defeat.*

In the decades since the campaign ended, numerous historians have accepted the values of 1916 and have treated the evacuation as a victory. Military historian John North observes caustically that the evacuation was the only successful military operation accomplished by British arms on the Gallipoli peninsula.† If as much care, forethought and

---

* The historian Llewellyn Woodward sees this clearly: 'The evacuation was not a victory but the last stage in a defeat . . . which by great forethought, resolution and ability on the part of the military and civilian authorities in control of the war, might have been avoided.'
† Major North was wrong. There were a few successful military operations, notably the Australian defeat of the Turks on 19 May,

brainpower had been applied to the offensive, North wrote, the Gallipoli peninsula could have been captured between dusk and dawn on any day of the week. I go further than North, for whom I have great respect, because the evacuation was not a military operation at all, except in the sense that it involved soldiers; in effect, it was a superb piece of organization. The evacuation was not difficult, since the distances were short, the ground over which the retreat was made was known to the inch by every man involved, and because the British ruled the sea. The evacuation was not tested as an operation of war because it was not *contested*.

When the evacuation was decided upon more than 134,000 men had to be removed from the peninsula. The principal credit for the meticulous organization which got them off goes to Brigadier-General C. Brudenell White, Birdwood's Chief-of-Staff after Colonel Skeen's evacuation from illness. Throughout the operation, at Anzac almost all important points were referred to White and many matters from Suvla came to him. From early morning to late at night he sat by his telephone, explaining, cautioning and advising, with a rare perceptive patience.

The Turkish command knew for months, from the British and Egyptian newspapers, that an evacuation was being discussed. Many German and Turkish officers believed that it was unlikely, but von Sanders ordered field commanders to be watchful and to report any signs of preliminary evacuation. The British Army, as well as 5,000 animals and 300 guns, had to be withdrawn in the face of the enemy, whose trenches were not more than 300 yards and in some cases only five yards from the British lines. Commencing on 10 December, 44,000 men, 3,000 animals and 130 guns were taken off

---

when they accounted for 10,000 Turks at a loss to themselves of 160, and in August in the battle of Lone Pine.

during the next seven nights at Suvla and Anzac by the many ships which appeared offshore when darkness fell. At Suvla during the day barges actually brought from ships *to the shore* guns, troops and stores; but early each night all were taken off again, ready for the same performance next morning.

A top-level order instructed units to pour away all alcohol, except that in casualty clearing stations; this was to obviate the risk of any man getting drunk and shouting out news of an evacuation or even attracting undue attention. No smoking or striking of matches was allowed in case sharp eyes picked up the glow as men left their posts to go to the beach for evacuation. The soldiers knew they had been defeated – even though some of them left in their trenches messages for the Turks, such as 'Don't forget, Johnny, we *left* – you didn't *push* us off.' The Turks have never been able to see the distinction.

After a week, 20,000 men were left at Anzac and 20,000 at Suvla – the maximum number that could be embarked in the last two nights. Twenty motor-lighters, fifteen trawlers, twenty-five steam and twenty-eight oared boats took the men to the old battleships, one transport and fourteen ferry steamers for passage to Mudros and Kephalos Harbour, Imbros. On 19 December the last 10,000 British and 10,000 Anzacs were in position to fight, if they had to, at least 100,000 Turks. The defenders went ahead with their programme of deception; the guns thundered as usual, and soldiers went from loophole to loophole firing rifles to give an impression of normal numbers. Others continued with their booby traps and delayed-action devices to set off rifles after everybody had left. That day the Turkish guns bombarded the Suvla piers and the night-collection point for the troops – and British tension rose.

The motor lighters arrived at the piers at 6.45 p.m. on 19 December while battleships and cruisers stood by to open fire if the enemy attacked. But, unmolested, the last boat shoved off from Anzac at 4 a.m. as a ton of high explosive went off under the Turkish positions. At Suvla the last troops were off by 5 a.m. As day dawned the beaches were empty and the sea deserted. Hours later the Turks discovered they were facing lifeless trenches.

Only Helles now remained, and here a curiously suspended state of warfare existed. The men of both sides were not inclined to be aggressive – the Turks because they thought the British would sooner or later leave of their own accord, the British because it did not make sense to die for a lost cause. On 21 December a curious incident occurred on the front of the Dublin Fusiliers, and Joseph Murray recorded it. A desultory battle had lasted for an hour when Murray and his mates realized that the fighting had ceased except for a personal bayonet fight between a Dublin and a Turk, 'strictly according to the rule-book'.

First the Dublin had a slight advantage, then clever footwork gave the advantage to the Turk. Both bayonets were pointing to the sky, then pointing to the ground. Advantage to the Irishman; the Turk pushed him away; both thrust, both parried – and so it continued until both men sank to their knees, absolutely exhausted. They faced each other, gasping for breath, with determination on their faces but no sign of anger. After a few moments we moved forward to collect our man and the Turks did likewise. We were within arm's length of each other but no one spoke. We, and they, hauled our men to their feet, both still holding their rifles at the ready. Both parties turned and walked slowly away to their respective trenches. Not a shot was fired from either line even though there were at least a dozen men ambling about at point-blank range. As we assisted our lad over the parapet, the boys gave a resounding cheer for the safe return of their conquering hero. I am certain I heard a similar cheer from the Turkish line.

The French division was withdrawn gradually during December, and the last 4,000 men were taken off by French warships on the night of 1–2 January; the Royal Naval Division took over the French trenches and the famous French guns, the 75s. Had they ceased to bark the Turks may have been suspicious.

Turkish officers at Anzac and Suvla had been fiercely criticized by their colleagues at Helles for having 'allowed' the British to slip away unmolested. The critics were told that if *they* allowed this to happen at Helles they would be doubly culpable. Yet, in about nine days, 35,268 soldiers were taken away from Helles without loss, as well as 3,689 horses and mules, 127 guns and 328 vehicles.

But the Turks did see some signs of evacuation, and on 7 January they laid down the heaviest bombardment of the campaign, exploded two mines and then tried an infantry assault. It failed because the officers could not drive the Turks *en masse* from their trenches; those who did climb out were instantly shot down by the watching British. The cruisers and monitors caused heavy losses in the Turkish lines; HMS *Edgar* alone fired 1,000 rounds of 6-in shell. The following day the Turkish artillery hardly fired a shot – though they could seriously have disrupted the final stages of the evacuation.

Because of high winds and rough seas, the last night, 8–9 January, was the most dangerous of all. By 1.30 a.m. the situation was critical at V and W beaches, and embarkation was twice stopped while engineers worked frantically in icy water to repair broken piers. The destroyers *Bulldog* and *Grasshopper* were brought alongside the blockship at V, where they embarked 1,600 men under difficult conditions. At W the heavily laden lighters, taking men to the destroyers *Staunch* and *Fury*, were unmanageable. The seamanship and steadiness of the naval officers and men mastered all problems and the anxious troops, many of them seasick, were got aboard.

The last man off at Helles may have been Major-General Maude, though the circumstances are hardly to his credit. He had left a bag on a stranded lighter at Gully Beach and missed it only when he had nearly reached W Beach, where he, with others, was to be taken off. It contained nothing of military importance, but Maude insisted on going back for it and a staff officer accompanied him. He thus risked the lives of the men packed onto the last barge, as well as risking discovery by the Turks. When the general had not returned in a reasonable time an officer set off to look for him. He found him caught in some barbed wire set up to catch the Turks. Back at the barge the anxious naval officer in charge said that he could wait no longer. Then out of the darkness appeared the rescue officer with the general. A delayed-action bomb set off one of the main Helles magazines and a man on the barge was wounded. Maude has been praised for his nerve in going back for his bag. More realistically, it can be inferred from this episode that senior generalship was stupid to the last at Gallipoli.

And the common soldier was human to the end, as we can see through the thoughts and actions of Private Charles Watkins, the large-eyed, big-hearted little Lancashire man who had tried to keep the reckless Australian sergeant from committing suicide some months earlier. Watkins and his mates were supposed to leave their trenches for the beach at 11 p.m., but at 10.45 he realized that he was alone amid an 'ominous silence' and was possibly the last man on the peninsula, left to the mercy of the Turks. Watkins' own account of how he felt and what he did on finding himself alone in the dark is vivid and moving.

Not a bloody soul in sight. It was obvious my mates had anticipated zero-hour, and instead of waiting for one another, had hot-footed it for the beach individually. Not that I blamed them, I was often tempted to do so myself these last two hours and now real panic set in and I followed their example. It was an eerie experience. I guess the first man who lands on the moon will feel like I felt that night. The loneliest man in all the world. And the most frightened. As I tore panic-stricken along the lines of trenches leading towards the gully and thence to the beach, it was like as if I was on a dead world.

The tortuous, twisting and now empty trenches, normally difficult enough to negotiate even when occupied, were now more than ever harder to struggle through in my panic urge for speed, and every few yards obstacles of discarded kit hindered progress. The untidy and hurriedly discarded equipment cluttering up the trenches told its own tale. An urgent line of silent moving men pressing hurriedly along the trenches toward the beach – moving relentlessly like lemmings – stopping for nothing.

Stumblng over valises thrown away, piles of blankets left in all sorts of odd places, tripping over rifles left sprawled across the trench – to my fevered imagination it seemed to take me hours to negotiate even a few traverses. But the strangest, the most eerie and the most frightening element was the absence of all human life. The trenches – normally full of men and now deserted. I felt as if I were picking my way panic-stricken through the deserted catacombs of a dead and long-gone civilization. Eerie! My God! I've never been so scared. The drifting heavy clouds over the moon's face alternate the night into an ever changing pattern of light and dark – an unnerving night of sinister forebodings, where every little sound I made seemed like the clatter of Doom. Not even a rifle shot anywhere – to remind me that somewhere, even if only in the Turkish lines, there is still some human life left on this earth.

Seawards, too, the absence of all life. Not even the comforting view of the lighted hospital ship. I guess she's made her last trip here and is now on the way to Alex.

Round the next traverse of the trench I come across a

soldier fast asleep on the firing step, head lolling to one side. Thank God at last for company, another human being besides myself on this nightmare planet. But it's the wrong sort of sleep. I shake him gently and he rolls flat on the trench floor, still and grotesque. There'll be no comforting chat with this chap. There's a bullet wound in his temple. He must have been killed very, very recently to have been left like that, probably in the mass press forward to the beach – probably killed through some silly sod not having adjusted the safety catch on his rifle properly. They'd no time even to pretend to bury him – he'd been left where he was. Oddly enough, even his body was some slight comfort – proof, this momentary companionship that other beings beside myself had recently occupied this now dead and silent planet.

At last I leave the trenches and attain the open deep gulley. Run soldier, run – you might still make it – you might still catch the last boat leaving the shore. Panting, swearing, falling flat on my face in the mud, sometimes in my urgent haste I stumble along the gully and eventually reach the beach and join a few others stood on the edge of the shore and hollering seawards. From out of the void of the night is a faint reply and now – God be praised – we espy a little pontoon-type raft being towed towards us. The raft already contains about a dozen men and we wade out and scramble aboard with them and the naval pinnace tows us slowly to the ship out at sea. The sea's a bit choppy and the raft alongside the ship bobs up and down dangerously. In the fitful darkness I discern with difficulty a little hatchway in the side of the ship and one by one we wait until the heaving raft is level with the hatchway of the ship, then jump the intervening few feet separating us. It's a tricky job, and the naval bloke keeps bawling out hoarsely the need for extreme care. The chap who jumped before I did was real unlucky. His iron-studded army boots slipped on the wet raft as he jumped and he slipped into the water and as the raft bobbed up and down he got his skull crushed between the raft and the ship's side. My turn now – a panic-stricken long-jump. I land stunned but safe on the iron footplates in the bowels of the ship.

Watkins sat at the stern of the rescue ship with his platoon sergeant. After a long silence the sergeant chuckled, 'Old Abdul'll get the surprise of his life in the morning. Not a bloody British soldier there.' He was quiet for a time and then said in a near-whisper. 'Except for the bloody thousands we've left there. An' they won't be givin' Abdul much trouble, Ah'm thinking.'

Watkins writes towards the end of his memoirs:

I guess it was the reaction of the last few hours, but I found myself wracked with unmanly sobbing. I'm not sure why. I don't think it was so much the thought of all the chaps I'd known as kids and now left there – all the thousands of the other blokes who'd never breathe the air again. I don't know what it was – it could have been grief. But most, I think, was the dreadful feeling of the shame of it all – the British Army having to evacuate the Peninsula like this, and after all this gigantic wasted effort. Such things hurt a soldier more than you'd think – even an amateur soldier like myself.

The official historian, Aspinall, was covering up the 'shame of it all' when he wrote that, 'In the world at large the tactical success of the withdrawal went far to counter-balance its admission of strategic failure.' The phrase 'tactical success' is as misleading as it is intended to be; this was no tactical success, but a fullblown retreat. Further to gloss over the unpalatable truth, the official historian quotes a military correspondent in the German *Vossische Zeitung*. 'As long as wars last the evacuation of Suvla and Anzac will stand before the eyes of all strategists as a hitherto unattained masterpiece.'

It was easy for the victor to be magnanimous about the vanquished, but the proposition goes too far in giving the impression that throughout the ages generals had been trying to bring off unimpeded retreats. In fact, the glowing language makes an evacuation seem almost desirable. The truth is that a retreat, almost by definition, has no part in strategy. Another truth is that the so-called tactical success did not counter-balance the failure. Germany and her allies were exultant, the Allies' friends were dismayed and the world at large lost much of their faith in British political and military will.

It can be said of the evacuation that it was a remarkable illustration of clever staff work, inspired deception and enterprising improvisation. It came off also because of plenty of luck and/or – depending on one's degree of faith – the help of Divine Providence. When reflecting on its success it must be remembered that immense quantities of stores were left behind; von Sanders said that it took two years to collect the booty. This was proof that the 'tactical withdrawal' was a retreat.

By the end of the campaign 410,000 English, Welsh, Scottish, Irish, Australian, New Zealand, Sikh and Gurkha soldiers and Russian and Syrian Jews of the Zion Mule Corps, had served at Gallipoli and 70,000 French, Senegalese and other French colonial troops. The total British casualties were about 205,000, including 43,000 killed or dead of wounds or disease; 90,000 were evacuated sick. Within these overall figures are 26,094 Australian casualties, including 7,594 killed, and 7,571 New Zealand casualties, 2,431 killed. These were grievous losses for nations with small populations. The French suffered 47,000 casualties, including about 5,000 killed.

In the casualty figures the official historian, who went to some pains to find consolation prizes to balance the defeat, found something to be pleased about. 'It is right to remember,' he wrote, 'that at the expense of a casualty list which was less than double that incurred on the first day of the Somme, 1916, the Mediterranean Expeditionary Force in Gallipoli detroyed the flower of the Turkish Army, safeguarded the Suez Canal and laid the foundation of Turkey's final defeat.'

This is unadulterated sophistry. To find any satisfaction in these statistics being 'less than double' those on the first day of the Somme offensive is an intellectual perversion. The contention of the Dardanelles campaign so weakened the Turks, by destroying 'the flower of the Turkish Army', as to make then easier to defeat in Arabia is questionable. The British, Australian and New Zealand troops who fought the Turks in Palestine were convinced that they were up against troops of high standard.

Turkish records were loosely kept. Von Sanders said that casualties totalled about 216,000, with something like 66,000 dead. One Turkish account places their casualties at 251,000; the British Official History comments that 'other Turkish authorities place the total losses as high as 350,000'. I have been unable to find any Turkish authority who goes higher than 251,000. It would be logical to assume that fewer Turks were killed in action than Allied soldiers for three good reasons: For most of the campaign the Turks had fewer troops on the Peninsula; they always held the higher ground, so they were less vulnerable to machine-gun and rifle fire; and they did less attacking than the British. Nearly always the attackers lose more men than the defenders.

14

Midshipmen's Courage: Admirals' Fear

The much publicized gallantry of the midshipmen and their boats' crews on the day of the landings, 25 April, has ever since obscured the simple truth that the Royal Navy failed in its primary and secondary tasks at Gallipoli. The primary task was to break through into the Sea of Marmara; the secondary one was to support the troops on the peninsula with gunfire. An associated simple truth is that the great majority of ordinary soldiers did not know that the Navy had failed – but many senior naval officers, most notably Commodore Roger Keyes, certainly knew.

There were some naval successes, but the only important one was that of the submarines which passed through the Straits. Also, it is obviously true that the Army could not have stayed on the peninsula as long as it did without being supplied by the Navy. That the warships were asked to carry out tasks for which their guns were not suitable and their gunnery officers not trained is one explanation for why the Navy failed the Army – it does not cancel out the failure.

The part played by the Navy is best dealt with in a single chapter – rather than by chronological insertions in the story of the land operations – because focus then becomes sharper.

And such sharp focus is necessary from as early as 4 April, seventeen days after the defeat of 18 March and still three weeks before the landings.

On 4 April eight *Beagle* class destroyers became operational as mine-sweepers. Infinitely better than the trawlers, they had heavy sweep hawsers to break a way through the mines, while the trawlers could only laboriously drag mines aside, one by one, into shallow water. Sweeping in formation, these six destroyers could have swiftly – at 14 or 15 knots – opened a passage for the battleships following close behind. While nothing in war can be certain, it is highly likely that such an operation would have succeeded. It was never tried. Admiral de Robeck had considered himself beaten once, and forever after he was inhibited and overcautious. Nevertheless, in his orders for 25 April, de Robeck stated without qualification that after the Army had made its position secure 'the Navy will attack the forts at the Narrows, assisted by the Army'. To the concern of many naval officers, this promise was not kept.

On that fateful 25 April naval gunfire was thunderous in some places, but in others the guns were strangely silent. The soldiers who so much admired the Navy were not to know that during the Helles landings the Navy badly let them down. With the exception of HMS *Implacable* the ships gave poor covering fire, and in some cases none. Because of *Implacable*'s gunnery, the landing at X Beach was the most economical and successful of the dreadful day. Elsewhere the shambles was made worse by naval inactivity.

Captain Eric Bush, who served at Gallipoli as one of the gallant midshipmen, has noted with personal distress:*

It was the paucity of firepower during the actual touch down which resulted in the appalling casualties on the

* In his book *Gallipoli*, George Allen & Unwin, 1975.

beach. Not only did bombarding ships stand too far out, whence they could see nothing, but they lifted their fire much too soon, which enabled the defenders to stand up in their trenches and pour murderous volleys into the men in the boats while our naval shells fell harmlessly inland.

Another sailor, Lieutenant-Commander Andrew Cunningham,* in command of *Scorpion*, has been equally honest in more damning recollections:

We destroyers lay off the beaches [on 25 April] . . . though for some incomprehensible reason we had the strictest orders not to open fire in support of the Army. I have never discovered who was responsible for this stupid edict, for many opportunities were missed of directly helping the landings by destroyers – so close inshore that they could even see the Turks bobbing up and down in their trenches.

The *Scorpion* itself lay stopped for a considerable time off V Beach, 500 yards off a trench full of the enemy firing on our troops, and unable to do anything. We could see our infantry lying flat on their faces on the beach under withering fire, and every now and then one or two men dashing out to cut the wire . . . only to be quickly shot down.

It was a tragedy and a mortifying situation for a well-gunned destroyer; but a few days later . . . an order that should never have been given was rescinded.

The order not to fire was directly responsible for the death of many soldiers. It caused the dreadful silence of HMS *Albion*, which was stationed at V Beach, and her failure to

* Later Admiral of the Fleet Lord Cunningham of Hyndhope and First Sea Lord. He tells his Gallipoli story in *A Sailor's Odyssey*, 1951.

provide covering fire from its impressive weapons – four 12-inch, twelve 6-inch and some 12-pounder guns, as well as machine-guns. Yet the official historian of the campaign has written that, 'The situation at V Beach was only saved from complete disaster by the machine-guns mounted in the bows of the *River Clyde*.' A couple of machine-guns doing the work of a warship's guns!

I have been unable to trace the original order, and it is impossible to imagine any rational reason why it should have been given. A few veterans, still bitter after fifty or sixty years, have suggested to me that the Navy did not want the landing to succeed; if it did, their reasoning goes, the Army victory would make the naval failure of 18 March all the more shameful. It is hard to believe that, even in the climate of stupidity prevailing at the time, any naval commander would have sent soldiers to their deaths for such a reason. It is equally difficult to understand why a warship captain, seeing British soldiers in such a desperate position, would fail to open fire on the Turks regardless of any order to the contrary. As Admiral Cunningham has said, it was a stupid edict.

The tremendous missiles flung from the battleships occasionally wiped out a Turkish company and their roar frightened the Turks, but a broadside that would have sunk an enemy ship did little against the enemy positions. Naval guns have a relatively flat trajectory, and caused little damage to positions on hills and none at all to those behind crests or in valleys or ravines. Churchill and others had a sublime but ignorant faith in the power and destructiveness of naval bombardments. What was needed were lobbing cannon, from heavy howitzers to trench mortars – weapons which could fire a shell high so that it would drop smack into an enemy position. These weapons were nonexistent early in the campaign and were in short supply throughout. A principal cause of failure was the technical inefficiency of naval gunfire. The British ships could hit fairly small moving targets at six miles, while the Turks' trenches were within a mere half mile at Helles, and one and a half miles at Anzac. But the ships' guns could not blast the trenches because naval gunnery technique was based on direct laying at visible targets. Gallipoli's cliffs and hills hid the enemy trenches from the ships, and it was not possible to direct the guns onto a specific point. There was also the constant danger of hitting British troops. For some unexplained reason indirect fire techniques were not used, though on 3 May Commander Dewar of the *Prince of Wales* presented a report on methods of indirect firing. No action was taken and a writer in *The Naval Review*, October 1957, suggests that the proposals were not forwarded 'perhaps because they might be interpreted as questioning the infallibility of the admiral'.*

Captain Dent of HMS *Edgar* used indirect firing methods on 15 November with great effect in helping a British attack at Helles. He had officers ashore as spotters, and at night used illuminated aiming marks on land. With the same technique the *Edgar* fired 1,000 rounds of 6-inch shell into the Turkish trenches at Helles on 7 January to support the evacuation.

The thrusting, energetic Keyes, Chief-of-Staff to de Robeck, was prepared to risk the ships for the sake of great pains, and was the senior officer most distressed about the Navy's lack of aggression. During a conference on *Queen Elizabeth* on 9 May he vehemently urged a new naval assault to Admirals de Robeck, Wemyss and Thursby. It would be a renewal of the attack of 18 March but made more purposefully.

Keyes wrote, 'I can think of nothing more detestable than to watch our troops being destroyed by rifles and machine-

* The captains of the Turkish ships *Barbarossa* and *Tourgood* used indirect firing techniques against HMS *Queen Elizabeth* and *Agamemnon* on 6 March, firing over the peninsula's hills, and they hit supply ships at Anzac on 25 April.

guns which, in spite of our great armament, we were powerless to silence; and to hear desperate fighting going on in the ravines and gullies, hidden from view by the formation of the land.'

According to Churchill, Keyes and numerous other naval officers were 'grieved beyond measure at the cruel losses that the Army had sustained', and 'they felt it almost unendurable that the Navy should sit helpless and inactive after the orders they had received and the undertakings made on their behalf' – that is, by de Robeck.

The aggressive French Admiral Guépratte also favoured direct assault. His telegram to the French Minister of Marine showed that he expected to be launched in decisive attack, and he asked for an additional and stronger ship to reinforce the French squadron.

De Robeck feared that if such an attack failed and the fleet was seriously damaged the Army would be stranded. What the Army might have felt about this was impossible to say, as no Army officer was invited to the conference, though Hamilton and Braithwaite were close by on *Arcadian*.

Keyes induced de Robeck to present his plan to the Admiralty, but de Robeck spiked it by his back-pedalling phraseology. 'It is improbable that the passage of the Fleet into the Marmara will be decisive . . . it is equally probable that the Straits will be closed after the Fleet [enters] . . . the forcing of the Dardanelles and the appearance of the Fleet off Constantinople would not of itself be decisive.'

The admiral was playing safe, leaving the decision to London and in particular to Churchill. The naval officers still believed that Churchill was important, but his power was running out fast, and the Conservative Opposition had him marked for removal. Despite the caution of the de Robeck telegram, Churchill asked for an attack on the Narrows forts – at least an operation large enough to clear the Kephez minefield. Fisher was dead against the idea, and he was increasingly exasperated with Churchill himself. He felt that the impetuous, patronizing and imperious Churchill was interfering in concerns which were properly those of the First Sea Lord and he was right. On 11 May he wrote Churchill a long letter, which ended:

> . . . Although I have acquiesced in each stage of the operations up to the present [because he had been assured of great political success for Britian if the Gallipoli venture succeeded] . . . I have clearly expressed my opinion that I did not consider the original attempt to force the Dardanelles with the fleet alone was a practicable operation. I cannot, under any circumstances, be a party to any order to Admiral de Robeck to make any attempt to pass the Dardanelles until the shores have been effectively occupied. . . .

Fisher must have felt himself justified in this view when, on the night of 11–12 May, a Turkish torpedo-boat under a German captain, Lieutenant-Commander Rudolph Firle, sank the battleship HMS *Goliath* in Morto Bay, with the loss of 618 officers and men. In fact, the sinking proved only that the naval screening of the big ships was poor.

The very next day *Queen Elizabeth*, considered too valuable to be risked, was withdrawn from the Dardanelles, a decision that angered Kitchener so much that he virtually accused the Navy of a stab in the back. This, in turn, further irritated Fisher, who had arranged for *Queen Elizabeth* to be replaced by old cruisers whose hulls were fitted with a protruberant anti-torpedo blister – it was called a bulge blister – and by monitors firing 14-inch shells. The monitors, squat and low-floating gun platforms, should have been on the spot from the beginning.

Forced by Fisher's hostile attitude to be cautious, Churchill replied to de Robeck's presentation of Keyes' idea on 13 May, 'We think that the moment for an independent naval attempt to force the Narrows has passed and will not arise again under present circumstances.'

If de Robeck – and Keyes – were still in doubt about the Navy's role, a forthright Admiralty telegram put them right: 'The role of the Fleet will be to support the Army in its costly [a dig at Kitchener?] but sure advance and to reserve your strength to deal with the situation which will arise when the Army has succeeded with your aid in this task.'

Churchill and Fisher, in a face-to-face meeting one evening, reached precise agreement on what naval forces would be sent to the Dardanelles. Fisher's anger when he arrived at the Admiralty next morning to discover that Churchill had already radically changed the naval dispositions on his own account can be imagined – and appreciated. Churchill was wrong in every sense – in morality, in tact, in Admiralty procedure, in strategy. It was an example of the very bad manners for which Churchill was becoming increasingly notorious, and it had a dramatic effect – Fisher's resignation on 15 May. The first sentence of his note to Churchill read – 'After much anxious reflection I have come to the regretted conclusion that I am unable to remain any longer as your colleague.'

Churchill did not at first take this letter seriously – a fact which says much for his armour-plated self-esteem. Asquith rejected the resignation and ordered Fisher, 'in the King's name', to stay at his post.

But Fisher was too old to be ordered about in language which might have cowed a young lieutenant, and matters came swiftly to a head. Not only the Dardanelles crisis but the 'shells scandal' and the bloody setback on Aubers Ridge in France made it impossible for the Conservatives to continue to support the Liberals without a new 'arrangement'. Under Bonar Law's insistence, Asquith agreed that the Government needed major rebuilding. The first step was taken on the evening of 17 May, with the request, to Churchill and others, for their resignation. Desperate, Churchill tried to reverse the inevitable by making Fisher an extraordinary offer – one which he had no power or authority to make: the offer of a seat in the Cabinet if he withdrew his resignation.

Such was Churchill's force of personality that despite his dismissal he was given a positon on the 'Dardanelles Committee' – the new name for the War Council. But it was a junior position; Sir Arthur Balfour was now First Lord, and Sir Henry Jackson was First Sea Lord. These two were able enough – and more significantly, they were 'safe'; nobody needed to fear anything dramatic from them, least of all the Turks.

Hamilton, thought that in parting with Churchill Asquith had 'chucked away his mainspring'. But this particular mainspring was overwound, and its removal was justified. In any case, Hamilton was being subjective, since he felt that Churchill, a personal friend, was the only person at the Admiralty on which he could depend. At one of the many times when Hamilton was worrying about his shortage of ammunition, he wrote:

Officialdom at the Admiralty is none too keen on our show. If we can get at Winston himself then we can rely on his kicking red tape into the waste paper basket; otherwise we won't be met halfway. As for me, I am helpless. I cannot write to Winston – not on military business; least of all on Naval business. . . . [because of the prevailing Service etiquette]

While the British were making up their minds not to mount a further naval attack on the Narrows, the Germans and Turks were contemplating attacks of their own. The spectacular but futile bombardments by the Royal Navy in February had alarmed the Turkish leaders as well as the German Ambassador, Baron von Wangenheim. The Baron and his German military advisers saw even more clearly than the Turks that the Narrows were vulnerable to a determined naval attack. A series of messages from Constantinople to Berlin urged the German High Command to send U-boats. Von Wangenheim's personal telegram warned that if the British and French forced the Dardanelles the effect on the neutral nations would give the whole war 'a turn unfavourable to Germany'. It is ironic that this assessment agreed with Churchill's understanding of the importance of the Dardanelles. Berlin's response was prompt – a large submarine, U-21, (Commander Hersing) was sailing from Wilhelmshaven, while five small U-boats were being sent in sections by rail for assembly in the Austrian dockyard of Pola (later Pula, Yugoslavia).

Hersing was quickly into action. On 25 May he torpedoed the battleship HMS *Triumph* off Anzac with the loss of three officers and seventy-two men. The sinking was a major blow to morale, for it was witnessed by every man in the Anzac sector.* In the previous month the Navy, merely by its presence, had given the troops their greatest sense of security. The troops did not talk about withdrawal, but they knew that, if the situation became critical, the Navy was there to save them by evacuation, just as it was always on hand with ammunition, food and water. To see *Triumph* going down was acutely distressing. In near panic, de Robeck recalled all his large warships to the safety of the harbour on Imbros Island. Even the dummy warships – old transports tricked out to make them look superficially like battleships – were withdrawn. This hasty retreat left the troops feeling abandoned. 'The Royal Navy has never executed a more demoralising manoeuvre in the whole of its history,' wrote Compton Mackenzie, who was on Hamilton's staff.

The Admiral, quickly made aware of the results of the

---

* Within hours it was known that the Australian and New Zealand soldiers were each offering a month's pay towards the cost of salving the ship.

fleet's running away, sent HMS *Majestic* to anchor off W Beach. But the smaller boats and torpedo nets which surrounded *Majestic* were useless, and Hersing torpedoed her on 27 May. And again he had a vast audience, every man silent and sick at heart. Worse still, *Majestic* remained upside down in full veiw of the shore until the coming of the November storms. This impotent, undignified wreck seriously disturbed the troops, and they were glad when she finally slipped out of sight.

On 30 May Hersing sank a dummy British cruiser and was seen and chased by the intrepid aviator, Commander C.R. Samson of the Royal Naval Air Service. Under British counter-submarine measures the U-boat menace declined. But not its effect. The British battleships mostly stayed in harbour, to be replaced by cruisers and destroyers – and no naval captain ever slept easily again. The soldiers never recovered from the shock of having the battleships removed from their sight. Their bombardments were more full of sound and fury than destruction, but their very rumble had been comforting. Conversely, the Turks' morale went up. The armada anchored off Helles, with scores of launches, pinnaces and tugs scurrying about the battleships had been an unnerving sight, a token of Britannic might. And now the big ships had gone.

The U-boat menace disrupted British High Command. Aboard *Arcadian*, anchored off W Beach, Hamilton had been in direct cable communication with his main subordinate commanders. But the Navy could not guarantee his safety with U-boats in the vicinity and de Robeck had insisted on moving *Arcadian* to Imbros, eighteen miles from Anzac and fifteen from Helles. On 31 May, GHQ went ashore on Imbros and remained there.

'What a change since the War Office sent us packing with a bagful of hallucinations,' Hamilton wrote wrily on Imbros. 'Naval guns sweeping the Turks off the peninsula; the Ottoman Army legging it from a British submarine waving the Union Jack; Russian help in hand; Greek help. . . . Now it is our Fleet which has to leg it from the German submarines. There is no ammunition for the guns; no drafts to keep my divisions up to strength; my Russians have gone to Galicia and the Greeks are lying lower than ever.'

If the U-boats had caused some distress among British naval commanders, the feats of the British submarines in the Sea of Marmara and at Constantinople caused fear and, on occasions, panic among the Turks. The achievements of the Royal Navy submarine captains in their incredibly dangerous expeditions have not been valued highly enough, except contemporaneously by Keyes and Churchill. These craft, then small and underpowered and with only brief underwater staying power, caused much destruction, forced the Turkish command to stop for a time sending troops to the peninsula by water, and caused immense damage to Turkish morale.

In December 1914, Lieutenant Norman Holbrook in *B-11* had torpedoed the Turkish cruiser *Messudieh* in the Dardanelles and the success of the Australian *AE-2* – the first submarine to get into the Sea of Marmara – (Lieutenant-Commander H.G. Stoker) has already been referred to. Lieutenant-Commander E.G. (Courtney) Boyle in *E-14* spent the period 27 Apri to 18 May in the Marmara, and did much to dislocate the build-up of Turkish reinforcements and supplies; one of his victims was a troopship carrying 6,000 soldiers, many of whom drowned.

On the very day that HMS *Triumph* was sunk off Anzac, Lieutenant-Commander M.E. Nasmith in E-11 torpedoed the storeship *Stambul* lying alongside the arsenal in Constantinople. This remarkable exploit caused panic in the city, for the Turks had believed that their farflung battlefronts and forts would always keep their ancient city safe. The loss of the *Stambul* was of no consequence, but even the Germans in Constantinople were alarmed by the damage to Turkish morale.

On 10 June, Lieutenant-Commander Courtney Boyle took *E-14* into the Marmara and kept the Turks on edge for twenty-three days. He was followed by Lieutenant-Commander A.D. Cochrane in *E-7*, who bombarded trains, a railway viaduct, the Constantinople Naval Arsenal and the Zeitun powder mills. The psychological impact on the Turks was tremendous, and gives further indication of what might have happened had a battleship rather than a weak submarine reached Constantinople.

Almost as if in retaliation, Commander Hersing brought *U-21* from Constantinople and torpedoed the supply ship *Carthage* off V Beach. She had been lent to the French and had almost completed unloading a cargo of ammunition when she went down. But U-boat successes were becoming more rare. Nets kept them out of large areas of sea and the big ships were only exposed when needed for some major co-operation with the Army, while the harder-to-hit destroyers kept up the day-to-day contact. The monitors with their 14-inch guns, some smaller monitors and four bulge cruisers were all on station by the end of July.

Meanwhile the British submarines continued their audacious rampage in the Marmara. One of the most significant sinkings was that of the Turkish battleship *Barbarosse Hayreddin*, sent specially across Marmara to raise the morale of the Turkish troops, then under great pressure from a British offensive. Near Bulair, on 8 August, the great ship was torpedoed by Nasmith in *E-11*; she went down with 253 of her crew and ammunition she was taking to the Turkish Fifth Army.

In all twelve British submarines made entry into Marmara, or attempted entry, and six were lost. Their collective bag was impressive: one battleship, one destroyer, five gunboats, eleven transports, forty-four steamers and 148 other vessels. In three spells totalling ninety-six days, Nasmith in *E-11* sank 101 of these Turkish ships.

The official German assessment of British submarine

warfare in the Marmara is significant: 'The activity of hostile submarines was a constant and heavy anxiety. They dislocated very seriously the conveyance of reinforcements to the Dardanelles and caused many disagreeable losses. If communications by sea had been completely severed, the Turkish Army would have been faced with catastrophe.'

Unfortunately, the undersea part of the naval effort was seen by the senior British leaders, both in London and at the Dardanelles, as a sideshow, undoubtedly heroic, but relatively inconsequential in winning the campaign. Hamilton wrote, 'The exploits of the submarines give a flat knock-out to [the] contention that excitement and romance have gone out of war.' Apparently he was more interested in this aspect of undersea war than with the submarines' war-winning potential.

Later, Churchill stressed the value of the submarine effort. 'Naval history of Britain contains no page more wonderful than that which describes the prowess of her submarines at the Dardanelles. Their exploits constitute the finest example of submarine warfare in the whole of the Great War.'

Unable to get near the British warships, the U-boats went for transports in the Mediterranean. Lieutenant von Heimburg, commanding *U-14*, forayed from his secret base in the Dodecanese Islands on 13 August to sink the transport *Royal Edward*, en route to Mudros with thirty-one officers and 1,335 men; less than 500 survived. On 2 September von Heimburg sank the troopship *Southland*, but most of the 1,400 Australians on board were saved.

While applauding the British submariners' efforts, which he wanted to intensify, Roger Keyes understood that they were no substitute for conventional naval assault. He was badly affected by what he saw at Suvla. After being a witness to the bloody shambles on Scimitar Hill, he was again angry. 'It is awful; I can't bear it when I think and believe that we could stop it all, and end the business in a few weeks. I had it out again with the Admiral on Friday and again on Saturday.'

The leading member of the 'Forward' school, during the summer Keyes made detailed plans for a naval operation and wanted desperately to be given a chance to put them into effect. He had the support of Wemyss, the Second in Command, but not that of de Robeck, who mattered most. Nevertheless, the Admiral, out of his liking for his dashing Chief-of-Staff, gave him leave to report to the Admiralty with his plan. His audacious concept, in keeping with Keyes' own personality, is worth looking at in detail to show that Keyes was no mere glory-seeking hothead, the impression that is sometimes given of him. The fleet would be divided into four squadrons, three to take part in the attack, the fourth to support the Army. The Second Squadron comprised about eight old battleships and cruisers, four very old battleships acting as supply ships, as many dummy battleships as possible and several merchantmen carrying coal and ammunition. All these vessels were to be fitted with 'mine-bumpers'. Preceded by four of the superior destroyer-sweepers, and accompanied by eight destroyers and two sloops, this Second Squadron, led by Keyes himself, was to enter the Straits just before dawn, keeping below the searchlight area until dawn. Then it would steam through the Narrows at full speed. Keyes believed that aided by smoke screens, darkness and surprise he would break through with more than half the squadron to above Nagara. The ships would then attack the Narrows forts from the rear.

Meanwhile, at dawn the First Squadron would simultaneously attack the Narrows forts from below the Kephez minefield. This squadron was awesomely powerful – *Lord Nelson*, *Agamemnon*, *Exmouth*, *King Edward*, *Glory*, *Canopus*, four French ships, eight sloops and ten destroyers for sweeping. The Third Squadron, consisting of two monitors, the *Swiftsure* and five cruisers, was to cover the Army and co-operate from across the peninsula in the attack upon the forts at the Narrows. Fourth Squadron was entirely committed to Army support.

The bombardment of the Narrows forts and the sweeping of the minefields – already breached by the Second Squadron – would go on continuously. There must be no break. Keyes' plan allowed for the operation to continue for up to three days if necessary before the First Squadron made its final advance through the Narrows. His thorough plan also included detailed arrangements to supply the ships in the Marmara while they were preventing supplies from reaching the peninsula.

The Army's role was to mount a major sustained attack to occupy the Turkish mobile artillery and prevent the guns from firing on the ships.

Inevitably, the Keyes plan still called for ships to attack forts in defence of the old naval axiom, but recognized the logic of the axiom and made due allowance for it. Thus the plan had every chance of success.

Kitchener liked the Keyes plan and so, for a time, did First Lord Balfour, who came under Churchill's guns on 6 October, three weeks before Keyes reached London. Trying to kindle a fire under his successor, Churchill wrote, 'You should not overlook the fact that Admiral de Robeck is deeply committed against this [an attack on the Narrows] by what has taken place, and his resolution and courage, which in other matters are beyond dispute, are in this case prejudiced by the line he has taken since the beginning.'

Keyes, wholly agreeing with Churchill, many times tried to inject some of his own vigour and ideas into the older de Robeck – perhaps he tried too hard and set up resistence. The Admiral's 'fear of having to do *anything* in the Straits ever since 18 March would be rather pathetic,' Keyes wrote, 'if it was not so distressing and had it not had such a ghastly effect on our whole policy and been mainly responsible for the miserable fiasco here. . . .'

The fear which Keyes discerned in de Robeck had infected the Sea Lords. They demurred at his plan, and demanded not only guarantees of military support but also a particular strength of Army backing. The Government had by now promised the French to support new operations at Salonika; this meant that all available reinforcements were needed for the campaign in the Balkans. Since the Army could not satisfy the Navy's requirements, the plan was rejected; Kitchener, informed of this by Balfour, noted with an acid sneer that the Navy was 'afraid to wet its feet'.

On 18 November, Keyes met Lord Kitchener in Salonika, after Kitchener's visit to Gallipoli. Kitchener said, 'Well, I have seen the place. It is an awful place and you will never get through.'

Keyes replied emphatically: 'The fleet *could* force the Straits and would do so if given the opportunity.'

Kitchener refused to discuss the matter further, but still Keyes persisted. The next day, on Imbros, he spoke to Birdwood, who had come there to interview Kitchener, but his attempt to persuade Kitchener through Birdwood to use the Army so that the Admiralty would use the Navy came to nothing.

In rapid and forthright succession Keyes saw General Davies, commanding at Helles, Birdwood again, and then Monro. He made little progress and wrote, 'Kitchener wanted the Admiralty to take the initiative in proposing the combined attack and the Admiralty insisted on the army asking for it, but what was really wanted was a MAN to decide.'

Finally, Admiral de Robeck did go on leave, leaving in command Admiral Wemyss, who had already told Keyes that he favoured an attack. Wemyss went further – he put pressure on the Admiralty for an attack on the lines suggested by Keyes. But in London, during that bleak December, de Robeck torpedoed the plan; he told the War Committee that there was 'no definite object to gain by it'. This ill-informed point of view truly shows de Robeck's lack of vision.

Wemyss and Keyes fought on. On 8 December Wemyss

reported to the Admiralty – in possibly the first fighting message from the Navy during the campaign – that the Navy would attack, penetrate and hold. And it asked nothing more of the Army than a synchronized land attack. Wemyss followed up this confident message with a personal persuasive telegram to First Lord Balfour. But now the Navy was not getting the support it needed from Birdwood, who rejected Wemyss' appeal to oppose evacuation. Monro, worried about the influence of Wemyss and Keyes, ordered Birdwood and the corps commanders not to discuss military matters with the Admiral, and even complained to Kitchener about Wemyss' persistent harrying of the generals to get them to back his scheme for a combined attack.

The Navy had left its run too late to avert what Keyes was to call 'one of the most disastrous and cowardly surrenders in the naval, military and political history of our country'. Even an historian accustomed to digging for the many sides to any question finds it difficult to disagree with Keyes, who, as the spirit of the great Zeebrugge raid, showed what thrusting courage could achieve. John North saw the opportunity: 'At any time during this long summer the sufferings of the troops on the Peninsula could have been cut short by a determined rush by the fleet for the Narrows and Bulair.'

The Navy was always ready to provide Hamilton and others with rapid transport to wherever they might want to go, but real combined operations were never undertaken. The problem of 'form' was often a handicap, and nothing better illustrates this than the difficulties over the Royal Naval Air Service. Hamilton found the constant feud between Admiralty and War Office over the RNAS 'simply heart-breaking'. In line with the etiquette of the day Hamilton, being a soldier, could not put his own case to the Admiralty about the aeroplanes. The best he could do was to hope for some co-operation from de Robeck.

Early in the campaign Commander Samson, the courageous

and enterprising leader of the RNAS No. 3 Wing, established a rough landing ground at Helles, but the risk of having his aircraft destroyed by enemy shells forced him to the island of Tenedos. The British troops had great respect for Samson and his pilots – and the Turks destroyed them. In their frail planes, the fliers made the Gallipoli skies their own, shooting up lines of troops on the march and bombing their camps. In most cases the destruction they caused was negligible – Samson had to fight to get a ration of one hundred 100-lb bombs a month – but on one occasion (2 May) Samson claimed that two bombs were dropped on a divisional camp, 'blotting out' eighteen tents and killing perhpas one hundred Turks. The effect on Turkish morale of the RNAS air raids was considerable.

The main job of the RNAS planes was observation and photography. Even allowing for the poor techniques which existed at the time, neither the Army nor Navy leaders made nearly enough use of Samson's planes. The pilots' reports were often not passed on, though the information was sometimes vital. The trouble was that many of these reports should have gone direct to the Army, but they were pigeonholed or ignored by naval officers who had no understanding of Army needs. 'Lieutenant Butler has taken wonderful photographs of the German positions which have proved to be a great value to the Army,' Samson reported on 2 May. They might well have been valuable, but there is no record to suggest that any Army HQ received or made use of these and other photographs. Surprisingly, the two-volume official history of the Gallipoli campaign gives neither the RNAS nor Commander Samson a mention.

The Navy was at its best, in the eyes of some ordinary soldiers, when it was providing them with arms and equipment they could not get through normal channels. For instance, the sailors of HMS *Cornwallis* were highly regarded because they made on board a hand-grenade containing

242

twenty-seven shrapnel balls – the Cornwallis patent. Since grenades were always scarce the *Cornwallis* bombs were prized, especially as they exploded on impact, thus obviating the risk of their being caught and thrown back. Half a dozen artificers could make fifty grenades a day, a pathetic quantity that could be used up in the first moments of repelling an attack, but they were much appreciated.

For other soldiers the Navy symbolized support and provided excitement. 'The strafes by the Navy were always interesting to the boys,' wrote Captain Walter Belford of the Australian 11th Battalion, 'and they were inspiring sights even if the material damage was often negligible. The troops had an excellent view, perched as they were on the bare hills. . . . It was a thrilling sight to see those great ships, often mirrored on the calm waters of the blue Aegean, rocking to the turmoil of the mighty guns, as the shells went tearing overhead . . . and then the vessels would be temporarily obscured by the billowing smoke from the discharge of their guns.'

Despite the rapport between the ordinary Tommy and Jack Tar, the final verdict must be that the Royal Navy was not allowed to do its job at the Dardanelles. Gallant though its officers and men were, its leadership was paralysed by hesitancy and indecision, and inhibited by Admiralty disputes and confusion in London. At Gallipoli the Navy displayed a lack of spirit – again apart from the boats' crews – completely out of character with Royal Navy tradition and attitude.

'The Admiralty were prepared for losses,' Keyes wrote, 'but we chucked our hand in and started squealing before we had any. . . . The responsibility for the ultimate failure of the fleet to force a passage through the Dardanelles lies on the shoulders of those who would not allow us to accomplish our task, after the cause of the check had been discovered, and efficient minesweepers had been provided.'

What might have been accomplished, had the Navy acted early enough and with the determination it showed in many other actions, is best described by US Ambassador Morgenthau, who must be regarded as one of the most reliable eye-witnesses of the Turkish scene. A keen observer, and in close contact with officers of the Turkish High Command, Morgenthau probably had a better understanding of Turkish attitudes and reactions than any other foreigner in Constantinople. He wrote:

> In giving his assent to a purely naval expedition Lord Kitchener had relied on a revolution in Turkey to make the enterprise successful. Lord Kitchener has been much criticised for his action but I owe it to his memory to say he was absolutely right. Had the Allied fleet once passed the defences of the Straits the administration of the Young Turks would have come to a bloody end. . . . As for Constantinople, the populace there would have wlecomed the arrival of the Allied fleet with joy, for this would relieve them of the controlling gang, emancipate them from the hated Germans, bring about peace and end their miseries.

Such a naval coup would also have ended the miseries of the British and Dominion soldiers on the peninsula.

Much later Roger Keyes wrote with emphatic deliberation: 'Nothing will ever shake my opinion that from the fourth of April, onwards, the fleet could have forced the straits, and, with losses trifling in comparison with those the army suffered, could have entered the Marmara with sufficient force to destroy the Turco-German fleet.'

15

The Guilty Men

General condemnations of the conduct of the Gallipoli campaign abound in the writing of ordinary soldiers, scholars, military historians, naval historians, journalists, politicians, novelists and senior Service officers.
To take an example of each:

The common soldier: Private Joseph Murray, Hood Battalion, Royal Naval Division: in his diary, 8 January, 1916: 'Perhaps as the years roll by we will be remembered as the expedition that was betrayed by jealousy, spite, indecision and treachery. The Turks did not beat us – we were beaten by our own High Command.'

The scholar: Sir Llewellyn Woodward, in his *Great Britain and the War of 1914–1918*: 'No single act of military incompetence [Gallipoli] had such far-reaching effects on the history of the war.'

The military historian: R. Ernest Dupuy and Trevor N. Dupuy, in *The Encyclopaedia of Military History*, 1970: 'With possible exception of the Crimean War, the Gallipoli expedition was the most poorly mounted and ineptly controlled operation in modern British military history.'

The journalist: Ellis Ashmead-Bartlett, in *The Uncensored Dardanelles*, 1920: 'No first-hand Power except Great Britain would have rushed bald-headed at the Dardanelles and

Gallipoli without months of reflection and silent preparation by a highly trained general staff, composed of the best brains of the army.' And: 'Never have I known such a collection of unsuitable people to whom to entrust a great campaign, the lives of their countrymen, and the safety of the Empire. Their muddles, mismanagement, and ignorance of the strategy and tactics of modern war have brought about the greatest disaster in English history.'

The politician: Sir Edward Grey, British Foreign Secretary at the time, writing in his memoirs, 1925: 'Nothing so distorted perspective, disturbed impartial judgement and impaired the sense of strategic values as the operations on Gallipoli.'

The novelist: Compton Mackenzie, in *Gallipoli Memories*, 1929: 'All our leaders suffer from an exaggerated sensitiveness over the feelings of other leaders.'

The senior officer: Major-General J.F.C. Fuller, an alert, enterprising and innovative general (he was also a military historian), in his *Decisive Battles of the Western World*, vol. III, 1957: 'There was no judgement; no clear strategical analysis of the initial problem; no proper appreciation of the tactical requirements; and no true attempt to balance the means in hand with the end in view.'

The naval historian: Stanley Bonnet, *The Price of Admiralty – An indictment of the Royal Navy*, 1968: '. . . the disaster of the Dardanelles, an example almost without equal of intrigue and indecision, illogical tactics and inadequate logistics.'

It is time for History to be more specific in appropriating the guilt – for guilt is more appropriate than blame or responsibility – and more precise about the errors and inadequacies of the principal figures involved. They appear in this 'charge sheet' in alphabetical order, since any order of guilt would be difficult to assess. The positions and ranks given are those which applied in 1915.

Lieutenant-General Sir William Birdwood, commanding at

Anzac. Aged fifty at the time of Gallipoli, Birdwood is the least guilty of all the generals who served at Gallipoli, with the exception of Major-General Walker. But some charges must be laid against him. Though an uncle-figure to his men he was lax about their health. Not until the end of July, with sickness reducing his force at the rate of ten per cent a week, did he realize that dysentery was the cause. Australian doctors offered many suggestions about improving the diet of his troops – oranges being brought from Egypt, cornflour from the south of France – but Birdwood was unco-operative.

He did not exercise enough personal control over the battles of 6 to 10 August; indeed, he failed to make himself aware of the serious problems. He confessed later that the objective he set Major-General Godley – the capture of Hill 971 – 'was a most difficult task – more difficult than I myself realised.' Most culpably, he was responsible for the bloody debacle at Hill 60, again in failing to study the problem adequately.

Birdwood has been called vain, boastful and overambitious, but there is nothing to show that these traits affected his performance or judgement at Anzac.

Major-General W.P. Braithwaite, Hamilton's Chief-of-Staff: For one grave error Braithwaite must take the blame – the separation of the General Staff and the Lines-of-Communication (or Administration) Staff. He had the notion that the administrators – who managed supply, shipping, water, hospital services and so on – were not really soldiers but businessmen. (And indeed they were; by 1914 war was far too complex a business to leave in the hands of the fighting generals.) Yet the administrative staff was left out of discussions 'to an incredible degree', C.E.W. Bean observes. When GHQ transferred from the *Arcadian* to the *Queen Elizabeth*, the chiefs of administration were left behind and were even deprived of the right to use the 'wireless telegraph'. It was up to Braithwaite to 'marry' GHQ and Lines-of-Communication HQ – and he failed.

Later the Lines-of-Communication staff was stationed in Mudros Harbour aboard RMS *Aragon*, formerly a cruise liner. An extraordinary extravagance, *Aragon* even had a permanent saluting guard for the benefit of visiting VIPs. For the lack of understanding shown by the staff aboard *Aragon* for the problems of the men ashore, Braithwaite must bear a large part of the blame.

A major part of Braithwaite's job was to shield his chief from interruptions and irritations which might prevent him from devoting all his attention to important matters, but he was excessively protective. When worrying reports came in he would often tone them down before showing them to Hamilton. A tactless man, he antagonized many senior officers, including Birdwood, and *he* was fairly easy-going. Wherever Braithwaite went he left a trail of resentment, though Hamilton seemed unaware of this.

He must be held responsible for inducing Hamilton not 'to interfere' in the progress of battles master-minded by other Generals when it was manifestly right for Hamilton to interfere. This was especially so on 25 April, when, by taking a hand in Hunter-Weston's landings at Helles, Hamilton could have materially influenced the result of the operation.

Maxwell, the GHQ chief censor, told Ashmead-Bartlett on 1 July that Braithwaite was determined never to allow anyone to have access to Hamilton except himself, that he tried his best to turn him, and to control the campaign'. Maxwell also complained of constant intrigues at GHQ.

Winston Spencer Churchill, First Lord of the Admiralty. Churchill, aged forty-one, was a victim of his own imagination and a puppet of his self-confidence. He had a brilliant scheme, possibly the only original idea of the war – the capture of Constantinople. And it was a feasible idea. Because it was so appealing and desirable Churchill leapt to the conclusion that successful accomplishment must follow. He did not carefully consider what forces were necessary to gain victory – and he did not weigh the consequences of failure. Many of his critics have criticized his 'strategy'. He *had* no strategy about the Dardanelles operation and his knowledge of tactics was virtually non-existent. What he did have was policy. And the policy was sound.

But his guilt is clear. He was guilty of exceeding his authority, and of alerting the Turks to the probability of attack when he ordered Admiral Carden's fleet to attack the Dardanelles outer forts on 3 November, supposedly to test the range of the forts' guns. This piece of pointless bravado was a strategical and tactical mistake of the first order, because it put the Germans and Turks on their guard. A little later Churchill was guilty of gross dishonesty when he misled Carden into thinking that the Government had decided on a major attack on the Straits.* One of Churchill's naval critics, Admiral Wemyss, has said that Churchill's name would be handed down to posterity as that 'of a man who undertook an operation of whose requirements he was entirely ignorant'. I would not dispute this view.

He exceeded his authority again and was guilty of deceit on 14 May, when he changed naval orders given by the First Sea Lord, Fisher.

On several occasions Churchill failed to inform himself as thoroughly as one would expect of a man in his high office. Ashmead-Bartlett, who dined with him on 10 June, 1915, said: 'He seems to have an imperfect knowledge of the facts

---

* Fisher was emphatic in his testimony to the Dardanelles Commission that the moving spirit behind the naval attack was Kitchener and not Churchill. According to Fisher, when Kitchener could not find the means to fulfil his promise to help the Russians he told Churchill, 'Look here, we must do something for the Grand Duke; you do something at the Dardanelles, I have no army, I have no troops.' (Dardanelles Commission Report; p. 191; CAB 19/33, London PRO.)

and not to realise that the fleet never even approached the principal minefields [in the defeat of 18 March after preliminary attacks on 19 and 25 February and 6 March] or that the Turkish forts, which were saving their limited ammunition, were never silenced.'

On 5 June he was guilty of a foolish breach of security when he made a speech at Dundee which alerted von Sanders to the probability of a renewed Allied attack. On numerous occasions before his displacement from the post as First Lord he used his persuasive eloquence to win people to his way of thinking, despite their better judgement.

Churchill was also guilty of character assassination, particularly in the savage way, with his usual facility with words, with which he dealt with Monro – 'He came, he saw, he capitulated.' He implied that Monro was a blimpish general with a sealed mind and no imagination. Churchill saw Monro's recommendation of withdrawal as a condemnation of the Gallipoli–Dardanelles project; he attacked Monro as a way of making his own case seem sound.

He was a great danger to his own side because he wanted to dictate strategy and take part in the war himself; since this was not possible he sought vicarious battle experience by playing bloody war games.

Admiral of the Fleet Lord Fisher, First Sea Lord. In that Fisher, aged seventy-three in 1915, was Churchill's victim, it is unfair to be hard on him. Fisher's main guilt lies in not speaking his mind on the so-called Carden plan at the War Council meeting on 13 January, 1915. At this meeting several members were obviously ill-informed about what a fleet could and could not achieve, and it was Fisher's job to explain matters. He knew, if nobody else did, that a naval expedition could not 'take' the peninsula – as was proposed. Fisher said later that as an expert he was present at the War Council to open his mouth only when told to do so – though the politicians inferred from a naval or military expert's silence that he was acquiescing in whatever had been put forward.

Fisher's silence at War Council meetings on 13 and 28 January – and that of Admiral Wilson – was the product, says a writer in *The Naval Review*, October 1957, 'of a pseudo-disciplinary naval training and environment which did not differentiate between obedience to orders, which is right, and thinking as ordered, which is wrong'.

Hypnotized by Churchill's eloquence, Fisher reacted by becoming irritable or angry. Had he been stronger and more incisive he would have been more effective. On 28 January he almost resigned, but was persuaded by Kitchener and then by Churchill to give his reluctant consent to the naval attack. It was extremely difficult for him, he explained later, 'to forbid . . . an experiment on which rested so many sanguine hopes'. Perhaps the truth is that he was too old a man to stand up against the twin steam-rollers of Kitchener and Churchill.

Major-General Sir Alexander Godley, commanding the New Zealand and Australian Divisions at Anzac. Godley was not popular with the New Zealanders, who for most of the campaign formed the major part of his command, because he regarded them as expendable war material. He had the same attitude to tactics as Hunter-Weston – 'hammer away'.

He was guilty of gross dereliction of duty in not attending the vital staff meeting during the August battles. Had he done so, and followed up by taking direct command – which as a divisional general it was his job to do – the battle for Chunuk Bair and Hill 971 could have turned out differently.

General Sir Ian Hamilton, commanding the Mediterranean Expeditionary Force. As Kitchener's victim Hamilton deserves deep sympathy, but this cannot protect him from charges of guilt in the conduct of the Gallipoli campaign or from a high degree of responsibility for its failure.

Compton Mackenzie has said that in April 1915 Hamilton

'did look like a leader, sound like a leader and act like a leader'. But the more experienced C.E.W. Bean noted that 'a certain artistic sensitiveness . . . appeared to rob him of the power of driving, or at least of over-riding at the proper moment, less active-minded subordinates with whom he was on terms of friendly intimacy.' And, John North suggests, Hamilton's great failure was his inability to get done those things which he saw must be done.

His operations were doomed from the start. They were too ambitious considering his slender resources, and they showed an ignorance of strategy, of the topographical features of the combat area, of the psychology of his opponents. And they revealed the time-honoured British contempt for the intelligence of the enemy.

Hamilton was often inhibited by strict orders from the War Office. In this he was fairly treated in comparison with Sir John French, who had the usual power of a commander-in-chief to decide on actions without the prior directon or consent of the War Office. Hamilton, though a commander-in-chief in theory, was not one in practice; Kitchener, not wanting another 'difficult' general like French, kept Hamilton on a tight rein.

Hamilton's defenders claim that he had every attribute of a commander-in-chief. He certainly had many of them, but he lacked that most vital of qualities in a commander-in-chief – incisiveness. He did not say, 'we will do this' or 'you will do that'. He suggested and he urged when he should have ordered. He left too much to his staff and he made the cardinal mistake of assuming that his senior subordinates were as intelligent as he was. He seemed to believe that in almost every set of circumstances a word to the wise was sufficient; it was only necessary to point out some obvious course of action and it would be taken. Nothing else – other than the etiquette prevailing among generals – can explain why he allowed Hunter-Weston, Stopford, de Lisle and others to commit such atrocious errors. One wonders why, when he found that these men were not intelligent, he did not then consider it his duty to be more authoritative. He had the will to push exhausted troops still further – a necessary part of a great captain's make-up – but he entirely lacked it when dealing with senior officers.

Few commanders-in-chief in history have had it in their power to win a battle and possibly the entire campaign with a quick on-the-spot decision. Ian Hamilton had that chance at Y Beach on the morning of 26 April. He understood the tactical significance of Y more clearly than anybody, and he had at hand half a dozen senior officers, any one of whom could have been sent ashore in minutes to assume command and take the offensive. Lacking the confidence of his own judgement, he did nothing.

Again, off Anzac on the afternoon of 29 April, Hamilton said to Commodore Keyes, 'Don't you think we might land and look at it?' [the situation]. His staff pressured him out of the idea, no doubt out of apprehension for his safety. But as John North observed twenty-one years later, 'It must be another eternal regret of history that General Ian Hamilton . . . did not yield to his natural inclination to get nearer to the smoke of battle.' Hamilton was the boss and could have done anything he wished – but he repeatedly deferred to subordinates.

Hamilton must be criticized for allowing himself to become a prisoner on Imbros Island; at times, when naval organization broke down, he was virtually marooned. Had he set up GHQ ashore he would have felt the various crises through his pores; as it was they came to him almost in the abstract. Despite being gravely inconvenienced several times by his isolation on Imbros, Hamilton did not move from it. Another of his faults was that he consistently sent overoptimistic and misleading reports to London.

Two incidents show the personal weakness which was to lose the campaign. The first was his reaction to Kitchener's suggestion – in one of K's rare moments of insight – that

Birdwood should take control of Suvla as well as Anzac. He was the one man who might have bullied the reluctant Suvla generals into action, and as his staff was so profoundly experienced he could have managed the two sectors. Hamilton rejected the suggestion, probably because Birdwood as commander of Anzac *and* Suvla would have responsibilities similar to and possibly overriding those of Hamilton himself. He was putting his own feelings before winning the campaign. (Birdwood expressed approval of the decision, but as he could have done little else the genuineness of his approval cannot be assumed.)

The second incident occurred on 20 August, when the battle-shy Admiral de Robeck visited Hamilton for a serious talk. He said that the 'people at home' (the Admiralty) would see him through if he found a way of using the fleet in an attack. He was handing Hamilton an opportunity – and Hamilton rejected it. 'Every personal motive urges me to urge him on,' he wrote. 'But I have no right to shove my oar in – no right at all – until I can say that we are done unless the Fleet do make an attack. Can I say so? No; if we get the drafts and munitions we can still open the Straits on our own and without calling on the sister Service for further sacrifice.' He told de Robeck, 'Do what is right from the naval point of view and as to what is right from that point of view, I am no judge.' But he should by then have been a very good judge; he was saying, in effect, that he had learned nothing about combined operations. In any case, he had every right to shove his oar in, especially as de Robeck was inviting him to do so. Hamilton had missed another chance.

Overrall, Hamilton's guilt is great. He was a commander-in-chief in name only. For the sake of the soldiers he professed so much to admire he should have taken steps which would have left many more of them alive. At Suvla he deferred too long to the poor judgement of his subordinates out of unnecessary consideration for their feelings.

Major-General Sir Aylmer Hunter-Weston, commanding 29th Division and later VIII Corps.

This general, in charge of one of the finest British divisions of the war, was the Butcher of Helles. Ashmead-Bartlett realized that there was something 'very wrong' with Hunter-Weston after the first conversation he had with him. 'His excessive optimism seemed to show a lamentable ignorance of what it is possible for infantry to accomplish in modern warfare.'

Hunter-Weston repeatedly ordered assaults without any fixed objectives; they were thus useless and costly. During his period of command at Helles the equivalent of three divisions were lost in front of Achi Baba and Krithia without any important position being won. His aversion to attacking at dusk, during the night, and before dawn, killed many of his own soldiers; he always marched them, in broad daylight, frontally against an enemy ready and primed to repel the attack. More than any other general under Hamilton, Hunter-Weston flouted the proven military maxim that after an attack has once failed it should not be renewed along the same line or in the same form.

The general is said to have been a charming man personally, but he awarded a Military Cross to a young officer who had summarily executed three men for alleged cowardice on the battlefield. That is, the general equated these executions with outstanding gallantry in the face of the enemy, for which the MC is usually awarded. The subaltern concerned may have shown some quality of leadership if, in shooting the three men, he rallied others who might otherwise have panicked and broken the British line (I do not know if these were the circumstances), but to bestow the MC upon him was an insult to the decoration, to the dead soldiers and to the young officer himself. It revealed the crudity beneath the 'charming' face of Hunter-Weston.

General Joseph Joffre, French Commander-in-Chief. Joffre had a cynical double standard towards the Dardanelles campaign, supporting it in public and 'in principle' while working against it behind the scenes. He said in July 1915 that an operation against Constantinople could only be justified by its complete success; half measures were so self-defeating that he would not send a force from France until he could make it big enough. But effectively, that meant it would never be sent because Joffre was a committed Western Front man with an appetite for gigantic frontal assaults, one of which, sooner or later, would smash through the German lines. It was necessary, Joffre told his President, 'to keep the troops employed otherwise they would deteriorate physically and morally'.

His true attitude to Gallipoli came out in a report to his Minister of War in August, when he said that even with the help of thirteen extra French divisions, success would not be certain. It would be 'profoundly regrettable' if the attempt were allowed. His reasons are significant: 'It was the English who took us to the Dardanelles. Today the abandonment of the attack would be an English defeat. Tomorrow, if we were to send reinforcements, and to claim the chief command, we would be faced, in case of failure, by a French disaster.'

Joffre's arguments and objectives, presented at a steady pace, wore down his political leaders; the massive French reinforcements never did arrive, and the campaign was doomed. Perhaps Joffre should be commended for refusing to support an offensive in which he did not believe, but he was nevertheless guilty of failing to support his British allies – who were supporting him to the hilt. It did not suit Joffre for the British to have a smashing victory in the Orient, for it would have undermined French prestige.

Brigadier-General F.E. Johnston, commanding the New Zealand Infantry Brigade: When Bean wrote his Australian official history in 1924 he had to be circumspect in his assessment of leaders. Of this officer he said, 'Had Johnston possessed the physical and moral qualities required of subordinate commanders entrusted with the lives of men and with vital enterprises, the history of that day's fighting [8 and 9 August] would have been written differently.' Bean was more blunt in another comment: 'Despite Johnston's bravery he was completely unfitted by habit and physique for withstanding prolonged strain.'

When Robert Rhodes James published his book on Gallipoli in 1965 he could be more direct, and said that 'doubts as to Johnston's capacities were widespread through the New Zealanders; they widely believed that he drank excessively [and] it has even been suggested that he was not sober on 7 August.' James quotes the British official historian, Aspinall, as saying, 'I did, of course, know the truth, though, as official historian, I could not blurt it out . . . it was nothing but a national calamity that he was allowed to continue in command.'

Field-Marshal Lord Kitchener, Minister of War. Kitchener's guilt is fundamental. He delayed in sending an attacking force to the Mediterranean for amphibious operations; he chose the wrong generals, including Hamilton, to fight the Gallipoli campaign. Having chosen them he kept them short of reinforcements, artillery and shells until too late. He was guilty of criminal negligence in not knowing what he was asking of his generals and troops; his unforgivable ignorance can be seen from his comment to Birdwood when, at last, he visited Gallipoli in mid-November, 'Thank God I came to see this for myself. I had no idea of the difficulties you were up against.'

Had he studied the problem he might not have refused Hamilton's request for landing craft. Large flat-bottomed boats, each with a capacity for 500 soldiers, had been built in Britain for a projected scheme in the Baltic. These boats had steel-plated sides and decks which were proof against bullets and shrapnel. Hamilton asked for them for the landings on 25 April, and they would have saved many lives. Kitchener must bear some of the guilt for the slaughter at Helles.

Kitchener is also to blame for rejecting the sensible advice of General Cowans, Quartermaster General to the Forces, to set up an efficient and professional Lines-of-Communication staff. Since Kitchener never condescended to give an explanation for this decision or any other, we are left with the conclusion that it was wholly arbitrary and whimsical.

Bean has said of Kitchener: 'Slow of thought, more intuitive than logical, he could yet see big truths; and when he saw them he acted with a simple directness which bore down all opposition.'

Churchill makes the same point in greater detail: 'Lord Kitchener's personal qualities and position played a very great part in the decision of events. His prestige and authority were immense. He was the sole mouthpiece of the War Office opinion in the War Council. Everyone had the greatest respect for his character and everyone felt fortified, amid the terrible and incalculable events of the opening months of the war, by his commanding presence. When he gave a decision it was invariably accepted as final. He was never . . . over-ruled by the War Council or Cabinet in any military matter, great or small. No single unit was ever sent or withheld contrary, not merely to his agreement, but to his advice. Scarcely anyone ever ventured to argue with him in Council. . . . The belief that he had plans deeper and wider than any we could see silenced misgivings and disputes. All-powerful, imperturbable, reserved he dominated absolutely . . . at this time.'

Lord Balfour told Ashmead-Bartlett that he could not understand why everybody was so afraid of Kitchener. He was a 'harmless enough old gentleman' – he was in fact only sixty-five – 'somewhat slow in grasping points'. He was also excessively secretive.

Hamilton lived in apprehension of Kitchener if not in outright fear, but saw through him finally and wrote in his diary, 'He has cut his own throat, the men's throats and mine, by not sending young and up-to-date generals' to run the new divisions at Suvla.

In 1934 Hamilton was still bitter. At an ex-servicemen's rally at Jedburgh, Yorkshire, Hamilton met some men of the Ross Mountain Battery, who had fought with old-fashioned 10-pounder mountain-guns at Gallipoli. He referred to the incident in an introduction he wrote for a booklet issued for a veterans' journey to the peninsula, and added: 'Were I to put down fifty pages of controversial talk about the Dardanelles, I could not bring home to German, French, Bulgarian, Swiss or Russian soldiers a better, truer idea of our War Office in 1915 than by making clear to them the fact that these museum pieces were sent by the greatest mechanical nation on earth so that their soldiers could maintain the honour and prestige of their country against modern artillery.' This was a direct condemnation of Kitchener, with whom he had pleaded many times for more and better artillery and a much greater supply of shells.

It is in the nature of military commanders to pass the buck but Hamilton had legitimate grievance against Kitchener, who is more guilty than most of having killed the Gallipoli campaign.

Lieutenant-General Sir John Maxwell, commanding the British Army in Egypt. An opponent of the Gallipoli venture. Maxwell did all that he could to sabotage it, by withholding reinforcements from Hamilton. Whenever Hamilton sought more troops from Egypt – which Kitchener had given him authority to do – Maxwell found some specious excuse for being 'unable' to supply them. He was jealous about the priority being given the Gallipoli expedition and he expressed his jealousy by being unco-operative with stores, shipping, base facilities and much else. Had he obeyed Kitchener's order in a telegram of 6 April – virtually a *carte blanche* authority for Hamilton to have whatever he wanted – the first week on the peninsula just might have had different results.

Maxwell is guilty of gross professional betrayal of a colleague at a moment of crisis.

Vice-Admiral John de Robeck, naval commander at the Dardanelles: It is difficult to study de Robeck's part in the drama without becoming deeply perplexed. The historian keeps framing the question, 'What was in de Robeck's mind?'

Churchill thought this mind was limited – 'The larger issues of war in general or of the Great War itself were to a serious extent beyond his compass.' So seriously limited was he that he saw the role of the fleet as being ready to give battle to the German High Seas Fleet and little else; it had to be preserved to this end. No doubt this thinking was partly responsible for his decision to break off the battle of 18 March. But why did he never again attack, even when the fleet was stronger and infinitely better prepared for an assault? John North was surprised that de Robeck was thick-skinned enough to withstand 'the impact of the human drama of the Dardanelles throughout the eight and a half months he was witness to it'.

While the Army endured dreadful suffering, often in plain sight of the Admiral, he remained at anchored immovability. Even when it became clear that naval gunfire could do little to help the army advance, de Robeck proposed no other action. He was prepared to let the Army go on suffering – as he demonstrated when he opposed evacuation. If the Army had held tight to its beach-heads throughout 1916, 1917 and 1918, I wonder if he would have continued to grace the scene with nothing more than his moral support while his crews went on ferrying whole soldiers in and shattered ones out?

He did offer Hamilton a chance to ask for naval help, but he also spiked the plans produced by Roger Keyes to break through the Straits. His inaction suggests that he disapproved of the Dardanelles concept and was prepared to see it die. When Churchill wrote, 'Not to persevere – that was the crime', he was accusing de Robeck more than others. That is where his guilt lies – in failing to persevere, a fault made even more obvious when compared with the determination and success of the submarine captains.

Lieutenant-General Sir Frederick Stopford, commanding IX Corps at Suvla. Birdwood has said of Stopford that 'he was not big enough to face up to the situation; it overwhelmed him'. This is a compassionate way of expressing the plight of this pathetic figure on Gallipoli's stage. Enough has been said of him in this book to show that he had not a single quality needed in a corps commander and that his vacillation caused the failure of Hamilton's Suvla plans. He deserves History's censure but also merits its pity, for he was another of Kitchener's victims. Simply because he happened to be senior by virtue of date of promotion, he was plucked from decent obscurity and handed a task for which he had insufficient intelligence and resolution.

Major-General Sir Henry Wilson, sub-chief of the General Staff, then principal liaison officer between the British and French GHQs in France. Wilson was a clever man who believed that he knew everything and that the politicians and most other generals were ignorant. Articulate, eloquent and persuasive, he was easily roused to anger by any opposition; he was a man who had to have his own way. A born intriguer, he plotted against Kitchener, Hamilton and the whole Dardanelles project.

As his biographer says, Wilson had 'the happy faculty of gaining the upper hand in any controversy that be became engaged in'. Wilson always maintained that possession of the Peninsula did not necessarily ensure control of the Dardanelles and he would illustrate his view with what his biographer calls 'characteristic originality'.

'It's just exactly like fishing rights on a river. I'm on one side – Gallipoli side. Johnny Turk's t'other side – Asiatic side. I have fishing rights on my bank and exercise them. Johnny Turk has fishing rights on his bank. Now, where are we? Why, don't you see, Johnny Turk may be able to spoil my sport, and I may be able to spoil Johnny Turk's sport. But – you may say what you like – *I can't prevent the blighter fishing.*' [Not my italics.]

That such a fatuous, spurious and misleading analogy could influence leaders of the time says little for their intelligence, but it was typical of the methods Wilson used at every opportunity to campaign against the Gallipoli operation. One of his *coups* was to persuade, on 1 July, three new Conservative members of the Cabinet – Bonar Law, Walter Long and Sir Edward Carson – to oppose sending any more troops to Gallipoli. A Western Front man, a friend of Sir John French, Sir Douglas Haig and General Joffre, he was opposed to what he considered 'sideshows'. Shifty and shadowy, he was the saboteur of the Dardanelles campaign and as such is guilty.

The politicians. Writing in the spring of 1918 H.W. Nevinson, who knew as much about the Gallipoli campaign as did Ashmead-Bartlett, but who was more temperate in his criticisms, said that the ultimate failure rested on the 'authorities at home'.

He was referring in part to Kitchener and the obstructionists at the War Office but also to the politicians. In scheming for party and personal advantage, the politicians took a long time to reach decisions – and each delayed decision made the job of Hamilton and his subordinates more difficult. Asquith, Grey, Haldane and Balfour must all be given a share of the blame, and later Curzon and Carson when the War Council became the Dardanelles Committee.

Asquith was particularly at fault in not making known to the War Council a report from Fisher, on 25 January, 1915, in which he gave his reasons for opposing the bombardment of the forts at the Dardanelles. It is true that Asquith was under pressure from Churchill not to do so, but as Prime Minister the decision was obviously Asquith's. The politicians were perhaps most at fault in their failure to press Kitchener (himself a politician at this time) and Churchill for objectives, details and plans, ends and means.

John North has said that he could never understand how politicians who, in wartime, persist in their political intrigues miss being strung up on lamp-posts when the soldiers get back from the wars.

Some of the other generals at the front merit little more mention than that already given them in this book, such as Mahon who, in pique, left his division while it was in battle, de Lisle, who so mismanaged the attack on Scimitar Hill, and Hammersley, commanding the 11th Division, whose standard of generalship was not much above that of Stopford.

The System

To blame the generals without at the same time condemning the faults in the system which produced them would be unbalanced. Bean, who knew most of the leaders personally, said that the failure of leadership was the result of 'the inveterate respect of the Regular Army for seniority'. He was always sad that not until the great effort had failed did Kitchener and the Army send younger and more vigorous generals.

Ashmead-Bartlett, with a war correspondent's critical judgement, said that the 'root of the trouble lay in our amateur system of conducting war' with no General Staff at the War Office. Most of the professional General Staff had gone off to France, leaving the conduct of the war in London to Kitchener and some retired officers brought back into service.

There are other dimensions to the problem. The generals thought mostly of past successes and had learnt little from past failures; the South African War of 1899–1902 was littered with failures of frontal assaults on hills held by the Boers; had these defeats been taken to heart surely fewer frontal assaults would have been made at Gallipoli.

Again, the generals were concerned with military etiquette and with doing 'the right thing' rather than with winning. As Hamilton demonstrated time and and again it was more important for him not to interfere with a subordinate general's decision once battle had commenced than to push past him when he had made a mistake or had been too slow. Such mindless observance of etiquette was ludicrous. The removal of a general from command was a matter of great distaste. Usually his equals and superiors repeatedly covered up for him until his mistakes became so gross as to be visible to everybody. In the meantime he could lose battles and kill his own men.

The Gallipoli generals never did seem to understand, any more than General Haig in France, the magnitude of the sacrifice they expected from the troops and their families. One searches their despatches, reports, letters and diaries in vain for some expressions of sympathy, remorse, distress or sorrow. In killing off so many soldiers senselessly they belittled their sacrifice.

Aubrey Herbert, the author and Member of Parliament, who served at Gallipoli, was bitterly critical of GHQ for cruelty in leaving many British wounded to perish between the opposing lines after major fighting. The Turks were usually willing to have an armistice to collect wounded and bury the dead and they asked for one at Helles after the Krithia attacks in June. GHQ refused, apparently because they feared it might give the Turks some advantage, though this was not possible. So wounded men lay mutilated in agony and parched with thirst in no-man's-land, and sooner or later they died.

It was the System again which caused such needless suffering. On the Australian front, as has been seen, the local commander had the initiative to arrange an armistice for collection of the wounded.

Bean has described how many Anzacs attributed the British

failure at Suvla to the 'senility' of the leadership and partly to the inexperience of the British troops, but largely to 'causes which lie deeper in the mentality of the British people'. They were critical of the established order which caused Kitchener to hand the expedition to unsuitable commanders just because they were senior. Most Anzacs had noticed that the British soldiers, though brave, decent, modest and orderly, floundered helplessly when left without leadership. This failing was all the more noticeable because among the Australians and New Zealanders virtually any individual soldier could and would lead.

Bean had no adverse criticisms of junior British leading and often defended English battalion officers against other peoples' criticism. 'The British officer, whatever his defects, knew how to die.' He might have added that dying was part of the establishment order – the System. It would have been better had the officers known how to fight and *live*. This required no less courage but rather more skill.

A major fault of the System was that bright or different ideas – or even ideas by which some project could be tested or improved – were not wanted in the corridors of Army or Navy power. The case of Captain H.W. Richmond, RN, the Assistant Director of Operations of the War Staff, shows this clearly. Richmond, a competent officer, saw that surprise had been lost at the Dardanelles by successive bombardments and the much publicized and ill-timed assembly of troops at Lemnos. So he sent a secret paper to Lord Fisher, on 8 April, suggesting an alternative to the Dardanelles: The Army could be diverted to Haifa for an advance on Damascus, then Turkish held, with every chance of success. He was at once ordered to leave the Admiralty for interfering in a matter that had already been approved. Richmond had made the mistake of questioning higher authority – even if it was on a subject which should have been within his scope as Assistant Director of Operations.

16

Credit Where Due

Since I am concerned here with senior leadership it is not possible to mention the many battalion commanders (lieutenant-colonels and majors) who did well, and only a few brigadiers (brigadier-generals) can be mentioned.

Only one divisional general of all who served at Gallipoli deserves unqualified commendation – Major-General H.B. Walker, commanding 1st Australian Division at Anzac from 15 May. He succeeded in whatever he was asked to do and his casualties were no higher than could possibly be avoided. Walker was unlike any other general at Gallipoli. He really cared for his troops and he became angry when he thought that his superiors were putting them into ill-considered actions. Walker asked a lot of his men – but only after he had given them every chance of fighting and winning. He hated 'glorious' frontal assaults of the old style. When officers failed in leadership Walker got rid of them promptly; he was full of sympathy for exhausted officers, but they too had to leave – an exhausted officer could not adequately lead his men. In no way awed by rank, Walker spoke to Birdwood in a way that startled other officers, particularly when he considered his plans faulty. In conversation with the rank-and-file Walker was extraordinarily courteous, even gentle, though when he needed to outswear a tough Anzac he did so.

Other senior generals did an adequate job, notably Major-General Sir W.T. Bridges who ably led the Australians until mortally wounded by a sniper on 15 May. Lieutenant-General Sir F.J. Davies, who took over VIII Corps at Helles on 8 August, was a competent leader, and Major-General A. Paris, though undistinguished, did his best for his overused Royal Naval Division throughout the campaign. Major-General H.V. Cox led the Indian Brigade efficiently at Helles and at Anzac. Major-General J.G. Legge, of 2nd Australian Division, was always efficient, but his division was not in position until September so he was unable to show his real ability. Brigadier-General John Monash, 4th Australian Brigade, and Brigadier-General H. Chauvel, 1st Light Horse Brigade, achieved great military fame later in the war: Monash commanded the Australian army in France and Chauvel led the Light Horse in their remarkable thirty-six victories in Sinai and Palestine.

Major-General W.R. Marshall at various times commanded the 29th, 42nd and 53rd Divisions, Major-General W. Douglas the 42nd and Major-General C.G.A. Egerton the 52nd (Lowland) Division. The three did as sound a job as possible under poor corps commanders. Of Generals F.C. Shaw, J.E. Lindley, F.S. Inglefield and W.E. Peyton – they were present.

Lieutenant-General Sir Julian Byng, Major-General F.S. Maude and Major-General E.A. Fanshawe arrived from France late in August and were not really tested in the Gallipoli furnace, though all did well later.

Only one naval commander stands out – the energetic Commodore. Roger Keyes. The spirit and conscience of the fleet at the Dardanelles, Keyes ran the risk of destroying his own career by his persistent attempts to get the Navy into action. Never content for the ships to be merely floating gun platforms, he fought to the last for the Navy to get a chance at a Nelsonian action. Aged forty-three in 1915, he may have been too reckless, as some of his critics have said, but if so this was in reaction to the overcautiousness of his chief, de Robeck. Keyes was the naval officer who showed the greatest sense of Army-Navy co-operation and of amphibious operations.

Vice-Admiral S.H. Carden, who commanded at the Dardanelles until evacuated sick on 16 March, just before the great naval defeat, was yet another of Churchill's victims. Deluded by Churchill's messages about British intentions for the Dardanelles, Carden gave Churchill what he sought – an 'expert' assurance that it was feasible to attack at the Dardenelles and break through. The Admiralty, on 11 March, told Carden that the time had come for a vigorous attack and that he could expect Admiralty support, even if he suffered heavy losses. In a report on 14 March Carden said he would attack with his whole force. And next day the ship's doctor placed him on the sick list. What Carden might have achieved instead of de Robeck is another of the tantalizing speculations about the Dardanelles.

Rear-Admiral Wemyss worked hard to make Mudros into a great base and was efficient throughout. When he finally succeeded de Robeck he tried to make one last joint naval-military offensive, and also opposed evacuation. Rear-Admirals Thursby and Christian carried out many landings, supply and administrative tasks usually with cool efficiency, though Christian mishandled part of the Suvla landing. Under de Robeck's dead hand neither of these admirals had the opportunity to demonstrate their purely naval skills.

In London the one man to emerge from the Gallipoli mire without a stain was the short-statured Royal Marine, Lieutenant-Colonel Maurice Hankey. Clear-headed, far-seeing Hankey kept his head when all around him was uncertainty, confusion, vacillation and intrigue. Honest and direct and yet discreet, he was afraid of nobody, though among the field-marshals, generals, admirals and cabinet ministers he was only a junior personage. Hankey had a wiser head than any of them – and he was wise enough not to tell them that fact. Before the campaign began he saw more clearly than anybody the hazards it faced and his predictions were accurate. At an informal War Council meeting on 6 April Hankey said that it would be difficult to land the troops, largely because of the ravines that intersected the peninsula, also because of the enemy howitzers. Churchill flatly disagreed, saying that he anticipated no difficulty in effecting a landing. With the expedition decided upon Hankey did his best to make it succeed. His assessments and reports were models of clarity. When he visited Gallipoli as Prime Minister's representative, Hamilton resented him and suspected him of being some kind of sinister agent. Within a week he was writing that he was 'very glad to have' Hankey. Later he wrote that it was 'good to have an outsider of Hankey's calibre on the spot'. He felt better after talking with Hankey, 'who can grasp the bigness of what we are up against and can yet keep his head'. Nevinson refers to Hankey's 'high reputation for intelligence and capacity'. Nowhere did he show his intelligence more clearly than in his early analysis for the campaign, which, if followed, might well have brought success.

Success would have been possible by other means. The notion that the problem of the Dardanelles was essentially so difficult that no attempt to solve it could ever have succeeded is wrong. Three times at least victory was within the Allied grasp – in the naval attack on 18 March; when the troops landed on 25 April; and during the Anzac August offensive combined with the landing at Suvla Bay.

It has been said that troops were not available in large enough numbers to give Hamilton the numerical superiority he needed. This, too, is wrong. The troops need not have come from France: British soldiers were in Egypt in large numbers; at the time the Gallipoli campaign was being fought several divisions of British and Indian troops were being wasted in a futile expedition up the Tigris in Mesopotamia

(Iran) – even the Tigris relief expedition had 21,000 casualties. Later, other troops were sent too late to Salonika. In East Africa, too, many Commonwealth troops were tied up in bush and desert operations which had no bearing on the outcome of the war.

As for the Navy. . . . When I stand on Chunuk Bair or Achi Baba and see in my mind's eye that awe-inspiring armada lying at anchor offshore or in the safety of the Aegean island harbours I feel infinitely sad. Here was the Senior Service idling away the greater part of a year without once, after 18 March, doing what British fleets have traditionally done.

At Gallipoli it is possible to see that the Army could have crossed the peninsula in 1915. I have walked from Gaba Tepe, near Anzac, on the Aegean side of the peninsula to Maidos (now Eceabat) on the Dardanelles side. It is an easy walk because the terrain is even and the gradient gentle. One wonders what would have happened had Hamilton got his men ashore at Gaba Tepe and pushed them resolutely across the finger of land. True, the Gaba Tepe–Maidos route has the Sari Bair Range on one side and the Kilid Bahr plateau on the other, but it cannot be called a defile; the troops would not have been advancing through Khyber Pass type of country. The Turks would have seen them, but I still contend that surprise would have won the day. Unhappily, Hamilton and his generals had been trained 'to take the high ground'. At Gallipoli they constantly attacked the high ground – though they never did capture it. Apparently the idea of attacking the *low ground* never occurred to them. In a genuinely imaginative surprise attack Hamilton and de Robeck could have provided the Army with a protective corridor of gunfire which to advance. I am the first to admit that this is victory by hindsight. The idea asks for more than the leaders of the time could imagine.

John North, writing in 1936, believed that an 'absolutely forthright' attempt to punch a passage clear across the peninsula with the vigorous and 'exceptional Australians' would have resulted in quick and total success. Like me, he concedes that this view is the product of later knowledge. But I wonder if both of us are not being too charitable to Hamilton and de Robeck. It might be argued that Hamilton could not have known that in the Australians and New Zealands he had exceptional soldiers. To this I would say that he had served in South Africa and must have heard something of the dash of these colonial daredevils. In any case, as Commander-in-Chief of a major expedition he should have made it his business to know the capabilities of the divisions under his command. On 19 May, when the Anzacs took on the Turks in the open – their one and only such opportunity – they accounted for 10,000 of them – by the Turks' own account – for 160 of their own men killed. Hamilton may then have realized what an opportunity he missed with these men in not using them in a bold strike across the Maidos plain.

Hamilton had another option which he never tried and apparently never even considered. Instead of attempting to strike at Suvla with untrained troops led by generals he did not trust, he could have tried to turn the Turks' right flank at Anzac by marching a large part of his force by night to the Suvla arena. Then he could have sent them against the hills which were to become the objectives of the Suvla landing. I doubt if anybody would argue that the Anzacs and Gurkhas would not have taken the Chocolate and W Hills, Scimitar Hill and the other high ground, then undefended. Stopford's reinforcements could have been landed to support the seasoned warriors.

Such conjecture and speculation will continue because it is the intellectual thread of the Gallipoli story just as heroism and hardship form the emotional thead. At the time of Gallipoli and for some time afterwards many people could not see the campaign in perspective, so that in 1917 A.T. Stewart and C.J.E. Peshall, in a book called *The Immortal Gamble*, could write that 'no greater feat of arms has been writ in our history; no more wonderful story of indomitable courage'. The first part of this discription is hyperbolic nonsense, but the second is true. John North, writing twenty-one years after the catastrophe, believed that 'as Gallipoli would always remain one of the great stories of the world it was sufficient reason for telling it again'.

17

The Eternal Reproach

Gallipoli today is a reproachful place. Reproach is in the air at the Helles beaches, on the Sari Bair heights, in the tortuous ravines and amid the scrub at Suvla. Knowing something of the campaign one cannot visit the peninsula without being conscious of the straining effort and the endurance, the sweat and the blood, and the pain and misery that was commonplace.

Whenever I visit Gallipoli I remember C.E.W. Bean's observation that never in history was a campaign richer in pure heroism and conscious self-sacrifice. But I am equally aware that never was a campaign poorer in leadership at the front and in support from England.

The tangible evidence of loss is in the thirty-two cemeteries of the Commonwealth War Graves Commission. Some are hard to find and can be reached only with difficulty, especially in the lonely country north of Suvla. On one occasion my wife and I were the first visitors, apart from CWGC officers, to reach a cemetery at Azmak in three years. On the ridge near Quinn's Post we searched for hours for the 4th Battalion Parade Ground Cemetery, and when we found it we realized that several times we must have been within a few yards of it. It is a measure of the twisted nature of the terrain, which so often frustrated patrols sent out in 1915 and caused major difficulties in attacks.

Inscriptions on many of the war graves are piquant, sentimental and very much in tune with the time they were written – just after the war.

On the grave of Gunner J.Y. Twamley, Royal Field Artillery:

> Only a boy but a British boy.
> The son of a thousand years

On a headstone in a Green Hill Cemetery:

> Died for the flag
> A clean young Englishman

Private P.H. Price, Worcester Regiment:

> He fell like a warrior
> He died at his post

Private G.R. Yuill, aged 19, 7th Australian Infantry Battalion:

> Dear is the spot to me where my beloved
> son rests, my Anzac hero

Trooper W.A. Baker, 9th Australian Light Horse:

> Brother Bill a sniping fell
> We miss him still
> We ever will

In some battlefields, such as on the Somme and even in Ypres, it is possible to imagine the soldiers of the First World War singing; certainly this impression is strong behind the lines on the Western Front, where the troops were billeted in villages and on farms. But you hear no singing at Gallipoli; there *was* no singing – and nobody made up any songs. And no 'back areas' existed, no farms, no villages. In practically every theatre of conflict in the First World War it was possible for the soldiers to get away from the war at intervals. This did not apply in Gallipoli; the farthest anybody got, short of being seriously wounded, was Lemnos, and that was no holiday island.

As my wife and I were resting at Lone Pine one day, a coach-load of Turkish tourists arrived to visit the large cemetery and see the Australian memorial. They had just come down the road from the New Zealand memorial and other cemeteries at Chunuk Bair. The Turks have some monuments, but on the whole of the peninsula there is only one war grave and that more of a symbolic one to a brave sergeant killed on the Sari Bair heights. Neither during nor after the campaign did the Turks bury their dead properly; bodies were piled in heaps and covered with soil or thrown into ravines, where the bones can still be found. So the Turkish tourists were curious about the many immaculately kept British Commonwealth cemeteries, with their trees, shrubs, flowers and neatly tended gardens, and about the several imposing memorials. An English-speaking tourist, a middle-aged man, said, 'We cannot understand you British. You lost the Gallipoli peninsula war, yes?'

That was undeniable, we admitted.

'You lost it but you have built monuments from the tip of Cape Helles to Suvla Bay,' he said. 'You have an individual grave for every soldier whose body you could find, and the name of every dead soldier and sailor is on a monument somewhere. And you care for them as if you expect them to be visited by thousands of British people. Why do you do all this when you *lost*?'

It is indeed a great irony that through the work of the Commonwealth War Graves Commission Hamilton's expeditionary force is more firmly established on the Gallipoli peninsula in death than it ever was in life.

Pressed for their most vivid memory of the 'great story', survivors have told me of 'sand and flies', 'the bloody sun', 'the smell of the dead', 'the feeling of being forgotten', 'never getting a good sleep', 'the futility of it all', 'the pain of being carried down a mountain with two smashed legs', 'the total exhaustion', 'the waste'.

One of the last veterans I interviewed about Gallipoli, at the very end of 1979, was Major H. Fellowes Prynne, who served with 2nd County of London Yeomanry in 1915. He referred three times to the 'demoralizing apathy that was allowed to prevail and which caused so much discontent'. He still remembered the mixed exhilaration and fear of being under shrapnel fire at Suvla. In 1979 the dominant memory for Fusilier Herbert Beaumont of the Royal Welsh Fusiliers was visible in his hands, mis-shapen from frostbite at Suvla sixty-four years earlier. He was evacuated to Malta, where surgeons were about to amputate his hands only to be distracted by the arrival of another hospital ship with more urgent cases. When the doctors came back to Beaumont they made some more tests – by poking a needle into his finger behind the nail – and found that he had feeling an inch or so down. In this chance way his hands were saved. But between 1915 and 1979 they were continuously cold. On the whole Fusilier Beaumont was lucky; he saw a comrade pull off his sock – and his frost-bitten foot came with it.

Last words about Gallipoli are best left to the instigator of the Dardanelles–Gallipoli operation, Winston Churchill, to the common soldier, represented here by Private Charles Watkins, Lancashire Fusiliers, and to the Gallipoli dead, in this case Lieutenant John Hugh Allen, a New Zealander, killed in action on 6 June, aged twenty-eight.

Churchill: 'It is impossible to assemble the long chain of fatal missed chances without experiencing a sense of awe.'

Watkins: '. . . What an amateurish, do-it-yourself cock-up the whole conduct of this campaign must have been. From the time of the last big push on the Cape Helles front our complete lack of confidence in our superiors made us cynical, despairing and savage. We did our duty, but from now on we did it without hope, without enthusiasm. And that's a hell of a rot to set in, with any Army.'

Lieutenant Allen, in a letter home six days before his death: 'Nothing can convey to you how dreadful is the sight of a suffering, badly wounded man – nothing can convey it to you. . . . I heard two short surprised coughs, and saw a man bend and fall. A friend darted to him, opened his tunic and said to him, "You're done, Ginger, you're done: they've got you." This frankness really seemed the most appropriate and sincere thing. . . . They bandaged him up. While I was with him he said some remarkable things. . . . "Shall I go to heaven or hell, sir?" I said with perfect confidence. "To Heaven." He said: "No, tell me man to man." I repeated what I had said. A little while later he made up a beautiful prayer – "Oh God, be good and ease my pain – if only a little." All the while it was unbearable to see what he suffered. And then, slowly drawn out: "I didn't mean to groan, but" – in a long-drawn-out-groan – "I must." . . . I went to see him this morning. He was in a trench just wide enough to take him, a piece of newspaper over his face, the sun beating down upon him. Passersby stepped over his body as they went on their way.'

Acknowledgements

My primary thanks must go to my wife who has been my companion on all my trips to Gallipoli; she read my manuscript in rough and made many helpful suggestions, and she typed the final version. Mr Jock Irving of the Commonwealth War Graves Commission helped us to find and reach inaccessible parts of the battlefield when he was the Commission's regional director based at Chanakkale.

Other people specially helpful in one way or another in the planning of the book or in obtaining material include Mr N.F. Flanagan of the Australian War Memorial, Mr John Suddaby of the Imperial War Museum, and Miss B. Spiers of the Royal Marines Museum.

I am especially grateful to my friend Mr Charles Watkins of the Lancashire Fusiliers for permission to quote from his Gallipoli reminiscences, privately published in a limited edition in 1970, under the title *Lost Endeavour*. Mr Watkins, a private at Gallipoli, was later commissioned as an observer in the Royal Flying Corps. His description of life at Helles is one of the most vivid in Gallipoli literature. My thanks go also to Mr Greville Cripps, MC, who served as a lieutenant with the Dublin Fusiliers, for some interesting unpublished episodes at Helles, and to Brigadier R. Rathbone, who was at Suvla with the 6th Loyal North Lancashires. Other incorporated material came from Mr J.M. Hollis (sergeant, Royal Field Artillery, Suvla) and Mr Walter Gifford (private, 10th Australian Battalion, Anzac).

The Gallipoli Association. The association was founded in 1969 by Major E.H.W. Banner, TD, who was also the chairman and honorary secretary. I have made much use of veterans' recollections published in the association's quarterly journal, *The Gallipolian.* Extracs are credited where they appear. In 1980 the youngest member of the association was Captain Eric Bush, RN, aged 80, an historian of the campaign. In January 1980 the association had about 350 surviving full members and 45 associate members. The secretary's address is 'Delphi', Maresfield, Sussex.

Other sources. I have read a large number of papers, journals, diaries and letters either at the Public Records Office, the Imperial War Museum Library, or privately owned, including material in my own collection. While I have directly quoted from only a few of these sources all helped me to obtain a thorough understanding of the campaign and the conditions under which it was fought. This applies also to Peter Liddle's *Men of Gallipoli,* an excellent book built on the testimonies of many men who served on the peninsula. Mr Liddle's collection of primary source material is kept in special Great War Archives at Sunderland Polytechnic.

I consulted innumerable divisional and regimental histories on matters of fact. Lieutenant-Colonel R.K. May, curator of the Border Regiment Museum, Carlisle, was particularly helpful in providing material and photographs concerning the battalions of the Border Regiment.

Others who helped include Lieutenant-Colonel Michael Whitehead of 6th Queen Elizabeth's Own Gurkha Rifles (for material about the gallant Major Allanson), Major D.M.O. Miller, and Dr Michael E. Hoare, Head of Manuscripts Section, Alexander Turnbull Library, Wellington, New Zealand.

Bibliography

Allanson, Colonel C.J.L.: *The Allanson Diary*, published by 6th Queen Elizabeth's Own Gurkha Rifles, 1977.

Armstrong, H.C.: *Grey Wolf–Mustafa Kemal*, Methuen, 1932.

Ashmead-Bartlett, Ellis: *The Uncensored Dardanelles*, Hutchinson, 1928.

Ashmead-Bartlett, Ellis: *Despatches from the Dardanelles*, Newnes, 1915.

Aspinall-Oglander, Brigadier-General, C.F.: *Military Operations, Gallipoli*, 2 vols and two sets of appendices and maps; (The Official History) Heinemann, 1929.

Bean, C.E.W.: *Official History of Australia in the War of 1914–1918*, Vols I & II, Thirteenth edition, 1944.

Belford, Captain Walter: *Legs-Eleven*, Perth, 1940.

Birdwood, Field-Marshal Lord: *Khaki and Gown*, Ward Lock, 1941.

Bonnet, Stanley: *The Price of Admiralty: An Indictment of the Royal Navy, 1805–1966*, Robert Hale, 1968.

Brodie, C.G.: *Forlorn Hope*, Frederick, 1956.

Burton, O.E.: *The Silent Division: New Zealanders at the Front, 1914–1918*, Angus & Robertson, 1935.

Bush, Eric: *Gallipoli*, Allen & Unwin, 1975.

Callwell, Major-General C.E.: *The Dardanelles*, Constable, 1924.

Cassar, George H.: *The French and the Dardanelles*, Allen & Unwin, 1971.

Churchill, Winston S.: *The World Crisis 1911–1918*, 2 vols, Odhams, 1923.

Corbett, Sir Julian: *Naval Operations*, Vol 2, Longmans, 1921.

Creighton, Revd O.: *With the Twenty-Ninth Division in Gallipoli*, Longmans, Green, 1916.

Cunningham, Lord: *A Sailor's Odyssey*, Hutchinson, 1951.

Cutlack, F.M.: *War Letters of General Monash*, Angus & Robertson, 1935.

Darlington, Sir Henry: *Letters from Helles*, Longmans, 1936.

Dixon, Norman F.: *On the Psychology of Military Incompetence*, Jonathan Cape, 1976.

Ermin, A.: *Turkey in the World War*, Oxford, 1930.

Fuller, Major General J.F.C.: *The Decisive Battles of the Western World*, Vol III, Eyre & Spottiswoode, 1957.

Gillam, Major John Graham: *Gallipoli Diary*, Allen & Unwin, 1918.

Hamilton, General Sir Ian: *Gallipoli Diary*, 2 vols, Edward Arnold, 1920.

Hankey, Lord: *The Supreme Command*, Vol I, Allen & Unwin, 1961.

Hargrave, John: *At Suvla Bay*, Constable, 1916.

Herbert, Hon Aubrey: *Mons, Anzac and Kut*, Hutchinson, 1920.

Higgins, Trumball: *Winston Churchill and the Dardanelles*, Heinemann, 1963.

Hogue, Oliver: *Love Letters of an Anzac*, Melrose, 1916.

Horne, Charles F. (ed): *Source Records of the Great War*, National Alumni, US, 1923.

Kannengiesser, Hans: *The Campaign in Gallipoli*, Hutchinson, 1927.

Keyes, Admiral Roger: *National Memoirs*, Vol I, Butterworth, 1934.

Knight, Frank: *The Dardanelles Campaign*, Macdonald, 1970.

Liddell Hart, B.H.: *The Real War 1914–1918*, Cassell, 1930, later published as *A History of the World War 1914–1918*.

Mackenzie, Compton: *Gallipoli Memories*, Cassell, 1929.

Masefield, John: *Gallipoli*, Macmillan, 1916.

Moorehead, Alan: *Gallipoli*, Hamish Hamilton, 1956.

Morgenthau, Henry: *Secrets of the Bosphorus*, Hutchinson, 1918.

Murray, Joseph: *Gallipoli 1915*, William Kimber, 1965.

Nevinson, H.W.: *The Dardanelles Campaign*, Nisbet, London, 1918.

North, John: *Gallipoli, The Fading Vision*, Faber, 1936.

Patterson, J.H.: *With the Zionists in Gallipoli*, George Doran, New York, 1918.

Perk, Major Kadri: *The History of the Dardanelles Campaign*, Military Review, Istanbul, 1940.

Price, W.H.: *With the Fleet in the Dardanelles*, Melrose, 1917.

Prigge, E.R.: *Der Kampf um die Dardanelles*, Germany, 1916.

James, Robert Rhodes: *Gallipoli*, B.T. Batsford, 1965.

Samson, C.F.: *Fights and Flights*, Benn, 1920.

Von Sanders, Marshal Liman: *Five Years in Turkey*, U.S. Naval Institute, 1927.

Smithers, A.J.: *Sir John Monash*, Leo Cooper, 1973.

Geoffrey Sparrow and I.N. MacBean Ross: *On Four Fronts with the Royal Naval Division*, Hodder, 1918.

Stewart, A.T. & Peshall, C.J.E.: *The Immortal Gamble*, A. & C. Black, 1917.

Thompson, P.A.: *Lions Led by Donkeys*, Werner Laurie, 1927.

Tubby, A.H.: *A Consulting Surgeon in the Near East*, Christophers, 1920.

Waite, F.: *The New Zealanders at Gallipoli*, Whitcombe & Tombs, 1921.

Wemyss, Lord Wester: *The Navy in the Dardanelles Campaign*, Hodder & Stoughton, 1924.

Woodward, Sir Llewellyn: *Great Britain & the War of*

1914–1918, Methuen, 1967.
Reports, anthologies, edited books, Service reviews.

The Anzac Book, written and illustrated in Gallipoli by the
   Men of Anzac, Cassell, 1916.
Dardanelles Commission: *First Report and Supplement*, 1917,
   and *Final Reports and Appendices*, 1919, HMSO.
Gallipoli, Memories, A Plain Diary by a Plain Soldier,
   published in Constantinople, probably 1920.
War Letters of Fallen Englishmen, Housman, Laurence (Ed.),
   Gollancz, 1930.
Naval Reviews, Numbers 2, 3 and 4 of Vol. XLV, for April,
   July and October, 1957.
New York Times Current History of the European War, Vol II,
   N.Y., 1915.
Reminiscent Sketches 1914–1919, by members of Queen
   Alexandra's Imperial Military Nursing Service, London,
   1922.
Uncensored Letters from the Dardanelles, by a French Medical
   Officer to his wife, Heinemann, 1916.
Turkish War College publications, published in 1920: *Mehat
   Bey, The Battles of Sedd-el-Bahr* (that is, at Helles);
   Selaheddin Bey, The Naval Battles of the Dardanelles;
   Izzedin Bay, The Battles of Ari Burnu (Anzac).

Notes on some of the authors

Henry Nevinson and Ellis Ashmead-Bartlett were able war
correspondents and their reports are of great historical value.
Nevinson was perhaps too sympathetic to Hamilton and the
staff while Ashmead-Bartlett was too critical. Dr C.E.W.
Bean, the principal Australian official historian throughout
the war, remains the source *par excellence* for the Gallipoli
campaign, particularly for the Anzac sector. I doubt if any
official historian of any nationality in any war approaches

Bean in depth and detail. The British official history is limited in comparison. Its author, Brigadier C.F. Aspinall-Oglander, is the same Aspinall who was a member of Hamilton's staff and is referred to in my book; after the war he adopted the style Aspinall-Oglander. Chaplain Creighton was killed in France in 1918; Major Oliver Hogue died during the influenza epidemic of 1919–1920 before returning to Australia; Admiral C.G. Brodie was the twin brother of Commander T.S. Brodie, captain of the submarine *E-15*, who was killed in the Narrows.

Index

INDEX